AF878441

The Guerrilla Guide to Filing for Social Security Disability

By Lawyer X

The Guerrilla Guide to Filing for Social Security Disability

By
Lawyer X

Published by Rebellion Books
www.RebellionBooks.com

Developed in the United States

ISBN -13: 978-1-7337988-0-8

Library of Congress Assignation in progress

READ BEFORE CONTINUING

Waiver

The information in this book is intended for educational and/or entertainment purposes only. It is not intended to be used as a substitute for competent legal advice from a licensed professional attorney and with whom you have an attorney-client relationship along with all the privileges that relationship provides. The law on this topic changes frequently and varies from jurisdiction to jurisdiction. The information and materials provided are general in nature, and may not apply to a specific factual or legal circumstance described in your circumstances. By proceeding further, the reader acknowledges the nature of this work, agrees that it is not advice, legal or otherwise, and agrees that if advice is desired, it will be sought from a licensed attorney practicing in their jurisdiction.

Send us an email to info@lessonsinlaw.com and we will let you know of any significant updates to the book. We do not give out our mailing lists so you do not have to worry about SPAM. We value your business and SPAM makes us just as mad as it makes you.

In addition, if you spot any typos or errors please let us know. We do our best but sometimes things are missed. When converting a document into PDF, Kindle, or Nook format, glitches can occur and get overlooked.

LessonsInLaw.com offers a full line of ebooks to help you get the basic knowledge you need to represent yourself in court. Our books are available in PDF (sold through our publisher at www.RebellionBooks.com), Kindle and printed formats (sold through Amazon at www.amazon.com/author/robertdbennett and Nook format (sold through Barnes and Noble).

Check out our other books on The Guerilla Guides to the Law series:

The Guerrilla Guide to Picking a Jury: Jury Selection and Voir Dire for Non-Lawyers

The Guerrilla Guide to Written Discovery (Civil Cases)

The Guerrilla Guide to Settling Your Car Wreck Case

The Guerrilla Guide to Legal Research: Finding the Law for Non-Lawyers

The Guerrilla Guide to How to Fight A Debt Collection Lawsuit

The Guerrilla Guide to Trial Objections

The Guerrilla Guide to Small Claims Court

Table of Contents

THE PURPOSE BEHIND THE GUERRILLA GUIDES TO THE LAW

The *Guerrilla Guides to the Law* were envisioned because there is a great need for people to have knowledge about matters that are usually hidden by the legal profession. Not hidden, as in some great conspiracy behind locked doors, but it may as well be.

Instead, knowledge about the law is hidden behind volumes and volumes of case law, statutes, and treatises, buried beneath long and archaic words and in some cases, even Latin.

Does it have to be?

No, most legal concepts and information (not all, but most) can easily and clearly be stated in small words and, with a little work from legislators and the people in the legal system, made easy to understand.

So why is it done this way?

Many people think it is an actual conspiracy, but in reality, it is done this way ***now*** because it was done this way in the ***past***. In addition, it helps to justify the high legal fees that a lawyer charges or the high salaries paid to judges (who work much less than you probably do and often are not as smart).

The *Guerrilla Guides to the Law* hopes to strip away many of these trappings and explain legal subjects in a way most people can understand. We cannot provide you the education going to law school would, but we're also a lot less expensive and we'll tell you things many lawyers don't even know.

The *Guerrilla Guides to the Law* are each about a separate topic. Although everyone is complete in itself, and due to the nature of the law, multiple topics are discussed throughout. Often we will refer you to another book in the set for a more complete understanding of a different issue.

For instance, when a Guerrilla Guide to the Law deals with a lawsuit, some information on discovery will be provided. However, for an in-depth study on the issue of discovery, we will recommend The Guerrilla Guide to Written Discovery. This is done both to keep the size and cost of each guide at a reasonable level as well as to not overwhelm the pro se litigant with information.

Also, and this is extremely important, we don't know and can't anticipate the facts of ***<u>your</u>*** case.

The Guerrilla Guides to the Law are aimed at teaching concepts which apply across the board but we cannot write a book aimed at your specific facts. We write these books assuming the readers are intelligent and willing to put the time and effort into their case to apply what we give them. If they are not willing to do so or need a step by step guide designed around the specific facts of their case, then they ***should not*** be representing themselves in the first place.

About the Author

Lawyer X is the pen name of a former attorney who now spends all of his time writing and consulting. While in practice, he was involved in both criminal and civil trials across the United States, including picking or helping to pick juries in many cases.

In addition to his work as a trial lawyer, Lawyer X wrote many legal articles, lectured at continuing legal education seminars, and was active in the legal community in many ways.

He maintains anonymity now so that he can provide knowledge from inside and express honest opinions and viewpoints that other members of the legal community would just as soon weren't shared.

His goal is to see changes in the legal system that would allow people to represent themselves in cases where lawyers are not needed or can't be hired for economic reasons, yet still have a stranglehold on the system.

This book is written by a former trial lawyer and is designed to help you not be intimidated by the Social Security Administration (SSA) system, the judge, or the rules and procedures.

Let us address for a moment what this book is not:

1) It is NOT designed to teach you how to be a lawyer;
2) It is NOT a substitute for a lawyer;
3) It is NOT filled with useless and/or arcane information designed solely to make the book longer so we can charge more and make you think it's worth more.

When we first started working on the *Guerrilla Guides to the Law* we had a choice. We could do what other companies have done and write books with a little good information and lots of useless stuff to make the book thicker so we can justify charging more or we could write books that contain a lot of useful information, little to no fluff, not worry about thickness and make them available at a reasonable price.

We chose the latter.

If you have read any of the other *Guerrilla Guides to the Law* then you already know that we do not include useless information, a lot of exercises (which no one ever uses), archaic history of the law, or other parts just to justify a higher price.

We publish books in the size they need to be to convey the necessary information and, usually, in formats for Kindle, Nook, and PDF. This enables us to keep the price down and allows us to make changes periodically if something new develops.

If you're looking for books to put on a shelf and make it look like you know what you're doing, then the *Guerrilla Guides to the Law* are not them.

If you're looking for books that will help you with a problem and get to the point quickly in a way that is easily understood, then we think you've made a good purchase and hope that when you finish this book you will agree with us.

One other thing: A warning!

As we discuss on the www.LessonsInLaw.com website, tricks are for kids. Get it?

The internet is filled with tricks and strategies to handle lawsuits and these are usually a waste of time and energy, and make you look foolish if you actually try to use them. They usually come from someone who never attended law school, does not understand theories behind law, and either heard about or tried some kind of trick once and believed it worked and will work every time when in reality they just got lucky and the judge ruled in their favor on some other point and they don't realize it.

As an example, one absolutely false attack I have heard of is a person arguing that if the flag in the courtroom has a yellow fringe then it means it is an admiralty court (dealing with the sea) and therefore has no power (known as jurisdiction in legal terms) to handle any other kinds of cases.

This concept is absolutely incorrect and the idiot who put this, and other rumors like it, out there on the internet has done a great disservice to people trying to represent themselves. While admiralty courts may have a yellow fringe on their flags (I have no idea whether that is true or not) in other courts that fringe is there for decoration and has nothing to do with conferring jurisdiction on a court. If you argue that to a judge or anyone else in the legal community, be prepared for them to look at you like you are crazy and from that point on they will stop taking anything you say seriously.

The "fringe" tactic, as well as others you might see which sound suspicious, likely came about because someone once made that argument and the judge dismissed the case on other grounds, like no witnesses, and the person who made the argument now thinks they have discovered an innovative legal tactic and are the next Clarence Darrow so they sit in their parent's basement wearing their bathrobe, eating Hot Pockets, and sharing their "wisdom" with the world.

Simply put, if someone is telling you what to do in court and they have never been to law school and never practiced law...well, let's just say you should be extremely careful about any information they provide and if you do follow their advice then you have no one to blame but yourself.

Each time we consider doing another legal topic for a Guerrilla Guide, we evaluate as many of the other books already available on that topic as possible. If the topic is already covered sufficiently, then we don't do our own book.

The Guerrilla Guide to Filing for Social Security Disability Without a Lawyer is no different. Once we began to consider a book on this topic we looked at what was already out there and were surprised at a number of things we discovered.

First, for a topic this important and so relevant there were a few, but not a lot, of books available.

Second, what few books which are available are either 1) designed for lawyers and filled with legal terminology that is incredibly difficult for the layperson to understand, and/or 2) were written by non-lawyers and contained material that is so far off base (aka ***wrong***) that using it would likely cause more harm than it would help, 3) were so stuffed with useless information it was almost impossible for someone to actually pick out the bits that are useful, and that is from the perspective of someone who has been involved in dozens if not hundreds of cases involving Social Security claims, or 4) were so simple and lacking in real information they provided almost no real help to anyone who was actually going through the process.

Some of the books even contained "advice" and suggestions which were not only a waste of time but which would likely cause you to lose your disability case and have to start over from the initial application stage.

This book, on the other hand, is designed to assist you in responding in a professional, effective manner using the rules, the law, and tactics developed over time to obtain a ruling in your favor. We assume you do not have fifty extra hours a week to dedicate to your claim and so we do not provide examples of how to act in a way that is not likely to work, unprofessional, or which “plays games” with the system because those aren't necessary. If you truly are disabled ***as that term is defined by the Social Security Administration*** and you present your "case" correctly, then you will likely be approved at some point in the process.

Let me rephrase and repeat, everything in this book is based on sound legal principles and tactics based on research and real experience in the Social Security system, not tricks and gimmicks which rarely, if ever, work.

We are going to try to avoid as much duplication as possible in this book. However, since we will be discussing the two types of Social Security Disability and many of the terms used are the same, a certain amount of duplication is unavoidable. It is also necessary because some readers will only be interested in reading about Supplemental Security Income (SSI) and others will only be interested in reading about Social Security Disability Insurance (SSDI) and they will not want to have to go back and forth between the sections to get answers.

Also, some terms will be used interchangeably such as "claimant" and "applicant", among others. The reason this is done is simple, it is the way it is done in the real world and the way the clerks, employees, judges, and lawyers talk. As you are reading through this book, keep a notepad or two and a pen handy. One notepad should be used to make notes of specific importance to your case, as well as the location where that information was found. However, If you come across a term in this book and you are unsure of the meaning, jot down the word, the chapter, and section where it was found and then drop us an email at info@lessonsinlaw.com and we will try to respond with the definition we were using when writing the book. In some cases, we may even add that definition to our website or edit the book to make the meaning more clear. People in the legal profession are taught from the beginning to use certain "terms of art" to mean something which takes a much longer explanation if everyday

English was used. That's why you see so many Latin expressions still in use in the legal world. Unfortunately, many of these "terms of art" become a natural part of our vocabulary and we forget most people don't understand what they mean. Add to that the "word fatigue" which comes after writing hundreds of pages of a book, which required reading and researching thousands of pages of material, and you can see why lawyers, paralegals, and others often word ideas poorly when they are intended for the general public.

The meaning of most of the words in the book should be obvious unless the SSA uses a special definition in which case we will try and provide that definition and usually a link to the SSA website page where the term is defined. When we use two different terms for the same concept, again an example would be "applicant" and "claimant", it should be obvious as well but if not, please let us know. We try and answer all of our emails and respond to any comments made on the LessonsInLaw.com website although sometimes it may take a few days.

Finally, there are a lot of links in this book designed to show you our source for the info and also to make it easier for you to use the actual SSA forms. However, the SSA changes constantly.

We try and update all of The Guerrilla Guides to the Law as changes are made in their topics but realistically, it will be extremely difficult to keep completely up to date on the SSA forms. We have seen them make multiple changes to the same page on the website within days of each other with the end result being almost exactly the same as the first attempt.

Because of this, we encourage you (if at all possible) to check the links we provide and use the forms that are online rather than making copies of the ones in this book. The one thing the SSA does well on its website is to remove the data and forms which are no longer correct. If you find a section which isn't working, usually the website will provide a link to the new page. We'd also ask you to drop us an email to editor@RebellionBooks.com and let us know so we can make the change.

Overview of the Social Security Disability System

This chapter is going to be an overview of the entire Social Security system as it pertains to "disability". It may be that you already know all of this and, if so, feel free to skip this section. However, it is usually a good idea to take a few minutes and read chapters like this because it contains many terms and concepts that are important to everyone. Look on it as a refresher rather than just skipping through the chapters. Many people, lawyers, and judges don't know as much as they think they know and even the most innocuous of materials can yield a tidbit which can make a difference.

Unlike some other books, we're not going to devote time to explain how the Social Security system was created, the history of the legislation, etc. If you want to know that information then there are a number of resources available for research into those areas.

For our purposes here, and in keeping with ***The Guerrilla Guides to the Law*** approach of not wasting time and pages just to make a book longer and more expensive, how the system developed isn't important and if any aspects of it are necessary to know, they will be included in the pertinent sections of the book.

What is important to know is the Social Security Administration is a federal agency, with offices in each state and most major cities. It is rare you would have to travel more than an hour to find a Social Security Administration office where you can ask questions, file your initial application, etc.

That's not to say the office workers will be much help. Just as with every other business or government agency you get some good and some bad. However, I can tell you the reports of the service provided by the "front line workers" at the Social Security Administration are probably the worst of any governmental agency. Rudeness is a common complaint as is incorrect information being provided. In addition, some of the assistance being given in filling out the forms actually causes them to be filled out incorrectly.

Luckily, however, it is now possible to do the initial application process online which requires no contact with the lowest rung of workers. This method does require that you understand the system thoroughly and that you be able to locate information yourself by using the internet and other resources, like this book.

Throughout this book, we may sometimes refer to forms by their numbers, titles, or other designations. However, an applicant should be aware that these are subject to change at any point and it is always the responsibility of the applicant to be sure the form they are using is the correct one for the task. Don't simply rely on the identification we use. We do our best to be accurate and, just as we do with all of the Guerrilla Guides to the Law, we will do our best to update the materials but occasionally form names and numbers are changed with no notification to anyone.

The Social Security Administration

What exactly does the Social Security Administration (SSA) do?

The Social Security Administration has a great website with lots of information and lots and lots of pages. Unfortunately, when you're trying to find a general statement as to what they do the website states their mission is to "deliver Social Security services that meet the changing needs of the public".

While it sounds good, that mission statement really doesn't tell you anything.

The local office of the SSA is where you can apply for Social Security benefits, whether disability or retirement, apply for SSI, black lung benefits and hospital insurance protection, check on your earnings record, enroll for medical insurance (Medicare), obtain forms you need to apply or maintain benefits whether they be for retirement or disability, appeal SSA decisions, receive assistance in applying for food stamps (in certain offices), and get information about your rights and obligations for services which the Social Security Administration provides.

For our purposes in this book, we are mainly going to discuss the Social Security system as it applies to disability. This chapter is going to be an overview of that part of the SSA.

Types of Disability Payments

The first thing to know is there are two types of "disability" payments provided by the Social Security Administration. There are additional types of "disability" provided by states and insurance companies but those are not the topic of this book and will not be covered.

The first type of Social Security Disability is Supplemental Security Income or SSI. These payments do not require a work history and are for disabled individuals with very limited income and assets.

The second type is Social Security Disability Insurance, also known as SSDI or SSD or just plain "Disability". For our purposes in this book, we will normally refer to it as SSDI. This type of disability payment requires that you have a minimum amount of quarters of work history and payments into "the Social Security system". These requirements will be discussed more fully later.

It is possible, but rare, that a person will qualify for both types of disability. If so, then the applicant cannot draw both types but has to make a choice. Normally the choice is pretty easy since SSDI usually pays substantially more than SSI.

Definition of Disability

Anyone applying for Social Security benefits needs to understand that the Social Security Administration uses very specific definitions when making their determinations. Just because a person has been found to be disabled by a private insurer, an employer, a division of a state or local government, or anyone else does not mean they will be found to be disabled under the definition used by the Social Security Administration.

Let's be clear what Social Security does not do:

- They will not decide if you are "disabled" based solely on how you look. In fact, many of the people who make the decision on your case will never meet you. However, the interviewer at Social Security does complete a form that asks about his or her impression of the applicant's abilities and appearance during the interview.
- They will not decide if you "deserve" the benefits. They look strictly at whether you are medically disabled. It does not matter if you are having a rough time finding a job or paying the rent or that you really deserve the benefits simply because you lost your job.
- They will not base their decision on what is fair. They follow their rules and procedures, not what seems right or fair. They realize you have been paying into Social Security for years, but that is not the issue.
- They will not care whether your doctor thinks you are disabled in a general sense. The applicant must meet the specific definition of "disability" as stated by the Social Security Administration (and set forth below).

The deciders at Social Security will look at the medical records, and based on the medical records, determine if you are disabled.

For Social Security Administration purposes "disabled" means a person is "unable to engage in any substantial gainful activity because of a medically determinable physical or mental impairment". In order to draw benefits, the disability must last or be *expected to last* for a continuous period of at least 12 months *or* be expected to result in death.

To qualify for SSDI or SSI benefits, an applicant or claimant must meet the specific definition of disability as stated by the Social Security Administration in order to be considered disabled. As stated by Social Security:

"We consider you disabled under Social Security rules if:

1. You cannot do work that you did before and we decide that you cannot adjust to other work because of your medical condition(s);
2. If you do work, you are unable to earn over Substantial Gainful Activity (SGA); and

3. Your disability must last or be expected to last for at least one year or to result in death."

We will remind you of this later, but the term "Substantial Gainful Activity (SGA) is defined as "a person who is earning more than a certain monthly amount (net of impairment-related work expenses) is ordinarily considered to be engaging in SGA." The monthly earnings amount are listed in Appendix I.

These definitions and concepts are often difficult for laypeople to understand so we will discuss these in more detail below.

INABILITY TO ENGAGE IN SUBSTANTIAL GAINFUL ACTIVITY (SGA)

For our purposes here "inability to engage in substantial gainful activity" means that if you *do* work then you don't earn more than a certain amount of money set forth by the Social Security Administration.

WORKING AND SSDI BENEFITS

For SSDI recipients, you can earn up to $880.00 per month (or no more than 80 hours per month if self-employed) **without affecting SSDI benefits**.

Note: As with anything else that relies on data or figures provided by the SSA, or any part of any government for that matter, the amount should be checked regularly and the SSA provides these numbers at https://www.ssa.gov/oact/cola/twp.html and in Appendix K.

For all earnings over $850.00 in 2018 or $880.00 in 2019, Social Security will place the recipient in a Trial Work Period. The Trial Work Period will test the recipient's ability to work for at least nine months. During that time the recipient will continue to receive the full amount of the Social Security benefits. The Trial Work Period will continue until the recipient has earned income more than $850 per month in 2018 or $880 per month in 2019 for nine months within a 60-month period.

After the Trial Work Period, the recipient has 36 months in which he/she can work and still receive benefits for any month in which earned income is less than "substantial".

The Substantial Gainful Activity (SGA) amount in 2019 is $1,220.00 of earned income per month (or $2,040.00 if you are blind).

This means for 2019, an SSDI applicant can earn up to $1,220 per month **while waiting for a disability determination**. Once you start earning more than $1,220.00 per month (or $2,040.00 if you are blind) you are considered to have Substantial Gainful Employment and generally are not eligible for SSDI.

See Appendix I for a complete list of monthly Substantial Gainful Employment amounts.

Working and SSI Benefits

For SSI, there are special rules used to determine the if the total monthly earned and unearned income is under the maximum allowable amount. Your SSI payments are based on how much income you have. When your income goes up, your SSI payments go down. If your only income is from SSI and your job, then the first $85 of your monthly earnings do not count. For every dollar over $85.00, your SSI benefit is reduced by 50 cents. More information on how SSI benefits are calculated can be found in this SSA publication https://www.ssa.gov/pubs/EN-05-10095.pdf or on page 12 of this SSA publication https://www.ssa.gov/pubs/EN-05-11015.pdf.

Regardless of your physical condition and your ability to work, since SSI is "needs based" you won't qualify to receive benefits if you earn more than the amount of the SGA. In addition, if you earned more than the SGA and then you stopped working and applied for the benefits you have to show either that your medical condition worsened or that any special assistance you had which allowed you to do the job was no longer available.

A final note on SGA. This is ***only*** the amount you get from working. It doesn't include inheritance, gifts, etc.

Medically Determinable Impairment

The Social Security Administration website offers the following definition for Medically Determinable Impairment:

> *A medically determinable physical or mental impairment is an impairment that results from anatomical, physiological, or psychological abnormalities, which can be shown by medically acceptable clinical and laboratory diagnostic techniques. The medical evidence must establish a physical or mental impairment consisting of signs, symptoms, and laboratory findings-not only by the individual's statement of symptoms.*

Unfortunately, that definition requires some additional definitions:

- disorder - an abnormal condition
- anatomical - body structure
- physiological - body function
- psychological - mental

Essentially, what the Social Security Administration is saying in their definition of a Medically Determinable Impairment is an impairment must be proven by clinical and laboratory diagnostic methods. Or, to put it in even simpler terms, it must be based on medical findings in addition to the patient's own complaints.

The SSA will rely on the test and records from the applicant's own physicians and medical providers. In fact, they are required to give greater deference to the actual treating physicians then they are to doctors employed by the Social Security Administration. However, this is often not the case in reality. The Social Security Administration has a huge number of positions and other medical providers as well as vocational rehabilitation consultants who do independent work for them. These experts often appear at the Social Security hearings either in person or, more commonly, by video conference or teleconference.

While complaints of pain are common, these complaints alone are insufficient to provide the basis for benefits unless there are some type of medical results, reports, or opinions which provide additional documentation of the cause for the pain.

A complete listing of Medically Determinable Impairment for adults used by the Social Security Administration is located on the Social Security website at https://www.ssa.gov/disability/professionals/bluebook/AdultListings.htm.

A complete listing of Medically Determinable Impairments for children is located on the Social Security website at https://www.ssa.gov/disability/professionals/bluebook/ChildhoodListings.htm.

NOTE: At some point in the process the applicant will be provided a form which allows him to describe the pain and symptoms in their own words. It is *extremely* important that the applicant be absolutely truthful in their assessment and description of their pain and other symptoms and to not downplay or exaggerate these. Many applicants go to one extreme or the other and doing so never helps their case.

Duration of Disability

The duration of the disability requirement is easy to understand.

To be eligible for SSI benefits the impairment must be severe enough for the applicant to be disabled for at least 12 continuous months or for the impairment resulted in the applicant's death.

While some conditions enable the SSA to make an immediate determination as to impairment, as an example if the applicant is in a coma and their application is being processed by their court-appointed guardian, most impairments will require that the applicant go through the entire process before being approved.

As to the potential for the impairment resulted in the applicant's death, there are no specific definitions or guidelines as to how to measure the possibility of death. However, some diagnoses, such as cancer, will automatically include a certain median life expectancy. With these illnesses, it is just a matter of checking the SSA guidelines and making the determination.

It is important to note that the 12 continuous months of impairment does not mean that you must have been disabled for 12 months prior to applying for SSI. The 12 months is the total minimum duration the impairment is expected to last. This 12 months can include the time prior to applying, while the application is pending, and after the application is approved.

When in doubt as to whether the severity of the impairment is sufficient to qualify for benefits a person should apply and let the SSA rule on their application. The requirements to be approved for SSI are less stringent as a person ages and thus a person who is 60 years old with an impairment may get approved whereas a person who is 40 years old with the same impairment may not. The only exception to the rule requiring a 12-month duration of the impairment is when the diagnosis is blindness. SSI claims based on blindness are not subject to any duration although if the blindness is cured then the ability to draw SSI will no longer apply.

SUPPLEMENTAL SECURITY INCOME (SSI)

This system has two initial requirements. The first is that the applicant or the members of the applicant's household have limited income and limited resources. The second is that the applicant is disabled or blind as that term is defined by the Social Security Administration.

INCOME AND RESOURCE LEVEL FOR SSI

First an explanation. When determining Income and Resource Level the SSA looks at:

- If single, the applicant's income;
- If married, the applicant and spouse's income combined;
- If a child, the income of the parents who reside in the same household.

Under SSI, this determination is actually the hardest to calculate even though it is based on an objective standard. To qualify for SSI benefits the monthly income of the applicant and their household cannot be in excess of an amount known as the Federal Benefit Rate (FBR). This is an amount set by law and usually increases annually. The amount can be found by doing a Google search using the following terms:

Federal Benefit Rate for (INSERT YEAR)

As an example, for 2015 there was a 1.7 percent cost of living increase which raised the monthly amount to $733.00 or $8,804.43 annually for an individual.

The numbers don't always match up exactly because the calculations use both rounded and unrounded numbers as shown below which is a portion of the SSA website addressing this issue.

SSI Federal Payment Amounts For 2018

Maximum Federal Supplemental Security Income (SSI) payment amounts increase with the cost-of-living increases that apply to Social Security benefits. The latest such increase, 2.0 percent, becomes effective January 2018.

SSI amounts for 2018

The monthly maximum Federal amounts for 2018 are $750 for an eligible individual, $1,125 for an eligible individual with an eligible spouse, and $376 for an essential person.

In general, monthly amounts for the next year are determined by increasing the *unrounded annual amounts* for the current year by the COLA effective for January of the next year. The new unrounded amounts are then each divided by 12 and the resulting amounts are rounded down to the next lower multiple of $1.

Calculation details

	Unrounded annual amounts for—		Monthly amounts for
Recipient	**2017**	**2018** [a]	**2018**
Eligible individual	$8,830.84	$9,007.46	$750
Eligible couple	13,244.80	13,509.70	1,125
Essential person	4,425.55	4,514.06	376

[a] The unrounded amounts for 2018 equal the unrounded amounts for 2017 increased by 2.0 percent.

Payment reduction

The monthly amount is reduced by subtracting monthly countable income. In the case of an eligible individual with an eligible spouse, the amount payable is further divided equally between the two spouses. Some States supplement SSI benefits.

The SSA doesn't count certain income/benefits when determining the amount of your income level for its purposes. For example, it doesn't count food stamps and housing assistance or utility company or governmental help with your home energy bills.

This is very confusing but if you think you might qualify and you aren't sure whether or not you meet the Federal Benefit Rate then just apply, be truthful in the amounts you enter, and they will tell you whether you qualify or not. You won't get into any trouble for applying so long as you tell the truth and are accurate on the numbers you enter.

Another issue that can disqualify a person from receiving SSI benefits, other than total income, is the value of the assets or "resources". The most current list at the time of the writing of this book states you will not be eligible if your assets exceed:

- $2,000 for a single person; or
- $3,000 for a married couple, even if only one of the couple are eligible or applying for SSI.

The Social Security Administration specifically excludes certain assets from being calculated in a manner to disqualify someone from receiving benefits. These exclusions include:

- the home you live in and the land it is on;
- household goods (e.g. your furniture, etc.) and personal effects (e.g., your wedding and engagement rings, clothing, etc.);

- burial spaces for you or your immediate family;
- burial funds for you and your spouse, each valued at $1,500 or less (See the SSI Spotlight on Burial Funds);
- life insurance policies with a combined face value of $1,500 or less;
- one vehicle, regardless of value, if it is used for transportation for you or a member of your household;
- retroactive SSI or Social Security benefits for up to nine months after you receive them (including payments received in installments);
- grants, scholarships, fellowships, or gifts set aside to pay educational expenses for 9 months after receipt;
- property essential to self–support (for more information see http://www.ssa.gov/ssi/spotlights/spot-property-self-support.htm);
- resources that a blind or disabled person needs for an approved plan for achieving self–support (For more information see http://www.ssa.gov/ssi/spotlights/spot-plans-self-support.htm);
- money saved in an Individual Development Account (IDA) (for more information see

http://www.ssa.gov/ssi/spotlights/spot-individual-development.htm);

- support and maintenance assistance and home energy assistance that does not count as income;
- cash received for medical or social services that do not count as income and is not a resource for 1 month;
- health flexible spending arrangements (FSAs);
- State or local relocation assistance payments are not counted for 12 months;
- crime victim's assistance is not counted for 9 months;
- earned income tax credit payments are not counted for 9 months;
- dedicated accounts for disabled or blind children;
- disaster relief assistance which is not counted as income;
- cash received for the purpose of replacing an excluded resource (for example, a house) that is lost, damaged, or stolen is not counted for 9 months;
- All Federal tax refunds and advanced tax credits received on or after January 1, 2010, are not counted for 12 months;
- The first $2,000 of compensation received per calendar year for participating in certain clinical trials;

- Some trusts (See the SSI Spotlight on Trusts); and
- up to $100,000 in a qualified Achieving a Better Life Experience (ABLE) account.

While this is a list of assets which can affect the resource level and thus whether or not a person is entitled to SSI it is important to note these can change at any time and, in addition, it is not a list which includes all possible assets or property.

The absolute ***most*** important rule to remember when addressing resources is to be honest! While an application may be denied because there are too many assets or the value is too high, an intentional failure to disclose assets can result in criminal charges. In addition, the applicant will be required to repay any monies they were paid as a result of the "fraudulent" application and the fraud can, potentially, cause a permanent bar to ever receiving these benefits in the future, even if the economic situation gets worse.

Citizenship and Residency Requirements for SSI

As you can imagine, SSI payments are, as a general rule, only available to U.S. citizens. However, like most rules, there are some exceptions. While you may agree with some or disagree with others on this list, these are the rules. I once heard an individual in a Social Security office loudly complaining because he didn't meet the guidelines but a non-citizen who was in the office did. His complaints, in addition to being insulting, did nothing to help his case, did nothing to hurt the case of the non-citizen, or accomplish any purpose other than the complainer being asked to leave.

The point of this is that the rules are the rules and the employees at the local Social Security Administration office have nothing to do with them being created or passed. If you want to complain, do so to your Congressman, not to the local office. From a former attorney's point of view I can tell you that you shouldn't even complain to your local Congressman until well after you have been approved and started receiving your monthly benefits as well as your past benefits (lump sum payment) because you may have to ask the Congressman's office for help at some point (more on that later) and you don't want to already be on their list of "naughty" constituents.

Now on to the list, all of which can be found under the various sections and subsections of 8 U.S.C. 1612.

Non-citizens can be entitled to SSI payments if:

- The non-citizen was legally residing in the United States during the first seven years due to special conditions such as being granted asylum, being a refugee, granted status as a Haitian or Cuban entry, or something similar.
- The non-citizen entered the U.S. for the purpose of permanent residence and has worked at least 40 qualifying quarters as that term is defined under the Social Security Act. In addition, in some situations, the non-citizen may be able to count the qualifying quarters of a parent, a current spouse, or a deceased spouse.
- A non-citizen's military service can also allow them to receive benefits. If a non-citizen was honorably discharged from the U.S. military, is currently on active duty in the US military, is the spouse of a veteran or person on active duty, the unmarried dependent child of a veteran or person on active duty, or the surviving spouse of a deceased veteran or purse on active duty and has not remarried then they may be eligible as well.
- The non-citizen was lawfully residing in the United States on August 22, 1996, and became disabled at any time.

- The noncitizen has been battered or subjected to cruelty in the United States by a family member.
- The non-citizen was lawfully residing in the United States and began receiving SSI benefits on August 22, 1996.
- The non-citizen is lawfully residing in the United States and is a Native American born in Canada.

Unfortunately, the exceptions to the residency requirements for purposes of being allowed to draw SSI benefits are often complex. Further, the regulations change periodically. If a non-citizen wishes to draw SSI benefits they should consult with an attorney specializing in Social Security cases to determine their eligibility.

In addition, SSI payments are generally restricted to only those persons residing in the 50 United States, the Northern Mariana Islands, or the District of Columbia. If a recipient of SSI benefits moves outside these areas after applying for and receiving the benefits they may be disqualified from receiving additional amounts in the future. There are some exceptions to this law for disabled children of parents who are in military service or for students. Again, to know whether you would be affected by a move outside the above described areas you should consult with a Social Security attorney and receive their advice.

SSI Payments

The payment of any type of benefits can drastically affect SSI payments since it is needs based and both income and assets can cause a loss or denial of benefits.

The amount of benefits a person receives each month will be based on income and resources. The monthly maximum Federal amounts for 2019 are $771 for an eligible individual, $1,157 for an eligible individual with an eligible spouse, and $386 for an essential person.

However, if the person is no longer disabled, if they work and have substantial gainful employment above a certain amount, or if they are incarcerated the benefits may be stopped either permanently or temporarily.

Effects of Other Types of Payments on SSI Benefits

The payment of any type of benefits can drastically affect SSI payments since it is needs based and both income and assets can cause a loss or denial of benefits.

Effects of Outstanding Felony or Arrest Warrant

An SSI recipient cannot receive a monthly payment for any month in which there is an outstanding felony or arrest warrant for:

- Flight to avoid prosecution or confinement
- Escape from custody or
- Flight-escape.

Effects of Incarceration or Confined to Correctional Facility

An SSI recipient cannot receive a monthly payment for any month in which the recipient is incarcerated or confined to a correctional facility for a full calendar month.

Social Security Disability Insurance (SSDI aka SSD aka Disability)

Most of the time when lawyers are discussing Social Security Disability they will be discussing SSDI and will simply refer to it as "disability". There are a number of reasons for this. First, most lawyers don't take SSI or Supplemental Security Income cases. The reason for this is simple, lawyers work for a percentage of back benefits they recover and in Social Security Disability or SSD cases, the Social Security Administration withholds that percentage from the past benefits check sent to the applicant and sends it directly to the attorney. With SSI cases, the past benefits are sent directly to the applicant and the attorney must try to recover their share from the person. Unfortunately, many applicants aren't as trustworthy as they might be, spend all of the past benefits check when they receive it, and the attorney never receives a share without having to go through a lawsuit and judgment against the client which is something every attorney hopes to avoid. When you add this inconvenience to the additional fact that the amount of benefits is usually substantially lower than in "a regular disability case" most lawyers choose not to take on the added burdens of SSI cases.

The SSDI system has two categories into which a disabled applicant must fall in order to be eligible for disability benefits:

- a disabled worker under the age of 65 or
- be the family of an eligible worker (known as Auxiliary Benefits).

Work Credits

To be qualified for Social Security Disability benefits a worker must have earned a specific number of work credits in a specified time. The number of credits and the amount of time depends upon the age at which the worker becomes disabled. There are four potential credits issued per year with each credit representing a work period of three months. In most cases, the worker must have earned at least 20 credits in the 10 years prior to applying for disability. However, since some people become disabled earlier in their work life, the required number of credits may be less. For instance, if a worker applies for SSDI benefits before age 24 then the worker will have needed to earn at least six credits in the three year period prior to when the disability began. For ages 24 to 31, the applicant will need credits for having worked half the time between age 21 and the time they became disabled. For age 31, and older the credits required are shown in the chart below. Unless the applicant is blind, the applicant must have earned at least 20 of the credits in the 10 years immediately before becoming disabled.

Born after 1929, Became Disabled at Age	**Number of Credits You Need**
Before age 24	Earned at least 6 credits in the three year period prior to when disability began.
24-31	Need credits for having worked half the time between age 21 and the time they became disabled
31-42	20
43	21
44	22
45	23
46	24

47	25
48	26
49	27
50	28
51	29
52	30
53	31
54	32
55	33
56	34
57	35
58	36
59	37
60	38
61	39

62 or older	40

In the year 2019 a worker must earn $1,360.00 (in 2018 the amount was $1320.00) in covered earnings to get one Social Security or Medicare credit or, phrased another way, a worker must earn $5440 to get the maximum four credits for 2019. It is important to note that you do not earn credits for pension payments or interest or dividends or any other type of investment income. You only earn credits on earned income.

Generally, anyone working a full-time job will have earned more than enough credits to qualify for benefits. Any credits earned in excess of the minimum number have no effect and do not raise the number of credits.

AUXILIARY BENEFITS

The SSA can also pay benefits (known as auxiliary benefits) to people who qualify based on family members' entitlement to disability benefits. In these cases, benefits are paid based on the earnings record of an insured worker. Auxiliary benefits do not require that the applicant be disabled nor that the applicant themselves have the work credits previously discussed.

Auxiliary benefits can be based on applicant status as a spouse, former spouse, child, or parent of a worker. In addition, auxiliary benefits can include the lump sum death benefit.

SPOUSE AND EX-SPOUSE BENEFITS.

To qualify for auxiliary benefits as a spouse or divorced spouse one of the following must apply:

An applicant may qualify for auxiliary benefits if they are at least 62 years old, have been the spouse of a disabled worker for at least one year, and the applicant is not entitled to a retirement or disability insurance benefit on their own that is half or more of the spouse's benefit

If the applicant is divorced from a disabled worker who is entitled to benefits, and the applicant is 62 years of age or older, and was married to the disabled worker for at least 10 years then they may be eligible to receive benefits.

A divorced spouse of an insured worker may be entitled to benefits if the worker has not filed a claim for benefits, the applicant is 62 years of age or older, the former spouse is 62 years of age or older, they were married for at least 10 years and have now been divorced for at least two years.

Benefits may also be available if the applicant is a disabled widow or widower, they are at least 50 years of age but younger than 60 years old, they are the surviving spouse or divorced surviving spouse of a worker who received Social Security Disability or retirement benefits.

If a surviving spouse, including a surviving divorced spouse, of a deceased insured worker, and is at least age 60 or older, they may be entitled to benefits.

A person may also be entitled to benefits if they are the surviving spouse, including a surviving divorced spouse, of a deceased worker who was paying into the Social Security program, and the person is caring for a child of the deceased who is entitled to benefits and who is either under age 16 or has been the disabled since before they were age 22. These benefits are also known as "mothers or fathers benefits".

CHILDREN'S BENEFITS

An application for children's insurance benefits can be made if a dependent unmarried child of a worker who was insured at death and the child is under the age of 18, the child is age 18 or

19 and a full-time student, or the child is an adult but has been disabled since before age 22.

Parent's Benefits

An application for parents benefits may be sought if the child was an insured worker who died while providing support to the parent; the parents are at least 62 years old; the parent is divorced, widowed, or unmarried and has not married since their child's death; the parent was receiving at least 50% of their support from the child at the time the child's death and the parent can provide evidence of the support within two years of the death. There are circumstances that allow the parent to be exempt from providing evidence of support in certain cases.

Citizenship and Residency Requirements for SSDI

Just as with SSI, SSDI payments are, as a general rule, only available to U.S. citizens or permanent residents. However, there are also exceptions when applying for this form of disability payments assuming that the applicant is lawfully present in the U.S. and meets the other criteria.

When applying for SSDI benefits the applicant will be required to prove that they are either a citizen, a permanent resident, or a resident alien. A complete list of the documents that the SSA will accept can be obtained from the SSA or their website. If an alien, then there will be additional documentation provided. Usually, the required documents will be something the applicant already has or which can be obtained easily.

Since the initial inquiry as to whether someone is able to qualify for SSDI is whether they have sufficient work credits, then legal status in the U.S. must be established. This differs from SSI since it is not needs based.

There are still certain requirements as to the payment of benefits while persons are abroad. An alien who receives benefits generally must return to the U.S. every 30 days or reside in the U.S. for 30 consecutive days during every six month period. This does not apply if 1) the alien is on active military duty for the U.S. or 2) there is a treaty between the U.S. and the alien's home country which sets forth a different standard. The U.S. currently has these types of treaties with Germany, Greece, Ireland, Israel, Italy, and Japan as well as the Netherlands.

SSDI Payments

The amount of benefits a person receives each month will be based on the average lifetime earnings of that person. The total household income, the severity of the disability or the total value of assets a person owns plays no part in the amount of benefits that will be awarded.

However, if the person is no longer disabled, if they work and have substantial gainful employment above a certain amount, or if they are incarcerated the benefits may be stopped either permanently or temporarily. In addition, the amount of their benefit may be reduced if they obtain disability benefits from other sources such as insurance.

Effects of Other Types of Payments on Social Security Disability Benefits

The payment of any type of benefits can drastically affect SSI payments since it is needs based and both income and assets can cause a loss or denial of benefits.

However, in the case of SSDI payments, other benefits won't have as drastic an effect.

If workers compensation payments, either periodic or lump sum, private disability, or other benefits, are made then those amounts can be deducted from the past due benefits (arrears) to be paid by Social Security. The fact that these benefits were paid or are being paid can also cause it to be much harder to locate an attorney to represent the claimant in their Social Security case. This is because lawyers are limited by the Social Security Administration to taking the maximum of 25% of the past benefits as their fee. If the past benefits are reduced it lowers the amount of the fee that can be collected directly from the SSA and may even mean the lawyer won't be paid at all.

Some payments do not count against the arrears. These payments include:

- Veterans Administration benefits
- Some federal benefits
- State and local government benefits if the work done to earn them was covered by Social Security
- Some private pensions or insurance benefits
- Supplemental Security Income (SSI) payments

Effects of Outstanding Felony or Arrest Warrant

An SSDI recipient cannot receive regular disability benefits for any month in which there is an outstanding felony or arrest warrant for:

- Flight to avoid prosecution or confinement
- Escape from custody or
- Flight-escape.

Effects of Incarceration or Confined to Correctional Facility

An SSDI recipient cannot receive regular disability benefits for any month in which the recipient is incarcerated or confined to a correctional facility for a full calendar month. However, any family members who are eligible for benefits based on the recipient's work may continue to receive benefits.

Monthly benefits are usually not paid to someone who is confined to an institution by court order and at public expense. This applies if the person has been found:

- Not guilty by reason of insanity or similar factors (such as mental disease, mental defect or mental incompetence); or
- Incompetent to stand trial.

Parole or Probation Violations

An SSDI recipient cannot receive regular disability benefits for any month in which a condition for probation or parole is violated.

The SSA uses forms that contain the same information whether you are applying for SSI or SSDI. You can see a copy of a current form for SSDI in Appendix A or on the Social Security Administration website at https://www.ssa.gov/forms/ssa-16-bk.pdf.

If you are applying for SSI (Supplemental Security Income), form SSA-8000-BK should be completed. You can see a copy of a current form in Appendix A or on the Social Security website.

While occasionally someone qualifies under both SSI and SSDI, it is unusual because most people have too many assets or are working and thus disqualified from being awarded SSI. Sometimes the forms have a section where you select which type you are applying for and sometimes they don't. When in doubt apply for both types and if you are approved for both then you can select which one you prefer. As we mentioned earlier, in almost all cases the SSDI benefit will be higher than the SSI benefit.

We will discuss the application form in more detail later but to start, take a few minutes and look over the forms in Appendix

A, just to know what type of information you will have to provide initially. Note that the paper forms may appear slightly different than the forms online but both will have the same questions and requests for information.

Again, the most important thing to know about applying for Social Security Disability, whether SSDI or SSI, is that the applicant absolutely ***must be honest***! Lying on the application will not only disqualify someone from receiving benefits but it is also a federal crime.

This doesn't mean that a claimant can't "spin" the information and put it in as favorable a light to them as possible but they must be truthful.

BEFORE THE APPLICATION IS FILED

Even before an applicant fills out their application for Social Security benefits they should start documenting all of their conditions. It is impossible to start doing this early as the more information and documentation of a condition that is available, the more likely a condition will be found to exist and to satisfy the 12-month duration requirement.

The most effective method of documentation for most people is through the use of a calendar and a small notebook with some type of binding to hold the pages together. Each day's notes should be made of any symptoms, complaints, activities that could be accomplished and that were tried but could not be completed, and any other information which reflects on the applicant's medical condition or general well-being. The same calendar can be used to track medical appointments and testing so it can be verified that the Social Security Administration has all the pertinent medical records when they begin the review. Additional notes with the names and telephone numbers of people with whom the applicant spoke, etc. can be made and kept in the bound notebook so there is always one central location with all of the information about the disability process.

The calendar can also be used to document when medications are taken, side effects of the medications, and any psychological or mental issues caused by the injury, impairment, or medication.

It is important that the applicant remember Social Security benefits can be based on the cumulative effects of all conditions and medications. What this means, in simple terms, can best be explained by an example. If a person has a heart condition which can be controlled by medication but the medication renders a person unable to engage in substantial gainful activity the Social Security Administration can still find the person is disabled even though the actual physical condition is controlled by the medication. Likewise, if there are multiple conditions which, separately, have a minimal effect but when combined asked to prevent the applicant from working that is also sufficient to receive benefits. Many people who choose to represent themselves often make the mistake of only addressing one issue or one condition rather than all of the health scenario and failed to properly document and explain the totality of their circumstances thus resulting in the denial of their benefits.

If a worker is still employed in either full-time or part-time capacity while seeking Social Security Disability benefits they should also document how their condition affects their ability to work and perform their tasks.

Essentially, a potential applicant should document anything and everything which could even potentially be of interest to the Social Security Administration or help convince the Social Security judge that they deserve to be awarded benefits.

How the Doctor Can Assist Prior to Applying

Unfortunately, most physicians and medical providers have no understanding of how the Social Security system works or what type of information is relied on by the Social Security Administration in determining whether or not to award disability benefits. We have provided a link to a good article to send to doctors explaining how they can help their patients. The link is http://practicalneurology.com/2009/04/PN0309_09.php

You should inform your physician that "although the enclosed article was published in the journal Practical Neurology, the same general concepts apply to all treating physicians regardless of their area of practice." This article helps to assist doctors in understanding how the system works. Some people are uncomfortable in providing this information to their physician while others take the position that they want to do everything possible to increase their chances of being awarded benefits. That is a personal choice on which we do not offer an opinion or advice. However, the information is available should you choose to use it.

Regardless, it is beneficial to ask any treating physicians to carefully and in detail document the symptoms which are reported over the course of time and to keep a thorough record of all issues.

It is also important to note that medical providers document almost everything which you discuss with them and, unfortunately, often leap to conclusions regarding your motivation in seeking treatment. Every attorney who does Social Security work or personal injury work can tell you of instances in which medical providers have to use the phrase "secondary gain syndrome" in their records. "Secondary gain syndrome" is a doctor's way of stating that they believe symptoms are exaggerated to some extent by a desire other than to be treated or make a recovery. In short, they think someone is exaggerating in order to enhance their chances of a monetary gain either in a lawsuit or by them getting Social Security benefits. In point of fact, most medical providers are absolutely unqualified to make this assertion and it absolutely should not be a part of someone's medical records. If you see this notation in your medical records we would suggest you contact a local attorney and discuss your options as far as forcing the physician to remove this notation as it can devastate your chances of being awarded benefits. There are a variety of options which can be examined or utilized to force this to be removed from the medical records but those are outside the scope of this book and need to be discussed with a local attorney.

Social Media

Social media is a phenomenon which is only recently become an issue as far as the legal field. To date, I have not heard of an episode where the Social Security Administration has done any type of investigation regarding an applicant's social media accounts. However, it is now commonplace for attorneys for both the plaintiffs and defense to look at social media in an attempt to find any casual posts which are inconsistent with a position taken in a lawsuit.

At some point, I would anticipate that this will happen with Social Security as well and certainly no claimant would want to be the first case in which someone was denied Social Security benefits because of a post they made on Facebook. Therefore from the time at which an applicant alleges they became disabled, which is likely before the actual application is filed, and at all times in the future care must be taken to avoid any material being placed on the Internet which is inconsistent with the claims being made or which will one day be made in an application for Social Security Disability benefits. For instance, if an applicant alleges they have a back condition which prevents them from doing any manual labor it would probably be a very bad idea for them to post pictures of themselves at a gymnasium working out with free weights even if that work out is a part of a physical therapy regimen. At the least, it could lead to some additional questions and a review of the physical limitations by a Social Security expert and at worst could result in a finding of no disability.

The Application Process

It was only a few years ago the only way to apply for Social Security Disability benefits was to visit a field office. However, with the advent of the Internet and improved telephone services, there are now multiple ways to start the application process.

We will discuss each of these in turn since they each work slightly in a different way.

Before applying using any of these methods, it would be wise for a claimant to use the "Benefit Eligibility Screening Tool" (BEST) available online at https://ssabest.benefits.gov/. The BEST will assist applicants in identifying all the different Social Security programs for which they may be eligible. As the website states, BEST will not screen for help with Medicare Prescription drug plan costs.

In addition, on the same starting page as BEST there is a link to www.benefits.gov which is a website offering information on more than 1,000 other benefit programs.

Applying in Person

Almost everyone will reside within an hour's drive of a Social Security Administration field office. Some of the larger cities may even have more than one.

First, it is not necessary to call and make an appointment to visit an office and to meet with one of the workers at the office. However, it is a better practice to make an appointment if at all possible. It is not uncommon when the offices are full of people waiting for their appointment for the waiting times lasting 45 minutes or longer. In addition, and as we've mentioned before in this book, there are probably more complaints about the "front line" workers for the Social Security Administration than any other government agency, and that's saying a lot. There are reports of rudeness, a seeming unwillingness to help, a complete lack of empathy, and a general lack of knowledge on the part of the workers.

These problems with the local offices cause many people to forego that method of application and to opt instead for applying over the telephone, which often results in many of the same complaints about the workers, or more commonly to use the online method.

Without a doubt some of the complaints are unjustified and anyone who has ever worked in a service industry knows many people are impossible to please. However, the sheer number of complaints about the SSA workers would indicate that the old maxim "where there's smoke there's fire" likely applies.

Even with all of the problems many people still prefer to apply in person and if they choose to do so being familiar with the process will make things easier.

Upon arriving at the SSA office the claimant should determine the office's method of "getting in line" and follow that procedure. There may be different sections that deal with retirement issues, Medicare, SSI, or SSDI. It is important to be sure that the applicant is "in line" for the workers get on with their particular issue.

After meeting with the initial clerk, the person will likely be scheduled to meet with an interviewer. This meeting may take place within a few minutes or can be scheduled days later. If there is an option to wait around and conduct the interview that day then an applicant would be well advised to do so since that lessens the chances of their request for the meeting being lost in the shuffle or set aside.

At this meeting, the interviewer will obtain information and evidence regarding the disability, assist in completing the application, and provide information on the rights and responsibilities of anyone applying for benefits. An applicant should make a note in the notebooks discussed earlier of the name and telephone number or extension of the interviewer in case it is later necessary to contact them for clarification or additional help.

Of course, being prepared prior to the Social Security interview can save lots of time. Take a few moments and go through the application forms shown in Appendix A and put together a packet of information which substantiates any answers to those questions.

While you can expect the workers at the SSA office to provide assistance the ultimate responsibility for procuring and submitting any evidence necessary to support the claim for disability rest solely on the shoulders of the person seeking disability benefits. The Social Security Administration workers should do their best to assist the applicant in any way possible it is ***not*** safe to rely solely on their assistance.

It is also not advisable to make any assumptions as to what the Social Security workers know about the case or will do to help support the claim.

However, the employees of the Social Security Administration can be very helpful in providing explanations, translators if needed, or especially in assisting in obtaining records from medical providers at no cost. There are specific forms used to request medical records for Social Security purposes and which state specifically that the medical provider is not allowed to charge for the records. If an applicant attempts to obtain records without using these forms then the medical providers will almost certainly charge for the copies and the price is often quite steep.

IMPORTANT NOTE: All forms necessary to apply for disability and to obtain records are available from a local SSA field office, online at one of the pages on www.SSA.gov, or by calling the SSA hotline at the toll free telephone number 1-800-772-1213, Monday through Friday (except for federally recognized holidays) from 7 AM to 7 PM. If the caller is deaf or hard of hearing, service representatives who are trained to help callers with those disabilities are available during the same hours by calling the toll free telephone number 1-800–325–0778.

ANOTHER IMPORTANT NOTE: An applicant must use the SSA forms for the application process except for those sections for extra information where the form specifically instructs the applicant to attach additional pages without specifically referencing a form number. The failure to use Social Security Administration forms will result in an automatic rejection of the application and the process must start over.

APPLYING BY TELEPHONE

As we mentioned above, the Social Security Administration has toll free telephone numbers which claimants may use to apply for disability payments. Those telephone numbers and the hours in which they can be used are listed in the previous section under **IMPORTANT NOTE**.

However, reports indicate attempts to apply over the telephone are even more difficult than going through the application process in person. There are several reasons why this may be true including an inability to properly ask or respond to questions, a tendency for both the representative of the SSA and the claimant to be less patient, and the fact that most people do better in face-to-face interactions.

The same rules regarding preparing ahead of time for the application and interview, an applicant being very familiar with their materials and information, and the burden being on the claimant to ensure the proper information is documented applies to telephonic applications as well as those in person.

APPLYING ONLINE

Applying online is likely the most common method of applying for disability benefits at this time, slightly more so than applying in person. This is only become true in the last couple of years both because of technological advances as well as claimant's willingness to use the online process.

When an applicant has gone through the BEST process as set forth above and is ready to begin their application they should go to https://www.socialsecurity.gov/disabilityssi/apply.html and began the three-step process.

This three-step process will include:

- reviewing the adult disability starter kit
- filling out the online application for Social Security benefits, and
- filling out the online adult disability report

Using the online process has several advantages one of these is that the applicant can work at their own pace without any pressure that many feel when working with an SSA employee. In addition, the application process can be paused at any point if additional information is needed or some interruption occurs. When the work is paused the SSA will issue a confirmation number which can then be used to access the application information when the claimant is ready to begin again.

Also, if at some point during the online application process the applicant hits a problem or needs assistance the work can become paused and the SSA contacted either in person at the local field office or over the telephone.

WHAT IS NEEDED TO PROCESS THE APPLICATION

THE APPLICATION

Of course, the first thing that is needed in the process is the application itself.

A couple of things. The application isn't formally called an application even though that is how most people refer to it. In Social Security Administration terminology this is called Form SSA-3368-BK, *Adult Disability Report.* An example of this form can be seen in Appendix B. The first thing the applicant may notice is while the form is designated as SSA-3368-BK on the first page of the instructions, in the upper right-hand corner of the form itself it states "Form Approved OMB NO. 0960-0579".

Why the difference in designation? That's another one of those topics that would take a lot of time to explain and would do absolutely nothing to improve the chances of getting a disability application approved. It is sufficient to know that sometimes forms would be designated in more than one way. This means it is important to be sure an applicant is using the correct form.

Social Security Number and Birth Certificate

An applicant will be required to provide the SSA with their Social Security number and their birth certificate or other proof of their age. If the application is being made for a different family member, such as a disabled adult child, the Social Security number and birth certificate of *that* person will be needed.

If the applicant submits an original record of any kind the SSA is supposed to return it to them after making a copy. However, most attorneys would never provide an original document to the SSA or any other government bureaucracy unless there is absolutely no way around it. Instead, a better solution is to submit a certified copy of the original record. "Certification" is just the process whereby an official swears that the copy is a true and correct duplicate of the original.

Certified copies can be obtained from:

- the official custodian of the record

- an employee of the SSA who is authorized to certify copies
- an employee of the State Department or a U.S. consular officer
- an employee of a state agency authorized to certify copies of original records in a state agency's files

It is permissible in cases where is the practice of the local birth registrar to issue uncertified photocopies of birth certificates to use them for disability purposes. However, it is safe to state an applicant would be likely to meet some resistance from the SSA employees when attempting to use an uncertified birth certificate under this exception.

In any instance in which the SSA needs proof of the applicant's age, the preferred evidence is a certified birth certificate or hospital birth record that was recorded before age 5, or a religious record such as a baptismal record that shows the date of birth and that was recorded before age 5. If these cannot be obtained certain other evidence can be used pursuant to 20 CFR Sec. 404.701-716. This includes:

- original family Bible or family record

- school records
- records of the U.S. Census
- a statement signed by a physician or midwife present at the birth (a notarized statement would be preferable)
- insurance policies
- a marriage record
- a passport
- certain employment records
- an immigration or naturalization record.

Medical Records

To obtain disability the Social Security Administration will need to obtain and review a variety of medical records. Often these records go back well beyond the time in which the applicant is claiming to be disabled and will include medical providers whose care was entirely unrelated to the condition which is causing the disability. A claimant can object to providing many of these records on the basis of their relevance or a privacy concern but any such objection is likely to cause additional delays in the processing of the claim.

At a minimum all disability claims will include the following information from medical providers:

- the name, address, telephone number, and fax number of the doctors, clinics, hospitals, pharmacies, and other medical providers
- the results of laboratory work and medical testing
- the names, dosage, and scheduling of all medications taken by the claimant
- medical notes, observations, and reports, etc. from all doctors, therapists, caseworkers, clinics, laboratories, and hospitals.

Most claimants only have a few, if any, of their medical records when they begin their application process. Providing a complete list of all medical providers will make the process move quicker without question. The main cause of delays in applying for disability benefits is obtaining a complete set of medical records. As we mentioned earlier while it may be faster for an applicant to seek you out and obtain copies of the medical records themselves, choosing to do so will result in an enormous out-of-pocket expenditure. If the claimant will provide the complete and correct contact information for their medical providers the DDS

(Disability Determination Services) will obtain the information at no charge.

The Social Security Administration field office is responsible for verifying non-medical eligibility requirements, which may include age, employment, marital status, or Social Security coverage information. The field office then sends the case to a "DDS" for evaluation of disability. The Disability Determination Services are state agencies which are fully funded by the federal government and are responsible for developing medical evidence for use in the disability process as well as making the initial determination on whether or not a claimant is disabled or blind under the law.

As the Social Security Administration website points out "... the DDS tries to obtain evidence from the claimant's own medical sources first. If that evidence is unavailable or insufficient to make a determination, the DDS will arrange for a consultative examination (CE) to obtain the additional information needed. The claimant's treating source is the preferred source for the CE, but the DDS may obtain the CE from an independent source. After completing its development of the evidence, trained staff at the DDS makes the initial disability determination.

Then, the DDS returns the case to the field office for appropriate action. If the DDS found that the claimant is disabled, SSA completes any outstanding non-disability development, computes the benefit amount, and begins paying benefits. If the claimant was found not to be disabled, the file is kept in the field office in case the claimant decides to appeal the determination."

The SSA does not send the application to any treating physicians for their input and they also advise the applicant not to do so either. If specific information is needed from the medical provider then the Social Security Administration will make that specific request and all the claimant would need to do is provide the contact information. At most, the applicant should do no more than contacting the medical provider's office and inquire as to whether they have responded to any of the Social Security Administration's requests.

However, it is highly recommended by those who are involved in the process of attempting to get disability benefits approved that a claimant request their medical provider to send them a copy of any report or other documentation the medical provider sends to the SSA. *It is extremely* important that an applicant review all of the records submitted by their medical providers as early as possible. In the event that the medical records contain information that is incorrect, the applicant can then request that the record is corrected to provide accurate findings. As an example, it is not uncommon for a medical provider to offer an opinion that a claimant is capable of performing tasks which, in reality, they are not. Whether this is based on an inaccurate assessment, a failure to properly evaluate the claimant's condition, or is just an error doesn't really matter. What *does* matter is that if the incorrect information is allowed to remain in the file then it could disqualify the patient from obtaining benefits to which they are actually entitled.

EMPLOYMENT HISTORY

The next area about which the Social Security Administration will want information is the applicant's employers, job titles, and job duties for the fifteen-year period prior to the application for disability.

It is important when filling out the sections of the Disability Report to not leave any sections blank. If the information is required but the applicant simply does not remember the information then the proper response is to write in the blank "unknown".

The questions regarding the employment history are extensive but fairly simple. The claimant will know most of the information off the top of their head. They are asked if the medical disorder affected their job and if so, how. The SSA asks if their work attendance or hours were affected and whether an employer had to provide special assistance for the employee to be able to do their job. Providing this information and providing it correctly may be critical to making the determination as to whether or not the employee is disabled and, if so when the disability began.

The application also ask about the type of business, job title, dates and days worked, and rate of pay. The claimant is also asked to describe the basic job duties and the amount and kind of physical activity required for the work. The physical activity questions include those about walking, standing, sitting, and bending. The SSA also wants to know about any lifting or carrying which were done on the jobs.

While the applicant can apply for disability benefits without being able to provide all of the requested information, failing to do so can result in a delay in the process and the information will have to be given to the Social Security Administration at some time before the ultimate disability determination is made.

Just as with any other section on the Disability Report/Application, if the claimant does not understand one or more questions they can contact an SSA employee at the field office or by telephone or speak to the disability examiner who has been assigned to their claim once the claim leaves the field office.

Daily Life Activities

Typically, the claims representative or the interviewer will ask the claimant to fill out a form which asked detailed questions about their Activities of Daily Living or ADLs. The main ADL form is titled *"Function Report – Adult"* which is Form SSA – 3373 – BK (which can be seen in Appendix D). While the form is designated as SSA-3373-BK on the first page of the instructions, in the upper right-hand corner of the form itself it states "Form Approved OMB NO. 0960-0681

The purpose of this form and the questions are for the SSI to form an impression of how the claimed impairment affects an applicant's daily life. The ADLs play a part in almost all disabilities including mental disorders. In fact, with mental disorders, the ADLs are often the best measure of the way the impairment affects someone.

Any questions about ADLs must be answered and should be answered in as much detail as possible. For some reason, people tend to downplay the effect of their condition on their daily life. While someone's choice to do that when speaking with friends or relatives is certainly within their rights if they take this approach in the disability process it greatly reduces their chances of being approved and can even result in the Social Security workers choosing to label the claimant who provides minimal information as uncooperative.

The ADLs are an area where people may be inclined to rely on their medical providers' assessments but to do so is a mistake since physicians almost never know what their patients actually do during the time they are not with them. It certainly doesn't hurt to discuss these matters with a physician as well as discussing how the condition which has led to the disability actually affects daily life but the most important information regarding these matters should be provided by the applicant to the Social Security Administration directly.

School Records

Normally the request for school records will only be important when applying for disability for a child, usually SSI. The Social Security Administration will either direct the adult who is applying on behalf of the child as to what records are needed or else they will request them directly from the school and the adult will simply have to provide a signature on some type of permission slip.

Information About Income and Assets

As discussed earlier, information concerning assets and income are only important when applying for SSI since there is an upper limit on the amount of these and anything over that amount is an automatic disqualification.

The Social Security Administration will direct the claimant as to what records are needed. These usually include a copy of the most recent W-2 form, tax returns, rent receipts, utility records, bank statements, and vehicle registration papers.

The Observations of the Field Office

For those people who choose to apply in person at the local field office, as opposed to applying online or over the telephone, there is an added issue of which they need to be aware.

Most applicants who apply in person are unaware that as they are filling out their application form and interacting with workers and others there in the Social Security office, the field office representative may observe them and make notes which are placed in their file. The worker will watch the applicant while they perform a variety of tasks which might relate to their impairment, condition, or claim. These can include the applicant walking, talking, sitting, reading, writing, hearing, answering, understanding, using their hands, and many other observations. This is yet another reason why it pays to be polite when dealing with the workers at the SSA field office since an applicant does not know who may be making notes which will go into their file and may affect the outcome of their claim.

While the observations of the SSA field office workers will not be dispositive on the claim they will certainly be considered along with all of the other data available.

Disability Onset Date

Another acronym which the claimant is sure to hear is an AOD, which is short for "Alleged Onset Date".

An applicant sets the date of the AOD when applying for SSDI. However, the Social Security Administration does not allow a claimant to receive benefits for any time in which they were engaged in substantial gainful activity and earning too much money to qualify for SSDI. So, for these purposes, the SSA determines an EOD which stands for "Established Onset Date". The EOD can be different than the AOD and is influenced by both nonmedical eligibility factors and the date the Social Security Administration considers the claimant to be unable to do substantial gainful work.

As for SSI, the onset date doesn't have any effect. SSI benefits are never awarded for a date earlier than the first day of the month following the date on which the claimant filed for disability benefits.

NONMEDICAL ELIGIBILITY REQUIREMENTS

This was mentioned in the previous paragraph and includes several different criteria. These must all be met before the Social

Security Administration will ever consider whether a claimant has a medical disorder that prevents them from working.

The field office determines whether or not a claimant satisfies the nonmedical eligibility requirements of SSI or SSDI which include age, employment, income, marital status, Social Security coverage, and other factors.

As an example, a nonmedical eligibility requirement for SSDI would be whether the applicant had worked the required number of quarters to be eligible for benefits. An example of a nonmedical eligibility requirement for SSI would be income level.

THE PROCESSING OF AN APPLICATION OR CLAIM

Once the Social Security Administration field office determines that an applicant meets the nonmedical eligibility requirements the file is then sent to the Disability Determination Service (DDS) to determine whether a medical disorder is severe enough to qualify for benefits.

Social Security Administration field offices deal with many different Social Security issues but the DDS deals only with determining the medical eligibility or disability benefits. When they receive the file the DDS workers collect any additional information needed, especially medical information. The office will acquire additional medical records by sending requests to the various medical providers based on the information already provided. They may also obtain nonmedical information such as details about the claimants work activities or skills.

The DDS examiner may also contact the applicant by telephone or in writing if they need information which is not contained in the documentation. The examiner may even go so far as to request the claimant undergo additional medical examinations or medical testing. These additional examinations or tests will be paid for by the Social Security Administration.

Healthcare Professionals and Their Role in the Social Security Disability Application Process

Medical providers and other healthcare professionals are inextricably intertwined with the Social Security Disability process. They have a number of roles and provide a variety of services including:

- Acting as medical experts who testify through reports or live administrative hearings,

- Act as consultants performing examinations or tests as needed to provide a complete picture of the applicant's physical condition and capabilities,
- Most often the medical providers act as treating experts by treating and providing medical evidence on behalf of their patients, and
- As medical consultants who review claims for the Social Security Administration.

Acting as medical experts who testify through reports or live administrative hearings

As we will be discussed more fully later when an application for disability benefits is denied the claimant can then appeal and ask to be heard by an Administrative Law Judge (ALJ). The ALJs work in a department of the Social Security Administration known as the Office of Hearings and Appeals. These ALJs often request expert testimony to help them understand and evaluate complex medical issues. These Medical Experts (ME) do not have any official authority as far as granting or denying benefits, their only duty is to testify and provide expert opinions on specific issues. These Medical Experts are paid by the SSA as independent consultants and review records only. They never actually examine the disability claimants.

Although the Medical Experts (ME) are supposed to be neutral and testify based solely on the records and with no bias for or against the granting of disability benefits, most Social Security attorneys are of the opinion that there is a very real bias shown against claimants. It is not at all unusual for the medical expert being paid by the Social Security Administration to have an opinion which directly contradicts that of the treating physician and other medical providers who are ***not*** "on the payroll" of the SSA. However, that is not always the case and I have, on more than one occasion, had an SSA medical expert render an opinion which was, I feel, one of the main reasons the ALJ granted benefits to my client.

Acting as consultants performing examinations or tests as needed to provide a complete picture of the applicant's physical condition and capabilities

Social Security examination consultants are most often used when an applicant's treating medical sources do not provide sufficient medical evidence for the DDS to make a disability determination. When this happens the DDS requests additional examinations or tests to be performed by health professionals. These health professionals can include physicians, osteopaths, psychologist, or others. In addition, audiologists can be retained to test hearing and the speech-language pathologist can be asked to evaluate problems with speech.

The consulting experts are paid by the Social Security Administration, must be licensed in the state in which the application for disability is being processed, must have the training and experience to perform the examinations or tests requested, and must have a thorough understanding of the Social Security Administration's disability programs as well as the evidence necessary to make a disability determination.

Most often the medical providers act as treating experts by treating and providing medical evidence on behalf of their patients

Generally, the Social Security Administration recognizes that a treating medical provider is the best source of medical information and medical evidence about the nature and degree of a claimant's impairment or condition. As such, a treating provider is usually the preferred person to perform any additional testing or examinations required by the DDS or SSA to process the claim.

However, the personal physicians of a claimant will not be asked nor will they be expected to decide if their patient is disabled as that term is used by the Social Security Administration.

Medical consultants who review claims for the Social Security Administration

This type of medical consultant is paid to do a "paper review" of the claim for disability benefits. They are usually licensed medical doctors and may be either a general practitioner or trained in a certain specialty. Their ranks will also include osteopaths and psychologists with a Ph.D.

Their work is normally performed either at a DDS office or at a regional or central office of the Social Security Administration.

PRESUMPTIVE DISABILITY PAYMENTS (SSI APPLICANTS ONLY)

The SSA recognizes that people who are applying for SSI are often in a very tough financial situation which, if they actually do meet the requirements for SSI, is absolutely not going to get better without the benefits. Because of this, there is a program which allows for up to six months of payments during the application process and while the application is pending. These payments are not available for SSDI applicants, only for those people who meet the income and asset requirements as well as the disability factor for SSI.

These interim payments are referred to as Presumptive Disability (PD) payments.

In addition to the payments, if a person is granted presumptive disability they would also be eligible to receive free medical care under Medicaid earlier than normal. Unfortunately, being granted presumptive disability payments is not a guarantee that the SSA will make a positive final determination for SSI benefits but, due to the stringent criteria, it is a positive sign.

Also, as long as fraud was not involved, if the ultimate outcome is that the SSI benefits are denied, the Social Security Administration can waive the requirement that the money is repaid.

Applying for Presumptive Disability

The application for presumptive disability should be made at the same time as the initial application for SSI and at the local Social Security Administration field office. While the SSA field office can grant presumptive disability for certain impairments most are forwarded to the state Disability Determination Services without the award being granted. If this happens the claimant should talk to the examiner at the DDS office about the presumptive disability claim.

Impairments Which Qualify for Presumptive Disability Payments

As mentioned above, the SSA field office can grant up to six months of presumptive disability payments at the initial application for SSI benefits if they have a reasonable basis for the belief that the applicant is suffering from a disabling impairment.

This initial granting of the payments is usually based on one of three types of evidence.

1) Observation

If, based upon the observations of the representative of at the field office, the claimant has one of the following disabling conditions the federal regulations allow for an immediate award for presumptive disability:

- Amputation of one leg at the hip, or
- Amputation of two legs.

2) Statements of the Claimant or of the Guardian of the Claimant

Since the award of presumptive disability is based on obvious and severe impairments when the evidence of these are statements of the claimant or the Guardian of the claimant, then the condition must be clear.

The disabling conditions which can be based solely on the statements made to the field office representatives are:

- total blindness or deafness

- bed confinement or immobility without an aid such as crutches, a wheelchair, a walker, etc. due to a long-standing and chronic condition
- diabetes that has resulted in an amputation of a foot
- Down syndrome with physical characteristics
- a stroke which occurred more than three months in the past in which has left claimant with continued difficulty in walking or using a hand or arm and such condition is more than moderate
- muscular dystrophy, cerebral palsy, or atrophy of the muscle characterized by marked difficulty in walking without aid, in speaking, or in the coordination of the hands or arms
- severe mental retardation in someone who is at least seven years of age such that the person depends on others for routine daily activities and personal care

Note that even with a statement being made as to these conditions, if the representative of the SSA field office believes that the allegations are false and/or has personal observation indicating that the allegations are false, then they may deny presumptive disability at the time of the application.

3) Disorders Requiring Additional Sources of Confirmation

If the field office agent is unable to substantiate the claimant's allegation, is unable to observe the alleged impairment, or believes the information which would normally entitle a claimant to presumptive disability is inconsistent and thus is unwilling/unable to grant presumptive disability payments immediately, the claimant may still qualify for PD after additional confirmation.

Some of the conditions which can qualify for PD but normally require additional confirmation are:

- infection with the human immunodeficiency virus (HIV)
- hospice services for a condition in which the claimant is expected to have six months or less to live
- a child six months or younger with a birth weight below 2 lbs. 10 oz., and a child six months or younger whose birth weight was as follows:

Gestational Age (in weeks)	Weight at Birth
37-40	Under 4 pounds 6 ounces

36	Under 4 pounds 2 ounces
35	Under 3 pounds 12 ounces
34	Under 3 pounds 5 ounces
33	Under 2 pounds 15 ounces

- allegation of a spinal cord injury producing an inability to ambulate without the use of a walker or bilateral hand–held assistive devices for more than two weeks with confirmation of such status from an appropriate medical professional;
- allegation of end-stage renal disease (ESRD) requiring chronic dialysis, and the file contains a completed CMS–2728-U3 End Stage Renal Disease Medical Evidence Report–Medicare Entitlement and/or Patient Registration;
- allegation of amyotrophic lateral sclerosis (ALS) known as Lou Gehrig's disease.

There are two other types of payments available from the Social Security Administration which are similar to presumptive disability benefits. These are emergency advance payments and immediate payments.

An emergency advance payment can be made to a new applicant who faces a financial emergency and who has been approved for SSI benefits but the benefit has been delayed or not received. These are only available one time and the maximum emergency advance payment is the smaller of the SSI federal benefit rate, the total amount of the benefits due, or the amount requested for the financial emergency.

If an emergency advance payment is granted this amount will be deducted from the monthly benefits in up to six monthly installments.

An immediate payment is available to those who are initially applying for SSI benefits or already receiving benefits and who are facing a financial emergency. The maximum amount of an immediate payment which can be made is $999 and the entire amount will be subtracted from the first regular payment due to the claimant.

The burden of proving an impairment is on the claimant. This is normally done through medical evidence such as records or testimony but it is not necessary for the applicant to actually obtain and provide the records, the SSA will get them directly from the medical providers once the applicant has provided the contact information and signed the appropriate forms.

When the ***existence*** of an impairment has been established the Social Security Administration will then move on to consider both medical and non-medical evidence to assess the extent/severity.

MEDICAL SOURCES USED BY THE SOCIAL SECURITY ADMINISTRATION

While many types of health providers, including practitioners of alternative medicine, may contribute records, only certain types are considered "acceptable" by the Social Security Administration.

A factor the claimant must be aware of but which doesn't arrive often is that the provider must be licensed or certified in the state in which they are practicing.

The following types of providers are "acceptable medical sources" as that term is used by the Social Security Administration:

Licensed Physicians - a licensed physician will have an M.D. degree and a valid license to practice medicine in the state in which they actually do practice. Their area of practice can be either general or in a specialty. Alternative health providers such as chiropractors, homeopathic practitioners, and naturopathic practitioners do not qualify as a licensed physician for the Social Security Administration disability purposes.

Licensed or Certified Psychologist - This medical source will hold a doctorate degree (Ph.D.) in psychology. For certain disabilities, a licensed or certified psychologist can include a school psychologist or another licensed or certified person with a different title who performs the function of the school psychologist in a school, public or private, setting. A psychologist also must be licensed in the state in which they practice.

Licensed Optometrist - An optometrist, who holds an O.D. degree, is considered an acceptable medical source only for the measurement of visual fields and visual acuity. The optometrist's measurements can then be used by a medical doctor or osteopath along with additional data to diagnose eye disease. An optometrist is *not* the same as an ophthalmologist.

Licensed Osteopath - A licensed osteopath holds a D.O. degree and must be licensed in the state in which he or she practices.

Speech/Language Pathologists - to be considered an acceptable medical source by the Social Security Administration a speech/language pathologist must be fully certified by the state education agency in the state in which they practice, must be licensed by the state professional licensing board, or hold a Certificate of Clinical Competence from the American Speech - Language - Hearing Association. A speech/language pathologist is only considered an acceptable medical source in establishing speech or language impairments.

Licensed Podiatrist - a podiatrist is an acceptable medical source under the Social Security Administration guidelines only to establish impairments of the foot or the foot and ankle. They must be validly licensed in the state in which they practice and hold a D.P.M. degree.

MEDICAL EVIDENCE FROM TREATING PROVIDERS

The Social Security Administration gives additional weight to the opinions and records of treating physicians so long as they are Acceptable Medical Sources as discussed above. While the regulations do not go into the motivation behind the special emphasis placed on evidence from treating physicians it is generally accepted the reasoning is due to a treating physician being better able to provide more detail and a more realistic long-term evaluation of the applicant's medical situation. In addition, the personal attention and interaction between a treating physician and their patient provide a different perspective than can be obtained from a "cold" reading of medical records or test results or even a one time, in person examination.

WAR STORY: We try to give as few "war stories" in the Guerrilla Guides as possible but in some cases they do help to illustrate a point.

In one case I handled, the claimant had lost at all stages of the process, then retained my office when the Administrative Law Judge ruled against them. At that stage, we proceeded through the remainder of the SSA procedures and then filed the civil lawsuit in the federal district court, which we won. The basis of the decision was the claimant's treating physician had put in their records everything needed to grant the benefits to the claimant and, instead, the SSA had relied on the report of one of their consulting experts who had never examined the claimant, only the records which had been relied on by the treating physician. The federal judge made it clear in their ruling that the opinion and findings of the treating physician were to be given "great deference" and that a consulting expert could not override the treating physician's findings in the event they had no additional evidence.

This "war story actually has two points. First, the treating physician carries a lot of weight. Second, if the claimant had seen fit to hire an attorney in the early stages they would have likely caught the mistake being made by the various entities in the claims process and been able to point out the treating physicians were not being given the proper consideration, thus shortening the waiting period before the claimant began receiving benefits. If someone is going to represent themselves in any legal matter, including applying for Social Security Disability, then they should be sure to be knowledgeable of the law and competent in the various issues.

While this book and the references given herein should contain the majority of what a claimant needs to know to win their case, they may also want to spend time reading case law from cases where the Social Security Administration has been sued in federal court. If you are unfamiliar with researching case law and legal research, in general, we would recommend you consider investing in The Guerrilla Guide to Legal Research: Finding the Law for Non-lawyers which is available at www.RebellionBooks.com.

IMPORTANT FACTORS CONCERNING MEDICAL RECORDS FROM TREATING PHYSICIANS/PROVIDERS

Timely Medical Records

Naturally, more recent medical records are particularly important with the SSA focusing on the six months prior to the application and the ones during the application process are generally viewed as key to the consideration. Older records can be important as well, particularly with a condition which progresses slowly. It is a good practice to identify more records rather than fewer although the obtaining of medical records is the reason most often cited for delays in the approval process.

Accurate Medical Records

Although the claimant is limited as to what they can do to assure the medical records are accurate, it is important the records be consistent as to the diagnosis, symptom(s), and condition. One thing the claimant does have control over is to try and follow the mainstream treatments and medical providers as much as possible. While many people believe in "natural" cures and methods of treating a variety of conditions the simple fact is that alternative health treatments are just not given as much credibility as traditional ones.

As an example, if a person is suffering from a disorder of the intestines, Irritable Bowel Syndrome for example, and prefers to be treated by a chiropractor as opposed to a gastroenterologist, then that is absolutely their right. However, they should be aware the examiner at the DDS or the Administrative Law Judge (ALJ) from the Social Security Administration are not as apt to take the chiropractor's diagnosis and treatments as serious as the treatments from the medical doctor. Thus, the claimant choosing to pursue alternative health treatments may hurt their chances, potentially severely, of being awarded disability benefits.

A claimant should never make the mistake of confusing their right to choose certain types of treatments with them exercising their right being the best course of action for their disability claim.

Adequate Amount of Medical Records

Unfortunately for many disability claimants, they only begin seeing a doctor and, thus accumulating records, when they decide to apply for benefits. Not only does this make it less likely the SSA will grant their application but it also limits the amount of time for which benefits could be granted. If the claimant had been suffering from the condition for months ahead of time then the benefits could have been retroactive to that time if records supported the time frame.

While the SSA will consider records recreated from the physician's memory, the officials aren't required to set aside their common sense and will almost certainly regard highly detailed records created from the memory of the physician with a degree of skepticism.

Still, records created from memory are better than no records at all.

Complete Medical Records

While doctors do keep notes of their visits with patients, the thoroughness of those records differs considerably from one doctor to another. Unfortunately, there isn't a lot a claimant can do to enhance the thoroughness of their doctor's record keeping. Doctors aren't well known for being receptive to suggestions from their patients and a claimant must always be aware that a request for more accurate records, more legible writing, etc. could end up getting a dreaded "secondary gain" notation in their records.

The best practice is to discuss the matter with the physician, making it clear that the applicant doesn't want to take up any more of their time than necessary, and explaining they are applying for disability. It is also a good opportunity to inquire as to whether the physician wants the claimant to keep a diary, notes, or some other method to track symptoms and a progression of the problems. It's been my experience that offering a great deal of deference to a doctor will go a long way. Like lawyers, physicians have large egos and often a little "stroking" of that ego will achieve the desired result.

An additional issue is that many applicants get mad at their doctors when they find the records aren't as complete or as legible as possible. Any lawyer who has done social security work to any degree has heard tales that of doctors being "paid off" by Social Security to prevent the claimant from receiving the benefits. Frankly, the allegation that this occurs is ridiculous when it comes to treating physicians. Not only would the SSA not perform such an act but, further, the physician would not endanger their license and livelihood by agreeing to perform such an act just as attorneys and judges don't get "bought off" by the other side to throw cases, or at least not to anywhere near the degree to which you hear the allegation being made by unsuccessful litigants.

What a claimant needs to remember is that the physician's job is to treat the patient for a condition and the records they make are for that purpose or, to a lesser degree, to provide documentation so the medical provider is paid by the insurance company.

So, all of this raises the question, "What can a claimant do to be sure the medical records are accurate and legible?".

The only step that is effective is for the applicant to review the medical records and make copies of any pages which contain sections that are not legible. The claimant can then highlight those sections, go to the physician's office and visit with the office manager and explain the situation. Once the office manager understand the situation and that the claimant is representing themselves they may be willing to type up any illegible notes or ask the doctor to clear up anything that is unclear.

A Patient's Right to Medical Records for Social Security Disability Purposes

A patient's right to have a copy of their medical records differs by state but as a general rule, it is a right although a patient would have to pay for the copies. Providers will require a patient to sign one or more forms to get their records, at least one of them being a HIPAA release form. While technically it isn't required when getting a copy of your own records, there is no way to convince the physician's office of this and no reason to waste the time trying. Signing a HIPAA form doesn't hurt a claimant in any way.

If a treating physician is reluctant to release the records, is rude or sarcastic, or generally not helpful then a claimant may consider looking for a new physician who is more receptive to the issues and the challenges faced by someone representing themselves in a disability claim.

Typically a medical provider will not have any objections to providing medical records to the Social Security Administration but, occasionally, there is an issue. Even when the physician agrees it can take months and, in reality, the SSA won't force the physician to provide the records since it involves them filing a lawsuit.

However, as has already been mentioned, the burden of proving the claimant is entitled to the benefits is on the claimant and therefore if the physician refuses to provide the records the claimant may be forced to hire an attorney to bring a lawsuit or to file a complaint with the state licensing agency for physicians.

Also, a claimant should be sure the Social Security Administration has the name and information of all medical providers and not just the treating physicians. This would include hospitals, laboratories where tests were performed, clinics, pharmacies, etc.

> ***Inside Trick:*** *It is often difficult for a claimant, or anyone else, to remember all of the different medical providers they may have seen or who performed services for them. One method used by lawyers to obtain a complete listing is to contact the medical health insurance provider and ask for a summary of benefits for all claims submitted, as opposed to claims paid, for the time period in which a disability is being claimed or in which a condition occurred which eventually resulted in a disability claim being made. This method usually provides as complete a listing as is possible to get from one source. To fill in the gaps the claimant can also go back through their bank records for the same period to look for canceled checks or debit card charges to medical providers. These two methods together can often give a complete record of the medical providers for the relevant time period.*

Records from Mental Health Professionals

Most states have an exclusion which allows mental health professionals to refuse to provide copies of their records to patients if, in the provider's opinion, the providing of the records could cause harm to the patient.

However, the professionals may not have an objection to providing a copy of the records directly to the SSA.

An additional option, if the mental health professional objects to providing the records to either the SSA *or* the patient, it is for the claimant to request that the mental health provider prepare a summary of their findings as they relate to the disability claim and provide that to the Social Security Administration. The summary should contain detailed information, findings, and comments about the information the SSA prefers to review when evaluating a mental disorder and should specifically address the requirements of the medical listing of the specific disability being claimed.

The final alternative, should none of these be acceptable, is to hire a lawyer to bring a lawsuit and force the mental health provider to furnish the records to the Social Security Administration.

Types of Information Needed from Treating Medical Providers

Rarely can a claimant provide too much information to the Social Security Administration but quite often they fail to provide enough. At a minimum the claimant should be sure their disability file contains the following:

- A medical history of the conditions which lead to the claim of disability. The time frame should include when the symptoms and complaints began appearing and not when they actually became disabling;
- Laboratory test findings and conclusion;
- The medical provider's (usually a doctor) prescribed treatment as well as any results or prognosis from that treatment;
- Any clinical findings including physical or mental examinations;
- The medical provider's opinion as to how the impairment or condition affects the claimant's abilities based on medical findings or observations. The report by the provider should specifically address any activities which would be involved with work such as standing, lifting,

sitting, carrying, etc. If the impairment is due to a mental condition then specific emphasis should be on the claimant's ability to understand, remember, and follow instructions and to interact appropriately with co-workers or superiors, customers, and the pressures of work.

NOTE: In the context of medical records and treatments a "complaint" is not a gripe which someone has, it is the description of a symptom, disease, or disorder or the symptom, disease, disorder itself. This is important to know so the claimant doesn't get defensive if the SSA workers, the DDS examiner, or anyone else in the disability process uses this description. It is a commonly used and is not meant in a derogatory fashion.

What to Do If the Medical Records Are Insufficient or Provide Evidence Which Is Not Helpful

In many cases the claimant becomes distressed when they review the medical records because it is obvious they are insufficient for the purposes of the Social Security Administration and the claim for disability benefits. This is not unusual and the records from many treating physicians suffer similar problems even though, the information contained therein is more than sufficient for a course of treatment of the patient. In addition, the medical file may not contain evidence of specific symptoms or issues either because the physician forgot to note them, did not consider them of importance in their plan of treatment, or, often, the patient simply forgot to mention them to the doctor.

Unfortunately, many medical providers detest doing paperwork even though it is required from the business end of their profession.

One of the things the claimant can do to prevent this from occurring is to discuss the matter with the treating physician as early in the process as possible. Let them know what the Social Security Administration will require as to medical evidence about the impairment and how the impairment affects the claimant's day to day ability to function. It should also be stressed to them that the SSA will require more than a simple letter stating the claimant has a disability.

Any letter from the doctor to the SSA should contain extensive detail about the impairment and its effect on daily life including walking, talking, the use of arms and legs and hands and feet, and many other issues potentially all the way down to breathing.

Instead of a letter, it is often a better idea for the doctor to send a Physical Residual Functional Capacity form (RFC). You can see an example of the RFC form in this book at Appendix E or on the Social Security Administration website at https://secure.ssa.gov/apps10/poms/images/SSA4/G-SSA-4734-U8-1.pdf. As with all other Social Security forms the RFC is subject to change and so it is best to run a Google search to find the current one by using the following terms:

Social Security RFC Form

It should be noted the form above is for a physical condition resulting in an impairment and disability. However, the Social Security Administration has a form which is slightly different and what should be used when the disability is due to a mental impairment. The Mental Residual Functional Capacity form can be seen at Appendix F or on the Social Security Administration website at http://ssaconnect.com/tfiles/SSA-4734-F4-SUP.pdf.

If the physician chooses to use an RFC form it would likely be extremely helpful for them to fill that out with the patient sitting there with them and able to answer any of the doctor's questions which may arise from the form. Many physicians, however, will be uncomfortable with that arrangement and it would not be a good idea for a claimant to push for this option with an uncomfortable medical provider.

Many physicians feel an ethical and moral obligation to assist their patients in every way possible and are more than willing to write a letter stating that the claimant is "permanently and totally disabled" regardless of the patient's actual condition. However, the physician's use of a generic term such as "disabled" without additional objective evidence is insufficient to meet the requirements or to show how the impairment limits the claimant's ability to function. It is possible to craft a letter which uses specific language and definitions from the Social Security Administration and which will increase the patient's chances of being approved (an example of such a letter can be found in Appendix G) but even then objective evidence must be contained in the file and records.

In conclusion, it's important for the claimant to bear in mind the physician is not the ultimate arbitrator of the question of disability under the Social Security Administration guidelines and doesn't make the final disability determination. Neither is the doctor an expert in job performance. However a treating medical provider does have an important part and a great deal of influence on the ultimate decision of a claim for disability benefits. This is through their providing medical evidence and information about the impairment(s) and the effect on the claimant's functioning both in life and at work.

THE ASSESSMENT AND OPINION OF YOUR TREATING PHYSICIAN

While we don't mean to be repetitious, it is impossible to stress enough how important your treating physician's statements and findings can be. The treating physician is so important to the process that the federal regulations require the SSA to accept their assessment unless the medical consultant of the DDS or the Administrative Law Judge (ALJ) can give a reasonable explanation for its rejection. Specific information about the claimant's condition will be given greater weight than the opinion of other doctors or even of the Social Security administration's own experts. The only exception to this is when the treating physician's opinion or assessment is not supported by the evidence or is directly contradicted by the evidence.

NOTE: While we have emphasized the importance of the treating physician's reports/opinions in this book, there are occasions when the treating physician does not believe the claimant is disabled, or, and this appears to be occurring more often, the physician simply doesn't like being involved in the disability process, or is skeptical about anyone receiving disability benefits.

If this is the situation then a claimant should first consider getting a new treating physician and, second, downplay the negative doctor's role as much as possible. Some doctors advertise that they do disability examinations and if the claimant can find one like that then a visit to them and a frank and honest discussion of their opinion on the process would be a very good idea.

Consulting Experts and Examinations in the Social Security Disability Process

While a person seeking Social Security Disability benefits would certainly have the right to hire consulting experts realistically this rarely occurs. So when we discuss consulting experts and examinations in the disability process were really talking about those experts retained and paid by the Social Security Administration.

Consulting experts are used by the SSA when they feel the records and other evidence provided by your treating medical professionals are inadequate to make a determination as to whether or not disability should be granted. While many people are opposed to the use of these experts, in reality, the claim would be denied if the SSA were only allowed to use the records of treating medical providers and those records were insufficient.

The SSA may use consulting experts or ask for a consultative examination in a variety of situations. These include:

- if the treating physician's records are not useful for disability purposes;
- if medical records of treating providers are not available for some reason;
- if the claimants do not have medical providers (for example in a case where the claimant simply couldn't afford medical care);
- in cases where the records from the treating doctors are too old;

- if the claimant has conditions or complaints for which they have never been treated.

In some cases, Consultative Examinations (CE) may be performed by a treating physician. However, that isn't as common as you might believe. Many treating physicians don't like to do the consultative examinations for a number of reasons. One of these is the physician is concerned there may be a strained relationship between them and the patient if the disability claim is denied and the CE is cited as a reason for that. Another reason may be simply that the SSA doesn't pay an amount for the CE which independent physician believes is sufficient.

Where treating physicians are unwilling or unable to perform the CE, the Social Security Administration then turns to an independent doctor called a Consultative Examiner to perform the required examination.

By definition an independent Consultative Examiner used by the Social Security Administration is considered an Acceptable Medical Source as that term has been discussed previously in this book. The Social Security Administration may use Consultative Examiners such as audiologists to round out a physician's reports or they may use physicians themselves. At this point in time, the SSA does not use alternative healers, chiropractors, naturopaths, or herbalists as consultative examiners.

While their duties and roles sound the same, Consultative Examiners as used by the SSA are not the same as Medical Consultants used by the DDS. To make it even more confusing, some SSA Consultative Examiners also serve as Medical Consultants to the DDS. While the identities may sometimes be the same the difference comes in their duties. A CE physician examines a claimant and then forwards their report and opinion to the SSA outlining what a claimant is able to do taking into account the claimant's medical condition. CE's do not make a medical disability determination. DDS Medical Consultants examine records, not claimants, and do have the authority to make a disability determination. The DDS medical consultants undergo special training by the SSA and DDS which teaches them how to make disability determinations.

Whether the individual is acting as a Consultative Examiner for the SSA or a Medical Consultant for the DDS the claimant doesn't incur any expense for the services. Both of these individuals, as well as any other CE's or MC's required during the process of making a claim for Social Security Disability benefits will be paid by the government.

THE CONSULTATIVE EXAMINATION REPORT

In the event a claimant undergoes a complete Consultative Examination the report will contain the following information at a minimum:

- A detailed history of the complainant's chief complaints.
- Important findings based on the examination, history as set forth by the claimant, and laboratory tests as related to the complaints. These can include positive findings shown by the test or by the observation of the Consultative Expert as well as a notation as to any expected findings which were not present.
- The results of any laboratory and other test performed according to the Listing of Impairments.
- The diagnosis and prognosis, in the consultative examiner's opinion, of the impairments.
- A statement regarding the abilities of the claimant in light of the impairments.

As stated earlier a physician who is not the claimant's treating physician who performs a Consultative Examination cannot decide whether the claimant qualifies for disability benefits and, while their input is useful in the disability process, it does not carry the same weight as the treating physician when supported by evidence.

In addition to the complete Consultative Examination, many CE's are *not* complete examinations but are, instead, specific in nature. When a Consultative Expert is requested to perform a narrow, specific test they are generally not requested to provide an analysis of what the claimant can and cannot do in light of their impairments.

If a claimant did not receive what they consider to be an adequate Consultative Examination then they have the right to complain. The complaint should always be in writing, even if accompanied by telephone call so that it can be placed in the disability file. If the CE took place while at the DDS level then the complaint should be made to the DDS examiner who arranged the CE. If the CE was done after the initial denial of disability and following an appeal to the administrative hearing level then the complaint should be made to the Administrative Law Judge assigned to the case. The claimant should not only set forth why they feel the examination was inadequate but should also request that they are sent to a different physician so they may be examined correctly. However, it should also be remembered this system involves professionals and any communications with the SSA, even those with complaints as to the Consultative Examination, should be done in a professional manner and with no vulgar language or expressions of personal feelings.

Symptoms of the Impairment(s)

During the Social Security Disability process, the claimant's life and the effects of the disability/impairment as well the symptoms will be examined as they relate to the claimant's ability to function in both daily activities as well as work.

Information about, and evidence of, the claimant's symptoms will be provided by a number of sources including treating medical providers, witnesses, records, and the claimant themselves. That information may include:

- Evidence of what a claimant does during a typical day
- How the symptoms and impairment affect the claimant's Activities of Daily Living (ADL's)

- A list of what activities or other factors may cause or aggravate the symptoms
- Detailed information about any medication taken by the claimant. This includes the name, dosage, side effects, and effectiveness of any medication (prescription or over-the-counter) used on a regular basis. In this context, medications include herbal or alternative medicine remedies whether prescribed or not.
- Other medical treatments used to relieve pain or other symptoms. An example of these might be hydrotherapy, acupuncture, physical therapy, etc.
- Anything the claimant does to relieve any symptoms.

An issue which is quickly becoming more common in Social Security Disability situations is the use of marijuana whether it is legal in the state where the claimant resides or not. At this time there is no clear advice which can or should be given regarding whether or not a claimant should report their use of marijuana to the Social Security Administration during the disability process. A claimant should be aware that, at least in the past, the SSA has taken the position it is compelled to consider marijuana use as a Drug Abuse or Alcoholism issue that could have a direct effect on the granting of disability benefits. Most lawyers will advise their clients not to voluntarily reveal marijuana usage but, at the same time, not to lie about it while under oath or in filling out any paperwork. A claimant always has the right to assert their Fifth Amendment privileges against discussing marijuana use with anyone from the Social Security Administration. Since this is an area of the law which is rapidly changing if a reader of this book is faced with a situation then they should take the time and visit with a local attorney about this issue before addressing it with the SSA.

SYMPTOMS AND THE SOCIAL SECURITY ADMINISTRATION

Symptoms are evaluated on a case-by-case basis. Because of this, it is extremely hard to prepare a game plan as to how best to present symptoms in any specific case to the Social Security Administration and the ability to make this evaluation and act on it is an area where an experienced attorney can make a great deal of difference.

The presence, or absence, of certain, specific symptoms will neither automatically grant the application for disability benefits nor result in their denial. The law requires the SSA to give considerations to each claimant's individual symptoms but the SSA examiners ***are not*** required to believe either that the symptoms exist or that they are as severe as the claimant may state. It is always best to have an Acceptable Medical Source provide objective evidence and findings which support the severity of the claimed symptoms. This can include testing procedures but even a mention of the symptoms in the notes of the AMS will certainly be of some assistance in evaluating the entirety of the disabling condition as well.

Additionally, evidence of the claimant taking measures to relieve the symptoms is, in itself, some proof of the symptoms. Likewise, the failure of a claimant to take any measures to address their symptoms may be taken as evidence that no symptoms actually exist or that the severity of the symptoms is less than now being claimed. In short, it is important for someone who is claiming a disability and claiming to have an impairment and symptoms from that impairment to take steps to treat the impairment and the symptoms. While, without doubt, there are many people who are simply unable to afford to obtain treatments from a doctor it is always better, as far as a claim for disability benefits, to have sought medical treatment.

The use of medication, both prescription and over the counter, to alleviate symptoms are in themselves some evidence that the symptoms exist. While many people dislike taking medication they should carefully consider what effect not taking the medication may have on their claim. While a person who has a low pain tolerance may find a condition to be so severe as to be crippling, that same situation could be alleviated through the use of some medication and if a doctor prescribes it then the claimant should not only follow the doctor's directions but should also be sure and discuss it on their next visit as well as look for alternatives which may also provide relief.

As discussed earlier, a disability claimant will at some point have to fill out a form describing how their symptoms, including pain, affects their Activities of Daily Living (ADL's). It is ***extremely*** important that a claimant not understate how their ADL's are affected by their symptoms. This is another place where the daily diary can come in handy. If, for instance, a claimant went to a movie theater to see a movie and had to leave an hour after the show began due to there being unable to sit for any longer than that it will be important to note that in the diary as well as on the information provided to the SSA. If the pain had gotten to the point they couldn't stand at the back of the theater to complete the movie but instead went home, took their pain medication, and then had to lie in bed for four hours before the pain subsided enough to allow them to move about it would be a good example of how pain affected a daily activity. An SSA representative would be less likely to believe a claimant had remembered the specifics of that situation, as well as any others, then they would be if the claimant reported they kept a daily diary and had noted the times and situation.

Once again, any notes in the records by the claimant's treating physician as to the severity of symptoms and their effect on the claimant would be good evidence.

We would stress that an exaggeration of symptoms or even outright fraud is more likely to hurt a claimant's case than to help it. Rarely is an applicant able to successfully fool their treating physicians, the Consultative Examiners, and the various employees of the Social Security Administration. There have been reports of claimant's renting wheelchairs, borrowing crutches or using someone else's walker when going for a Consultative Examination yet there is no notation in any medical records of a treating physician recommending or prescribing these devices.

This is the easiest way for a claimant to lose their disability case. Likewise, a person may be under observation from the time they enter an office to the time they leave. I once sat in a waiting room and watched through a full-length window as a person get out of their car and briskly walked across a parking lot and then, just before entering, suddenly slowed and bent over as if they couldn't walk except in a hunched position. That person then maintained that posture until they left again, not realizing that one of the experts in their case was sitting in the waiting room as well. I saw the expert make notes and while I don't know what happened in their case, I think it is a safe assumption that the expert's view was influenced a great deal by what they observed.

OTHER EVIDENCE

A part of the theory behind The Guerrilla Guides to the Law is using methods and resources which are unusual or a result of "outside the box" thinking. One area where this will come into play in the context of the Social Security Disability process is claimants looking for additional ways to prove their disability as well as places from which they can get evidence to support their claim.

It is not at all unusual to see an application for Social Security Disability benefits taken through to its conclusion, good or bad, and in which the applicant or lawyer has provided no evidence other than a list of the treating physicians. The "Guerrilla" method would require the claimant to look for additional sources primarily in the area of people who are willing to be a witness for the claimant or, at least, write a letter on their behalf. These sources could include relatives, social workers, babysitters, members of the claimant's church, clergy, fellow employees, employers, friends, and even the cashier or "bag boy" at the local grocery store if the claimant sees them regularly and they are familiar with the claimant's physical problems. In the same notebook discussed earlier in this book and used to track the various information involved in the disability process, the applicant should consider making an ongoing list of people who can testify to any condition which supports their claim for benefits. Naturally, before calling them as a witness the claimant wants to be sure that the person will not say anything which hurts the claim for disability. For instance, in a case in which a back injury is at issue, a claimant might call the bag boy as a witness to testify that for months he has been using twice as many bags for the claimant's groceries to keep the weight of each individual bag at a minimum. However, the same bag boy would ***hurt*** the case if he were to testify he had recently seen the claimant unload a 50-pound bag of dog food from the shopping cart into the trunk of their car.

This example is also a good one to demonstrate that a claimant who chooses to represent themselves in the disability process must "think like a lawyer" and evaluate not only what they will ask a witness (no matter who the witness is) but also what else the witness may say and how the claimant will need to react to any potential remarks.

When looking for witnesses to support their case the claimant must always keep in mind that while any type of evidence may help their case, nothing is as beneficial as evidence from the claimant's treating physician or from an Acceptable Medical Source recognized by the Social Security Administration.

What Information Matters Most

While all medical records are necessary for SSA to render a finding of disability, the claimant's age, education, and work experience play a large role in the decision.

If the claimant has an impairment, but not severe enough to meet the definition of a disability, the SSA will then consider vocational factors such as the claimant's age, education, and work experience to determine if that person can be classified as disabled.

The SSA uses the Medical Vocational Guidelines (MVG) tables (found in Appendix C) in conjunction with the RFC to determine disability. Table 1 is used for claimants who perform sedentary work. Table 2 is for claimant's who perform light work and Table 3 is for medium work. Heavy work is not included in the tables.

The Medical Vocational Guidelines are only used if the claimant is physically restricted from returning to work. These rules also help to determine if you can perform any other type of work.

Age

A claimant's application will be evaluated under the following age groups:

- Younger - Under 50 years old
- Closely Approaching Advanced Age - 50-54 years old

- Advanced Age - 55 and older
- Closely Approaching Retirement Age - 60 or older

The age of the claimant is important in relation to the ability to adapt to a new work situation. This means the older the claimant the greater the chance the claimant will be found disabled. Typically the age of 55 and over have a higher chance of a disability determination than under 55.

Residual Functional Capacity

After the age group is confirmed, the claimant will be evaluated for Residual Functional Capacity or RFC. The RFC determines what abilities you have after the onset of your condition or disability. The RFC can be sedentary, light work, or medium work.

For example: If the claimant was a construction worker before he hurt his back and after he hurt his back all he could do is sit or lay down even when taking pain medication, then his RFC would be sedentary.

If the claimant was a teacher who hurt his back and takes pain medication but the medication makes the person dizzy and not function correctly, then his RFC would be sedentary.

Education

Education is defined as formal schooling or training is used as a factor. When completing an application for disability the applicant will be asked about education. The SSA will accept what you submit and typically does not question it.

An Education Category will be evaluated as:

Illiteracy - someone who is unable to read or write a simple message such as instructions

Marginal Education - someone who has sufficient ability to reason, solve simple math calculations, and possess language skills to perform unskilled types of jobs.

Limited Education - someone who has some ability in reasoning, math, and language skills, but not enough to do perform complex job duties in a semi-skilled or skilled job. This is typically some whose formal education ended between seventh and eleventh grade.

High School Education and Above - someone who has completed high school and may have more education. This person has abilities in reasoning, math, and language skills. The

SSA generally considers this category to be semi-skilled through skilled work.

Work Experience

Work experience is the skills you have acquired through your past work. Your work experience is relevant to your ability to transition to another job. Your experience could contain skilled, semi-skilled or unskilled work.

Skilled work typically involves advanced education and the mental ability to perform such work. Skilled work requires judgment, dealing with people, working with facts and figures, reading blueprints, or relating complex ideas.

Semi-skilled work requires some skills but not complex ideas. This can include alertness, focus, inspecting, testing, guarding property or materials, and other activities.

Unskilled work is work that needs little to no judgment. It includes simple tasks that can be learned on the job. Typically if the job can be learned in 30 days it is unskilled work.

Transferrable Skills are skills learned from your past work which could be used in other work. If your skills can be transferred to other work, then most likely your application for disability will be denied. Transferrable skills is only for semi-skilled and skilled work.

To use the Medical Vocational Guidelines table (found in Appendix C) first locate the table which corresponds to your Residual Functional Capacity (sedentary, light work or medium work).

Next, search for the line that contains your age, education, and skills. The last column will refer to the disability determination.

THE "DECIDERS" IN THE SOCIAL SECURITY DISABILITY CLAIMS PROCESS

It is often quite difficult to read the actual materials of the Social Security Administration. However, knowing who will be involved in this section of the claims process is extremely important and therefore the actual website pages for the "Deciders" will be attached as Appendix H. Feel free to look those over before beginning this section.

As we've discussed, the initial step in the Social Security Disability process is a determination that the claimant has met the basic, non-medical eligibility requirements to receive benefits, usually that they have worked and earned a sufficient number of credits. This is done first since if the claimant hasn't worked a sufficient number of quarters then they are absolutely disqualified and there is no need for the Social Security Administration to spend funds, time, and effort in evaluating the medical situation.

However, if the initial requirement is met then the file is sent to a new agency to evaluate and make a decision on the application. The agency responsible for this is called the Disability Determination Services (DDS). They will receive the initial application which was filed as well as any medical records or other relevant paperwork in the file.

Although the DDS offices are operated by the states, their budget is provided by the federal government and, as such, they are required to follow all federal statutes, regulations, and laws.

The Disability Determination Services task is to handle the various types of disability claims. These types include:

- **New applications** (aka initial claims). It is important to note that if a claimant is turned down at all the different levels they can then refile another initial claim. There is no limit to the number of initial claims a person can file.
- **Reconsiderations.** A reconsideration (if the claimant has been turned down and requested that the agency reconsider the denial)
- **Continuing disability reviews**. These are where the DDS reviews a file of a claimant who has previously been awarded disability to see if their condition has improved.

NOTE: *When a person is involved in applying for disability but is too sick or hurt to continue the process the DDS can* *put a hold on the process, known as "diarying a claim", until such time as the person can continue. The need for the claim to be diaried does not have to relate to the condition for which disability is sought.*

DDS Employees

Administrative workers

Of course, as in almost any office, many DDS workers are administrative personnel. These include secretaries and clerks. While the disability applicant may see or talk to some of these individuals, they generally don't interact with the public to any extensive degree.

Claims Examiners and Vocational Analysts

A DDS claims examiner is assigned to an applicant's file very quickly after it arrives at the DDS office.

The claims examiner has a myriad of duties, but normally they review the application and make sure that all of the medical records are either in the file or on order, establish contact with the applicant, and do any other work necessary to get the file ready for review.

Another part of their job is to handle most of the non-medical issues involved in a claim. This can include ensuring the file contains the age, education, and work experience necessary to determine an applicant's potential and possible vocational courses of action. The claims examiner is also the person who arranges for consultative examinations and makes sure the applicant is aware of the date and time and interacts with the DDS medical consultants. A part of this interaction is often requesting advice on medical impairments as well as determining what type of additional medical evidence is required for the file and to make a decision on the claim.

One of the hard parts about being a claims examiner for the DDS is simply keeping up with the ever-changing rules. To stay up to date they rely on a publication called the *Program Operations Manual System* (POMS), which is a multi-volume tome that is online at https://secure.ssa.gov/poms.nsf/home!readform as well as going to their supervisors, who can then ask their supervisors, etc.

In addition to the claims examiners, and in a job which initially seems very similar, are the vocational analysts.

While most people only meet or talk to the claims examiner assigned to their case, the vocational analysts can also call if they have specific questions about work history or a claimant's education.

> ***IMPORTANT NOTE****: Occasionally a person finds themselves in the position of being in the process of applying for disability while at the same time there is a lawsuit pending regarding the incident which caused the disability or other bodily injuries. If the applicant is represented by an attorney and they receive calls from anyone purporting to be involved in the Social Security process or in any way are asking questions about their condition, disability, work history or prospects, etc. the applicant should contact their attorney. There have been cases where people misrepresent themselves to obtain "inside information" about a person for use in the lawsuit.*

Of course, when dealing with the DDS there is also a good chance you will speak with secretaries, assistants, and other administrative personnel. You are certainly entitled to be addressed and spoken to with respect but the DDS, as well as the Social Security Administration in general, are huge bureaucracies and are a part of both the state and federal government and thus the workers are subject to demands from every side. If you feel the DDS worker isn't doing something correctly on your case, is treating you rudely, or you have some other real concern then you are entitled to ask to speak with someone higher up, whether that be a direct supervisor or even further up the chain of command. However, most experts will agree that the nicer a person is, the better the chance any "judgment calls" will be decided in their favor as far as their file and its contents.

Another important piece of information to be aware of is that while the Disability Determination Services play a key part in putting together the information for review by the Social Security Administration's medical consultants, disability hearing officers, and, perhaps most importantly in the overall plan, the Administrative Law Judge, DDS doesn't actually *make* any of the decisions as to whether an applicant will or will not be granted disability subject to the restrictions in the next paragraph about the Disability Examiner. They are included in this section on the Deciders, simply because they can decide what information is missing or makes it into the file.

Disability Examiner

It's a little unclear whether the Disability Examiner is also the Claims Examiner or exactly how the distinction is made. However, what is not unclear is that the Disability Examiner performs many of the same functions as the Claims Examiner and can, under a specific set of circumstances, actually deny an application for disability. The circumstances when this can occur are set forth in the Roles and Responsibilities of the DE, MC, PC, and MA section of POMS which can be seen in Appendix H.

The POMS manual states specifically:

The DE alone may make the disability determination in the following situations:

No medical evidence exists in the current file or in any prior files and (despite making every reasonable effort) the DDS is unable to obtain any medical evidence that may exist and one or more of the following situations exists:

- *the claimant refuses or fails, without a good reason, to attend a CE as explained in DI 23007.009 and DI 23007.010;*

- *the DDS curtails CE development after establishing the claimant's failure or refusal to cooperate as explained in DI 23007.004E and DI 23007.005H; or*
- *the date last insured or other technical factor is in the past, and there is no possibility of setting an onset prior to the end of the entitlement period. (For additional information about technical factors in the past see DI 25510.006G.)*

The DE has single decision maker (SDM) authority in a prototype or SDM II DDS and the claim meets SDM requirements as explained in DI 12015.100B.1.

The DE has the authority to use the procedures for quick disability determinations (QDD) and compassionate allowance initiative (CAL) determinations as explained in DI 23023.001.

What is most important about this section is the Disability Examiner is allowed to reject an application ***if*** there is no medical evidence in the file ***and*** the claimant/applicant refuses to cooperate in attending a Claims Examination, fails to see experts selected by the DDS and/or SSA, and, in general, refuses to assist in the information gathering process.

In reality, this process of denial is rarely seen, but the most likely scenario is when the Disability Examiner has requested the claimant to see a physician assigned for the purposes of determining impairment and the claimant simply refuses to do so. At that point, there appears to be almost a presumption that the person seeking disability is trying to hide information, a presumption with which most lawyers who have dealt with similar situations would likely agree.

Medical Consultants

This is one of the most important people with whom an applicant will have contact, either in person or through paperwork, in the disability process.

The term "Medical Consultant" is very general and all-encompassing and can include almost any category of physicians as well as a mental health professional if they have a Ph.D.

In most cases the Medical Consultant will render their opinion purely on their evaluation of the file, never meeting or actually examining the applicant.

The Medical Consultant's determination of whether a person qualifies for the disability benefits includes:

- Conducting an evaluation of the medical evidence to determine if the impairment claimed by the applicant meets the requirements in the Listing of Impairments
- Describing the applicant's residual functional capacity (RFC), the manner in which the impairments cause limitations in abilities as well as assessing the severity of the impairments

Unfortunately, many people representing themselves and seeking disability benefits look only at the reasons the benefits should be granted. They make a severe tactical mistake by not taking into account the reasons the benefits might be denied and preemptively addressing those. That's the reason attorneys usually have a higher rate of getting people approved. They are trained from the first day of law school to look at both sides of every case and lower any damage negative information can create.

NOTE ON TERMINOLOGY: From this point on in the book we may use DDS (Disability Determination Services), SSA (Social Security Administration), or refer to the SSA office interchangeably unless the specific name makes a difference. Most people who apply for disability never realize they are dealing with various entities since most of the information comes to them on papers with the Social Security Administration letterhead. If they are required to fill out a form they do so on the SSA website or at the local SSA office, and if they reach the point where they go before an Administrative Law Judge, all the signs and information pointing them to the room mention Social Security. This is another of those instances where almost everyone in the process on the claimant's end just say Social Security even when they are talking about the DDS.

It is important to understand the reasons for the denial of benefits since the denial can come into play at any stage in the proceedings. The initial denial can be made by the DDS after looking at the records; a denial can come from the Administrative Law Judge (ALJ) after the hearing process (discussed in the next section); a denial can come from an appeal of the ALJ order to the Appeals Council; or, finally, a denial after filing a federal lawsuit.

The following are the most common reasons for the initial denial of a claim for disability benefits:

Too Much Work (Substantial Gainful Activity) (SSDI Only)

This section is ***only*** dealing with SSDI, or the type of disability you can draw based on prior work history and ***is not applicable*** to a claim for SSI, which is needs based.

The most obvious, and likely the most common, reason for the denial of disability benefits (SSDI) is simply that the applicant is still working to such an extent that the Social Security Administration (SSA) believes they do not meet the definition of being disabled. As a reminder, the SSA uses the following definition:

> " To meet our definition of disability, you must not be able to engage in any substantial gainful activity (SGA) because of a medically-determinable physical or mental impairment(s): That is expected to result in death or that has lasted or is expected to last for a continuous period of at least 12 months."
>
> https://www.ssa.gov/redbook/eng/definedisability.htm

As mentioned elsewhere in this book for SSDI applicants who ***are no***t blind, the limit on earnings from substantial gainful activity (SGA) at the time of the publication of this book is $1,180.00 per month. If the applicant ***is*** blind then the limit on what can be earned from SGA is $ 1,970.00 per month. This number is reevaluated on a regular basis and can change from year to year so it is important that the applicant is aware of the amount. The current figure can be found in Appendix I or on the SSA website at https://www.ssa.gov/oact/cola/sga.html.

Unlike some state and private insurance disability plans, with disability benefits from the SSA, it is an all or nothing proposition. If you earn more than the amount allowed for the month, then you receive no benefits. If you earn the set amount or less, you receive full benefits.

This is an important concept so we'll give a simple example here of the amount of SGA which can disqualify a claimant who is not blind, but assuming their medical condition is otherwise disabling:

If at the current numbers described above, the applicant earns $1,175 in a month, then they are disabled and will draw a full benefit check.

If instead, the applicant earns $ 1,181 each month, then they have exceeded the limit and will not receive any SSA disability benefits for that month.

TOO MANY ASSETS (SSI ONLY)

Just as the ***last*** section dealt with SSDI claimants only, ***this*** section deals only with SSI, the type of disability due to a medical condition as well as the claimant having limited or no resources.

The rules regarding SSI and the monthly income limit is different and much, ***much*** more complicated to calculate than with regular disability. There is a complete explanation of the various considerations in Appendix J and on the SSA website at https://www.ssa.gov/ssi/text-income-ussi.htm .

The SSA does have strict definitions on what is deemed income or assets. These are defined on the page set forth in Appendix J and the link above. The following section is taken directly from that page:

What is Income?

<u>Earned Income</u> *is wages, net earnings from self–employment, certain royalties, honoraria, and sheltered workshop payments.*

<u>Unearned Income</u> *is all income that is not earned, such as Social Security benefits, pensions, State disability payments, unemployment benefits, interest income, and cash from friends and relatives.*

<u>In–Kind Income</u> *is food or shelter that you get for free or less than its fair market value.*

<u>Deemed Income</u> *is the part of the income of your spouse with whom you live, your parent(s) with whom you live, or your sponsor (if you are an alien), which we use to compute your SSI benefit amount.*

Why is Income Important in the SSI Program?

Generally, the more countable income you have, the less your SSI benefit will be. If your countable income is over the allowable limit, you cannot receive SSI benefits. Some of your income may not count as income for the SSI program.

What is particularly helpful to the applicant, and a little surprising, is the SSA states "*not all income will count for SSI purposes*". The website gives a complete list, which can change at any moment, but at the time of the writing of this book the income that does not count for SSI purposes includes:

- the first $20 of most income received in a month;
- the first $65 of earnings and one–half of the earnings over $65 received in a month;
- the value of the Supplemental Nutrition Assistance Program (food stamps) received;
- income tax refunds;

- home energy assistance;
- assistance based on need funded by a State or local government, or an Indian tribe;
- small amounts of income received irregularly or infrequently;
- interest or dividends earned on countable resources or resources excluded under other Federal laws;
- grants, scholarships, fellowships or gifts used for tuition and educational expenses;
- food or shelter based on need provided by nonprofit agencies;
- loans to you (cash or in–kind) that you have to repay;
- money someone else spends to pay your expenses for items other than food or shelter (for example, someone pays your telephone or medical bills);
- income set aside under a Plan to Achieve Self–Support (PASS;
- earnings up to $1,8200 per month to a maximum of $7,350 per year (effective January 2018) for a student under age 22;

- the cost of impairment–related work expenses for items or services that a disabled person needs in order to work;
- the cost of work expenses that a blind person incurs in order to work;
- disaster assistance;
- the first $2,000 of compensation received per calendar year for participating in certain clinical trials;
- refundable Federal and advanced tax credits received on or after January 1, 2010; and
- certain exclusions on Indian trust fund payments paid to American Indians who are members of a federally recognized tribe

If the source of income is only what is earned from working and the SSI payments then the total monthly earnings for 2018 could be up to $1481 per month to a maximum of $ 7200 per year. However, as you can see from the definitions and examples above, the calculation is considerably more than that and any decisions should be based on the formulas provided by the SSA on the above referenced webpage or an amount provided, in writing, by the SSA. The reason I specifically mention "in writing" is that any oral representations made by the employees of the SSA can't really be counted on as evidence.

Whether someone is trying to draw or is actually drawing, SSI or SSDI, earning income doesn't automatically mean a disqualification from benefits. The Social Security Administration will usually allow a trial period during which they will be allowed to draw benefits. The trial period is usually 9 months, consecutive or not, during a 60 month period. Historically, the amount used for the trial period has changed nearly every year. Beginning January 1, 2019, that amount was set at $880 but, as with anything else that relies on data or figures provided by the SSA, or any part of any government for that matter, the amount should be checked regularly and the SSA provides these numbers at https://www.ssa.gov/oact/cola/twp.html (also in Appendix K).

Duration of Disability Is Too Short

Another frequent reason for the denial of benefits is there is no, or not enough, evidence to convince the SSA that the condition(s) causing the disability is severe enough to last at least 12 months or result in your death. As explained earlier, this is absolutely required to be eligible for disability payments to be approved, unless the applicant is blind and applying for SSI only.

While the claimant may be convinced, and may even have been told by medical providers, that their condition will last more than the minimum time required, this must be documented and proven for an award of benefits. Claimants attempting to represent themselves forget to do so and accordingly the claim is denied.

FAILING TO RESPOND TO REQUESTS FROM THE SSA

Incredibly, many claimants, even those represented by attorneys, do not appear to take the process with the seriousness it deserves. Whether this is because they believe their disability is so clear the benefits cannot be denied, an inability to follow through, or in some cases, simple laziness. The failure to respond to a request from the Social Security Administration is likely the easiest way to have benefits denied (more about this in the following section).

Unfortunately, many people lose their disability cases by moving and failing to notify the SSA of the address change so they can be notified of any requests or proceedings. Unlike many

things involving the SSA, changing your address and contact information is relatively easy. The changes can be made by visiting the local SSA office, being sure to get some kind of written confirmation of the change, by logging into your "***My Social Security***" account and go to the **My Profile** tab, by calling 1-800-772-1213 (TTY 1-800-325-0778) Monday through Friday from 7 a.m. to 7 p.m., or by following the instructions on the following webpage:
https://faq.ssa.gov/link/portal/34011/34019/Article/3704/-How-can-I-change-my-address

FAILING TO COOPERATE

As was referenced earlier, a claimant is under an affirmative duty to cooperate with both the Social Security Administration and the treating physicians.

Further, any attempt to appeal the case further than the Administrative Law Judge process (which will be discussed in the next chapter) can be summarily dismissed if the claimant has ignored requests or orders to provide additional materials, submit to examinations, or in any way has failed to cooperate.

While there are some exceptions or excuses which can be used to explain away what appears to initially be a failure to cooperate, it is still a risk. A claimant going through the efforts of being willing to do what the SSA asks ranks just slightly harder than changing the contact address.

The SSA often requests additional paperwork be completed either due to an incomplete file, an evaluation of the file which revealed what they believe to be insufficient information or a new set of forms having been required by the powers that be. Anyone who has ever dealt with government bureaucracies will agree it's substantially easier just to do what they want than it is to try and get the rules changed. While, certainly, a person is entitled to stand by their principles at some point they may have to make a decision on whether those principles are worth a delay in receiving benefits or possibly even a denial or loss of those benefits.

A similar decision, principles versus benefits, may have to be made with other topics as well. Every lawyer who does Social Security Disability cases has had clients who have strongly opposed following certain recommendations of their treating physicians, not wanting to meet with "experts" retained by the Social Security Administration, or something similar.

If a treating doctor has made treatment recommendations and the claimant refuses to follow them, the SSA will almost certainly make the assumption the reason is the claimant is more concerned with not recovering and instead, stretching out the time to draw benefits or reinforcing their position as to their disability. This assumption can usually be reinforced by the opinion of an expert who is paid by the SSA, although everyone would like to think this isn't the way the system works.

However, there are some excuses or exceptions which can provide a claimant at least a possibility of it being considered a legitimate objection. The SSA has even devoted a section of its website to discussing reasons for a Failure to Follow Prescribed Treatments. The pertinent areas are listed below and you can review the entire section at https://www.ssa.gov/OP_Home/rulings/di/02/SSR82-59-di-02.html .

"Under circumstances such as those described below, an individual's failure to follow prescribed treatment will be generally accepted as "justifiable" and, therefore, such "failure" would not preclude a finding of "disability" or that disability continues.

1. Acceptance of prescribed treatment would be contrary to the teachings and tenets of the claimant's or beneficiary's religion. A finding of disability would be in order where the evidence establishes that the disabled individual rejects prescribed treatment on the grounds that he or she is a member of a church which teaches that healing may be accomplished only through faith or prayer.

In such a case, the claimant or beneficiary must be asked to identify church affiliation. In addition, a statement or other information from either church authorities or other members of the religious order must be obtained to substantiate that the individual is a member of the church. Additionally, the church's position relative to medical treatment must ordinarily be documented (see note below for exception) by obtaining either church literature or a statement from church authorities concerning the teachings and tenets of the church.

NOTE: In Christian Science cases, it is not necessary to develop church teachings since it is well established that such teachings proscribe acceptance of medical treatment. In these cases, a statement by a Christian Science practitioner or church authority verifying the individual's membership suffices.

2. Cataract extraction for one eye is prescribed but the loss of visual efficiency in the other eye is severe and cannot be corrected through treatment.

3. In an unusual case, a claimant's or beneficiary's fear of surgery may bc so intense and unrelenting that it is, in effect, a contraindication to surgery. If a treating source who had advised surgery later decides that the individual's fear is so great that the individual is not a satisfactory candidate for surgery, there is no issue of "failure."

Where fear of surgery is suggested to be extreme, but the treating source has limited contact with the person and is unable to indicate the significance of the fear, an independent examination by a psychiatrist may be warranted as a means of resolving whether the fear contraindicates surgery.

Attendant to allegations of fear, it is not uncommon to see surgery refused on the grounds that the absolute success of such treatment has not been "guaranteed." No physician can guarantee the results of a major surgical procedure since any surgery generally entails some degree of risk. An individual may also attempt to justify refusal of surgery on the grounds of alleged personal or third party knowledge of persons who did not improve, or perhaps worsened, following surgery similar to that recommended to the individual by a treating physician. However, such reason(s) for nonacceptance of surgical treatment will not, in and of itself, negate a finding of "failure."

4. The individual is unable to afford prescribed treatment which he or she is willing to accept, but for which free community resources are unavailable. Although a free or subsidized source of treatment is

often available, the claim may be allowed where such treatment is not reasonably available in the local community. All possible resources (e.g., clinics, charitable and public assistance agencies, etc.), must be explored. Contacts with such resources and the claimant's financial circumstances must be documented. Where treatment is not available, the case will be referred to VR.

5. Any duly licensed treating medical source who has treated the claimant or beneficiary advises against the treatment prescribed for the currently disabling condition. Thus, if a person has two treating sources who take opposing views regarding treatment, one recommending and one advising against the same treatment, failure to follow the recommended treatment was justifiable. (Where an individual chooses to follow treatment recommended by one treating source, to the exclusion of alternative treatment recommended by one or more other treating sources, the issue of "failure" does not arise.)

6. The claimant or beneficiary is presently unable to work because of a condition for which major surgery was performed with unsuccessful results, and additional major surgery is prescribed for the same impairment.

7. The treatment carries a high degree of risk because of the enormity or unusual nature of the procedure (e.g., organ transplant, open heart surgery).

8. The treatment recommended involves amputation of an extremity (e.g., amputation at or above the tarsal region).

The specific reasons listed above are not all-inclusive as acceptable justifications for refusing to accept prescribed treatment. A full evaluation must be made in each case to determine whether the individual's reason(s) for failure to follow prescribed treatment is justifiable."

An additional reason that isn't covered well in the quoted sections above or elsewhere on the SSA website, likely because it doesn't happen often, is when the claimant doesn't have a treating physician. If a claimant has only seen a doctor a few times and the doctor makes a recommendation as to treatment, that recommendation could be challenged on the basis that the relationship between the claimant and the physician isn't of sufficient duration or hasn't been detailed enough for the doctor to have a thorough knowledge of the patient's condition(s).

Also, the physicians and consultants performing the examinations on behalf of the SSA are not considered treating physicians and therefore an objection could be raised if the SSA takes the position the claimant is going to be disqualified for not following their recommendations.

Disability Based on Drug or Alcohol Addiction

Up until 1996, alcoholism or a dependency on drugs could form a basis or be a contributing factor to a disability of determination. Unfortunately, in that year the infamous "Contract With America" was passed and beginning on the day of enactment, SSA ceased to award SSI payments and SSD benefits to new applicants. Some people who were already in the process or had been awarded benefits under the old laws and definitions would continue to draw benefits...for a while. If you want more of the history of the legislation and the results you can see a detailed explanation at https://www.ssa.gov/policy/docs/rsnotes/rsn2001-02.html .

While it looked like these rules may have been slowly changing again in favor of the applicants, those changes came to a screeching halt with the Congress and Presidential elections of 2016. As lawyers well know, the ease with which applications are granted varies tremendously depending on what political party is in control of the government.

However, as the law stands at the time of the writing of this book, the SSA will not grant disability benefits, either SSDI or SSI, if alcoholism or drug addiction is a ***"contributing factor"*** to the disability. For brevity's sake, we will refer to the substance abuse initials/acronym used by the Social Security Administration, "DAA" for Drug Addiction and Alcoholism.

So what is the definition of "contributing factor"? Unfortunately, there is no clear definition on the SSA website. What we can find however, is the test they use to determine if DAA is a disqualifier. The SSA states:

> "[T]he key factor we will examine in determining whether drug addiction or alcoholism is a contributing factor material

to the determination of disability is whether we would still find a claimant disabled if he or she stopped using drugs or alcohol."

So, what the SSA is essentially saying is they will not grant benefits if the primary reason for the disability is the applicant cannot stop drinking or using drugs. However, this means a claimant can still be granted benefits if their prior history of drug addiction or alcoholism has caused conditions which are now disabling. One example of this would be if a person's substance abuse had caused cirrhosis of the liver and damage to such a point the liver was unable to repair itself, leaving the claimant weak, his blood not clotting properly, and other conditions which would be disabling regardless of the cause and if any further substance abuse were stopped, the results would not improve significantly.

How The Evaluation for DAA is Done

First, a determination is made, separate from the disability determination, as to whether the DAA is relevant to the impairment(s) causing the disability. The relevancy to the disability will only be found to be true if the medical impairments are severe enough to be disabling.

The DAA determination is based on medical evidence sufficient to meet the requirements for that condition found in the Diagnostic and Statistical Manual of Mental Disorders published by the American Psychiatric Association. This publication, depending on the edition, is commonly referred to as the DSM-III, DSM-IV, etc. and describes the standard diagnostic criteria used to make a determination of any mental impairment but specifically in this section the finding of Drug Addiction or Alcoholism.

The medical evidence to support the finding that the claimant has DAA is provided by an acceptable medical source such as a medical doctor, licensed psychologist, etc.

One of the few factors working in the applicant's favor is that statements by the claimant are not, in themselves, sufficient to establish DAA. There must be independent corroborative evidence of the disorder or condition. Having said this, it is better not to say things like "I am a drug addict" or "I am an alcoholic" when a person knows those statements may be recorded in the medical or other records. Technically, the determination of drug addiction or alcoholism is a medical diagnosis and a claimant shouldn't be diagnosing themselves. The claimant should, however, answer truthfully about their consumption of alcohol or drugs since that information can assist in diagnosing other conditions or allow for proper care.

Does The Determination of DAA Prevent Approval of Benefits?

Once the SSA has found that the claimant is disabled, the claimant has a drug addiction or alcoholism, and that the DAA is relevant, the next determination to be made by the Social Security Administration is whether DAA is a contributing factor to the disability. Remember, the determination of whether it is a contributing factor simply means an answer to the question, "If the claimant stopped drinking or using drugs, would they still be disabled?"

A medical consultant will usually be used to answer the two following questions and the answer to these will determine whether the DAA is a contributing factor:

1. Which of the current physical or mental limitations would remain if the claimant ceased the use of drugs or alcohol?
2. Would the limitations which remain still mean the claimant was disabled?

While a medical consultant will likely be retained by the SSA to answer these two questions, the claimant may be able to head this off by having their treating physician answer these two questions in either a notation in the medical records or in a letter to the Social Security Administration. Even if the SSA still uses their medical consultant, there is case law stating the SSA and/or the Administrative Law Judge is to give greater weight to the opinions and findings of treating physicians than it is to their retained experts.

Many people, including some who are a part of the SSA disability process, get confused at this stage of the proceedings so it is extremely important for the claimant to understand what is ***not*** a disqualification. The law ***does not state*** a person cannot draw disability benefits if they are disabled due to the permanent damage(s) done to their body by drug abuse or alcoholism.

So, to summarize this section, even if damage has been done to the claimant's body by DAA, those damages have caused a condition which will last for more than 12 months or result in their death, the damages prevent the claimant from engaging in any substantial gainful activity, and ceasing the use of alcohol or drugs (other than prescription medications), then the claimant should be awarded disability benefits.

The three pages of the SSA website which set this forth, and which can be used to argue the claimant's case if anyone in the disability process uses the wrong standard, can be found at:

https://www.ssa.gov/OP_Home/cfr20/416/416-0935.htm

https://www.ssa.gov/OP_Home/rulings/di/01/SSR2013-02-di-01.html

https://secure.ssa.gov/poms.nsf/lnx/0490070050

CONVICTION OF A CRIME

The legislature often tries to disqualify people from various types of government benefits simply because they have been convicted of certain crimes. To date, they have been unsuccessful in most of these attempts, with one exception, to completely prevent the award of benefits from the SSA in these types of cases. We will cover the three main situations where the question arises including the one set of circumstances which results in a complete disqualification.

Felony Convictions

While a felony conviction, alone, won't disqualify a person from receiving SSA benefits assuming, of course, they meet all of the requirements to be considered disabled. However, a person cannot draw benefits for themselves while they are in jail or prison after a felony conviction. There are a number of publications available on the internet and for sale which state otherwise but they are absolutely incorrect in the general information. There is an exception which may apply if the person is in a rehabilitation program which has been approved by the court and which is likely to result in the convicted person getting a job when they are released if the anticipated release is within a reasonable period of time. There is little guidance on when this situation applies and in 20+ years of dealing with Social Security Disability claims we've never heard of this applying. Nonetheless, it is a possible exception although, with this one, the claimant should seriously consider hiring a lawyer to help them since it is such a rare situation, these facts are almost certainly going to mean an initial denial and then an appearance before an ALJ at a hearing, and the matter should be thoroughly researched and briefed since the Administrative Law Judge is likely to have either never had a case involving this issue or, at best, will only have had a few.

Disabling Injuries Occurred While in Prison or Jail

If the injuries or impairments resulting in a disabling condition occurred or an existing impairment was worsened while the claimant was in prison or jail, the person cannot draw benefits while in prison or jail. However, the claim for benefits could be started while still incarcerated but benefits could not be drawn while incarcerated nor could the time in prison be a part of the "retroactive benefits" or "back pay".

Disabling Injuries From Committing a Felony

The one absolute exclusion under this section is where the disabling injuries occurred during the commission of a felony for which the person was convicted. If this occurred, then the claimant can never use those injuries as the basis for receiving disability benefits. It is extremely unlikely this section of the law will ever change although there could, potentially, be some creative ways around the exclusion. This is another situation that is rarely seen and to be successful in making this claim would almost certainly require the services of an attorney and a complete review of the medical records before the initial application for benefits was ever made.

Commission of Fraud in the Application Process

If a claimant engages in fraudulent activity, either alone or with the assistance of others, which enables them to draw benefits then upon discovering the fraud the SSA can immediately stop the benefits, require any previous benefits paid to be reimbursed to the government, and can also result in a federal prosecution for fraud.

Appealing the Denial

While the exact numbers are hard to determine, many of the publications and experts estimate 65-70% of the disability applications are denied initially by the Social Security Administration offices. Personally, we believe that number may even be a little low with the actual number being closer to 80%. However, of the applications which are then appealed, the number of approvals jumps to around 75% although, as we indicated earlier, this can change based on the political party controlling Congress and the White House.

There are a number of reasons for such a high rate of initial rejections. Many initial applications do not involve attorneys and therefore many of the applications are denied due to simple errors such as filling out the papers incorrectly or inadequately, failing to identify the disabling conditions in such a way that the SSA workers can make a correct decision, and failing to provide sufficient documentation to support a finding that the claimant is disabled.

Many of these flaws can be corrected at the next stage of the process when the initial denial is appealed to a hearing before the Administrative Law Judge.

In the event the decision of the ALJ also goes against the claimant they can then appeal further by a written appeal to the Appeals Council and, finally, if the decision of the Appeals Council isn't favorable the claimant has the ability to file a lawsuit in federal district court asking the federal judge to overturn all of the prior decisions.

One thing most people do not realize is the amount of time which can be involved in the process of applying for SSA benefits. It can take anywhere from a few months to a year to get the initial approval or denial from the first application, the one done by the SSA reviewing the forms and medical records. This time period should not be considered as starting until all of the records and forms have been provided to the SSA.

Like many government offices, the SSA has a huge backlog. When government spending is cut, the number of employees are reduced either by outright terminations, transfers or by not replacing employees who leave. Fewer employees mean it takes more time to process the files.

As we mentioned elsewhere, if the SSA denies the initial application, the next steps will take over a year and sometimes two or even more. So a claimant needs to be prepared for this. It is an unfortunate reality of the system. The person seeking benefits will not help themselves or speed things up by calling the SSA office, going by there, sending emails, or making a nuisance of themselves. An old lawyer saying applies here..."If it won't help, then it can only hurt".

SHOULD THE CLAIMANT APPEAL

One question which is often asked by claimants who have had their disability denied is "Does it cost to appeal further?" The answer to this is no, not to the Administrative Law Judge and not to the Appeals Council. If the claimant should eventually file a lawsuit in the federal district court then there are filing and service fees. In addition, if at any point an attorney is retained then usually the lawyer will expect some form of compensation. In the stages before the federal court, lawyer's fees are set at a maximum of 25% of the past-due benefits you are awarded, up to a maximum of $6,000, plus costs, unless they apply to the Social Security Administration and request an upward deviation and a larger percentage. These types of deviations are rare and most lawyers are satisfied with the 25% and the costs. This amount is withheld by the SSA and sent in a separate check to the attorney and there is a standard contract promulgated by the SSA and which would be required to be signed and in the file.

If the case is pursued to the federal district court, the attorney is allowed to charge extra for this, and typically will, since the workload is increased and the work is different. The attorney's fees for this are not paid out of the past-due benefits and most attorneys will either charge them up front or work out some kind of regular payment.

Another factor to be considered is the reason for the denial. If SSDI was denied due to not having a sufficient amount of time worked (usually referred to as "work quarters") then if the dates the SSA is relying on are accurate it is a denial based on a basic requirement and the chances of winning are essentially zero. Certainly the applicant can continue, but it is almost, if not actually, impossible to win these.

If the denial is based on the impairment not lasting a year, then an appeal is worth pursuing since it can take a year or two to get a hearing set and a final decision will allow the additional time to be considered as well as any other developments which occurred. So, if it turns out the condition lasted for a year and two weeks and the claimant then went back to work, they would be likely to win the appeal and receive back pay for the time they were off even if they are now back at work, which could result in a nice sum of money to help them catch up on any debts incurred during the time they were disabled.

Statistics show an older applicant (55 or above) stands a greater chance of winning in front of an ALJ than a younger claimant unless the condition is seriously disabling. In addition, with advancing age other conditions begin manifesting. Since disability can be based on a cumulative effect of multiple conditions and medications, the older a claimant gets the greater the chance they will be able to add conditions and medical records to reach the "disability" threshold.

A claimant also has to take into effect their level of education and work experience. When the SSA experts begin looking into whether work/jobs exist in significant numbers in the national economy the expert has to consider the education and work experience of the claimant. This is often an area where good arguments can be made on appeal that the combination of limitations caused by the disabling condition or its treatment, combined with these two factors means that, in reality, there are no jobs in significant numbers which the claimant can actually perform.

In reality, if the claimant has already invested in this book and is willing to spend the time necessary to conduct the appeal correctly then there is rarely a reason not to appeal since there are no additional costs. Even the records from medical providers are required to be provided free of charge by using a specific SSA form to make the request.

The Different Levels of Appeal From the Initial Denial

The SSA provides a web page on this issue as well, although it is both a little simple in places as well as a little confusing. However, in the interest of too much information being better than too little, we'll provide the link: https://www.ssa.gov/pubs/EN-05-10041.pdf

If the initial application is denied, there are four levels of appeal. Some are rarely effective and add to the time which will pass before the claimant receives benefits if they win at one of the later stages but it is still worth trying them, particularly if you notice a mistake was made in the denial. An example of such a mistake might be where the denial was based on the claimant not providing a form, which was actually provided.

The four levels of appeal, in the order they would be used, are:

1. Reconsideration of the initial claim by the DDS;
2. A hearing before an SSA Administrative Law Judge;
3. An appeal of the ALJ's denial to the Appeals Council; and
4. A review in the federal district court by a federal judge.

How to Ask for a Reconsideration of the Claim

Filing an appeal for Request for Reconsideration is the first step in the appeals process.

The reconsideration request means an entirely new person with DDS who did not take part in the initial denial will review the file and records and issue their own decision. It is even possible to provide additional evidence if the claimant has received something which was not previously in their file and if the reason for the denial was the medical condition has improved, the claimant may request a meeting with an SSA representative to explain why they believe this is incorrect.

Unfortunately, this type of reconsideration is rarely successful unless there has been a clear mistake made in the initial denial or there is compelling new evidence which didn't have the chance to make it into the file before the denial.

The method of asking for a reconsideration will be set forth in the notice or letter of denial from the SSA but it must be done within 60 days, can be done through the SSA website, mailed to the SSA, or hand-delivered. It is advisable to get a receipt from the SSA for all hand-delivered documents. Once the documents are received at the SSA office, they will be digitally scanned and saved in the SSA computer system. All SSA personnel working on the case will have access to these documents.

Reconsideration of the initial disability claim is the first step in the appeals process. You must file for reconsideration within 60 days of receiving the denial notice from the SSA. If you do not submit your request within the allotted time, then you will need to begin the application process all over again.

Once the paperwork is filed for a Reconsideration of the Claim, the process can take anywhere from six weeks to several months to receive a decision.

Denied for Medical Reasons

If the claim was denied for medical reasons, then a request for an appeal or reconsideration can be made online at https://secure.ssa.gov/iApplsRe/start.

The appeal can also be made by printing and completing the following forms. (The number and name of the forms to request a reconsideration are correct ***at the time this is being written***. Always check the SSA website to ensure the forms are the same. These forms are also available in Appendix L):

- Form SSA-561, Request for Reconsideration
- Form SSA-3441-BK - Disability Report - Appeal- ,
- Form SSA-827 - Authorization to Disclose Information to the Social Security Administration

This information regarding the forms and links can be found at https://www.ssa.gov/forms/ssa-3441.html , which is also a page with a link to appealing the decision online as well as links to various PDF documents with additional information. That web page also has additional information from the SSA on the appeal process as well as a link to a new section of the website which allows the claimant to check up on and follow the status of their appeal.

After you print out and complete all three forms, mail the forms to the local Social Security office. All three forms should be mailed in the same packet to speed up the time to reconsider the claim.

If you do not have a printer then you can call the toll free number at 1-800-772-1213 and explain you do not want to use the online appeal process but you do want to appeal the decision made in your case. An SSA representative will send you the forms or schedule an interview.

If you live outside the United States or its territories, then contact the nearest U.S. Social Security Office, U.S. Embassy or consulate.

These forms should be sent to the local Social Security Office by both certified mail, return receipt requested and regular U.S. Mail. Include a cover letter explaining what is being included with the letter inform them of the two methods of mailing.

If the claimant is not sure whether they should file a Request for Reconsideration or a Request for an ALJ hearing, or has questions on how to fill out any of the forms they should contact their local SSA office or, even better, the national "hotline" number at 1-800-772-1213 which is open on weekdays, except federally recognized holidays, from 7 a.m. until 7 p.m.

Denied for Non-Medical Reasons (sometimes called a Technical Denial)

If you disagree with the non-medical reason denial decision then you can request an appeal online at https://secure.ssa.gov/iApplNMD/start.

The appeal can also be made by printing and completing the following form. (The number and name of the form to request a reconsideration is correct ***at the time this is being written***. Always check the SSA website to ensure the forms are the same. This form is also available in Appendix L):

Form SSA-561 - Request for Reconsideration

Some examples of a “non-medical” denial decision are:

- Did not work long enough
- Not enough recent work credits
- Denied another type of benefit, such as retirement
- Conviction or incarceration
- Earning too much money

After you print out and complete all the form, mail it to the local Social Security office.

If the applicant does not have a printer then call the toll free number at 1-800-772-1213 and explain you do not want to use the online appeal process but you do want to appeal the decision made in your case. An SSA representative will send you the form or schedule an interview.

If the applicant lives outside the United States or its territories, then contact the nearest U.S. Social Security Office, U.S. Embassy or consulate.

This form should be sent to the local Social Security Office by both certified mail return receipt requested and regular U.S.

Mail. Include a cover letter explaining what is being included with the letter and inform them of the two methods of mailing.

If the claimant is not sure whether they should file a Request for Reconsideration or a Request for an ALJ hearing, or has questions on how to fill out any of the forms they should contact their local SSA office or, even better, the national "hotline" number at 1-800-772-1213 which is open on weekdays, except federally recognized holidays, from 7 a.m. until 7 p.m.

How to File the Appeal from the Denial to the ALJ

If the Request for Reconsideration is denied then an appeal should be made for a hearing before an SSA Administrative Law Judge. This is the second step in the appeals process.

The odds on the denial being reversed on a reconsideration at a hearing by the Administrative Law Judge (ALJ), also known as the appeal to the ALJ, are substantially higher than at any other point in the process. The number of reversals granted by ALJs is 60% or above. In some cases, ALJs have even been questioned about why the rate of approved of claims were so high and the figure used was above 70%. We will spend more time on this section of the book than any other specific topic since it is the claimant's ***best chance*** for winning, and also where experience and knowledge which only comes from being in these types of proceedings can play the biggest part.

When the claimant receives the initial notice denying the benefits, there will also be information on how to appeal the decision. At this time, the appeal must be filed within 60 days of receiving the notice of denial and the SSA operates under the assumption the notices were received by the claimant by the 5th day from the date at the top of the letter. If the appeal is not filed within the time limit then the claimant likely loses the right to appeal. There are a few, very limited reasons in which the SSA will allow the filing of an appeal past the deadline but it is not worth the chance of a rejection so most lawyers try to file the appeal within 30-45 days so there is a little leeway in case something goes wrong.

As in the previous step, requesting the appeal is simple. The appeal can be filed online at https://www.ssa.gov/benefits/disability/appeal.html. Be sure and print or save the screens in some way showing the appeal was filed if you file online.

The appeal can also be made by printing and completing the following form. (The number and name of the form to request a hearing by the ALJ is correct ***at the time this is being written***. Always check the SSA website to ensure the forms are the same. This form is also available in Appendix M):

Form HA-501, Request for a Hearing by Administrative Law Judge.

If the applicant does not have a printer then call the toll free number at 1-800-772-1213 and explain you do not want to use the online appeal process but you do want to appeal the decision made in your case. An SSA representative will send you the form or schedule an interview.

If the applicant lives outside the United States or its territories, then contact the nearest U.S. Social Security Office, U.S. Embassy or consulate

This form should be sent to the local Social Security Office by both certified mail return receipt requested and regular U.S. Mail. Include a cover letter explaining what is included with the letter and inform them of the two methods of mailing.

If the claimant is not sure whether they should file a Request for Reconsideration or a Request for an ALJ hearing, or has questions on how to fill out any of the forms they should contact their local SSA office or, even better, the national "hotline" number at 1-800-772-1213 which is open on weekdays, except federally recognized holidays, from 7 a.m. until 7 p.m.

This information regarding the forms and links can be found at https://www.ssa.gov/forms/ssa-3441.html , which is also a page with a link to appealing the decision online as well as links to various PDF documents with additional information. That web page also has additional information from the SSA on the appeal process as well as a link to a new section of the website which allows the claimant to check up on and follow the status of their appeal.

Filling Out the Forms

Form SSSA-3441-BK, Disability Report

This report is essentially the same form the claimant has filled out before but the purpose of it is to update the file and to give the person doing the review, or the Administrative Law Judge, a quick rundown on claimant's current condition without having to wade through and read every report or medical record in the file.

The next section on here which is important and which special attention needs to be given is **Section 2 - INFORMATION ABOUT YOUR ILLNESSES, INJURIES, AND CONDITIONS.** There are three subparts here, A, B, and C, which allow the claimant to tell the SSA and the Administrative Law Judge about any changes in their condition(s), any new limitations, or any new conditions. If more space is needed it is provided in Section 10 of the form. It is extremely hard to tell a claimant what to write in this part of the report since it varies tremendously from one person to another. The only really helpful comments that can be made is to tell the truth and to be as complete as possible without being repetitious.

The Disability Report and the file will contain one or more Disability Reports before the claimant ever gets to the appeals stage, also provides places to list any new medical providers which have been seen or will be seen, any locations which may have more records, medications which have been taken since the last Disability Report or which are still being taken, additional testing which has been done, along with requests for much more information. The form is about 10 pages long.

Form SSA-561, Request for Reconsideration

Most of the form sections are self-explanatory, just as they were on the original forms. However, on the Form SSA-561, Request for Reconsideration there are a couple of blank sections we need to discuss.

The first is, on the current form, Section 8, which has the following wording:

> "I do not agree with the determination made on the above claim and request reconsideration. My reasons are:
>
> ____
>
> ____
>
> _______________________________________"

In this section (and if this is being done on a paper form additional information can be written on the back) the claimant will explain why the decision was incorrect.

As an example, if the decision stated "the claimant showed the ability to lift up to 50 pounds" and the doctor has actually said "the patient cannot lift more than 5 pounds", the response might be "The decision misstated the treating doctor's limitations on the amount of weight which could be lifted. The records indicate there is a maximum of 5 pounds lifting and the decision was based on an incorrect reading of the records."

The claimant could also choose to disagree with the interpretation contained in the decision, could have additional records which need to be added to the record, etc. There is no "magic language" which must or should be used by a claimant representing themselves and they shouldn't try to "talk like a lawyer". They should present their reason(s) for disagreeing with the decision in a clear and concise manner without indulging what seems to be a tendency to over-explain.

The next section which needs to be covered is Section 9, which only applies to a request for SSI benefits at this time and simply asks which type of review is requested. A Case Review is where a new DDS team which is made up of a medical consultant and a DDS examiner reviews the decision and makes a recommendation. An Informal Conference is likely to be over the telephone, and a Formal Conference is usually in person. The claimant indicates their choice by checking the box next to the type requested.

None of these seem to be any more or less likely to yield better results than the others but I would tend to choose a conference as opposed to just a case review and that way the claimant can be sure they emphasize the strong points of their case. Before the conference takes place, the claimant should take the time to write out a checklist or an outline of what they want to cover as well as any specific exhibits they wish to point out and then be sure and mark them on the page as they are covered during the conference. This is an easy way to make sure nothing important is missed.

Even the formal conference is still relatively informal and non-confrontational. The DDS examiner will be going over documents in the electronic record and so the claimant should have requested a copy of the record in advance since it is very difficult to review them at the office immediately prior to the hearing. Usually, the SSA office will send a complete copy of the file on a CD if the claimant requests it and they are allowed to require a slight payment for this, although I've never seen them charge. The file can also be reviewed online at the web page for the appeal which, at this time, can be reached through the "My Social Security Account" at https://www.ssa.gov/benefits/disability/appeal.html. If that link doesn't work for any reason, and as I indicated earlier it is a new feature, then the claimant can call the toll free number set forth above and they can provide the updated location to review the information online. However, I'd suggest using the CD version as the claimant can then use various free software programs to make notes on the pages in their personal copy of the file.

Form HA-501, Request for a Hearing by Administrative Law Judge

At this point, it can be assumed the claim has been denied or else a hearing in front of the ALJ would not be necessary.

The request to have the case heard by the ALJ must, as with the other deadlines, be made within 60 days of the denial of the reconsideration.

The form for this can be found at https://www.ssa.gov/forms/ha-501.pdf and in Appendix M of this book. Of all the forms which a claimant will use with the SSA, this is likely the shortest and easiest one, consisting of just over half of a page.

Much of the information requested in the form will have already been used in an earlier form and the hardest questions are 5, 6, and 7.

Question 5 simply asks why the claimant is requesting the hearing and why they disagree with the earlier decision. Most attorneys use a standard explanation such as "I believe the earlier review(s) did not consider or evaluate my doctor's statements and evidence and, if they had done so, the records clearly show I am disabled" or something similar.

Question 6 just asks if the claimant has additional evidence to submit. This could be an additional witness, more medical reports or records, etc.

Question 7 asks whether the claimant requests to appear at the hearing or not. Technically, it shouldn't make any difference whether the claimant appears or not but most attorneys believe, and we're in agreement, that it is beneficial to have the judge consider the facts in light of a face and a person, rather than just papers in a file. Using this reasoning, the best choice is to appear at the hearing and therefore that would be the box to check.

Once again, the claimant will have to submit an updated Form SSA-3441-BK, Disability Report. While it should only be required to submit changes, it is a better idea to fill the form out as completely as possible.

These forms need to be sent to the local Social Security office by certified mail, return receipt requested, along with any new evidence the claimant has and wishes to be included in the file and reviewed by the judge. It is also a good idea, at this stage as well as any other stage, to keep copies of anything sent to the SSA.

Prehearing Conference

The ALJ can hold a prehearing conference and one can be held at the request of the claimant. If the judge orders the conference, then the claimant must appear or stand a chance of having the request for the hearing dismissed. Once again, there are exceptions considered as good cause for missing the conference but it is not worth the risk of missing the conference unless the claimant is physically or mentally unable to attend.

Prehearing conferences are usually by telephone but the judge can require they be in person. However, the reality is these are rarely ordered at all and, if they are, it is because the judge believes something is missing from the file or is considering modifying the issue somehow, usually to make them simpler, or believes the file doesn't have all of the medical records and is trying to confirm what should be there.

Occasionally, instead of the ALJ conducting the prehearing conference, it may initially be handled by an "Attorney Advisor" to the judge. This Attorney Advisor helps to lighten the judge's workload and has full authority to overrule the decision of the DDS which would mean that claimant won without the necessity of the actual hearing.

If the judge conducts the prehearing conference, it will be "on the record" which usually means a recording will be made instead of a court reporter being present as was normal "in the old days".

It is also possible the judge will make a favorable decision at the prehearing conference.

THE ALJ HEARING

While we will discuss in detail the ways to handle hearings, there are a few things to cover first.

The rules require a claimant be given at least 75 days notice of the hearing. Any new evidence which the claimant wants to be considered must be submitted at least five days before the hearing. The evidence must be submitted in its original form with no changes or edits by the claimant.

While the SSA has removed a lot of the discretion the ALJ has in scheduling hearings, their workload is so high that it is not unusual for it to take a year or more for an actual hearing to be scheduled. As we mentioned above, there is no need for the claimant to try to speed things up by making calls, writing letters or complaining. The SSA is not going to move one claimant's case ahead of the others on the schedule.

The one area in which the claimant can make a difference in the scheduling is by agreeing to or refusing a video hearing. Typically, the video hearings occur faster than a live hearing and the claimant has a right to refuse the video hearing and instead insist on the live hearing but they should know it will likely delay matters.

Video Hearings

The video hearing may occur:

- With the judge at the hearing center with the claimant.
- With the judge at their office and the only person present with the claimant is a technician in charge of ensuring the equipment is performing correctly.
- With experts at their offices or at the judge's office (rarely). They could also be at the hearing center with the claimant or at another hearing center with video capabilities, or any combination of those.

Regardless of the locations, the claimant and judge should be able to see and hear everyone involved. The hearings are not recorded on video but an audio of the proceeding will be made and kept as a part of the record.

Hearings Conducted in Person

The hearings where the judge and claimant are there live may have the experts appear by video or by telephone.

These hearings will be held at a location as convenient to the claimant as possible. They are usually held at the federal courthouse, an office complex leased by the SSA, or even, occasionally, at the conference center at a hotel (which used to be very common in rural areas).

While the ALJ hearings are much less formal than a regular court, they are still court and the judge is still a judge and should be addressed as "Your honor" or "Judge (insert last name)". It is both expected and a matter of formality.

While the order of presentation is clearly set forth in the regular courts, in the ALJ hearing the judge has almost unlimited discretion. Normally, they will advance the case by presenting or discussing the SSA information first. This would include employment history, education, medical records, all of which would be followed by the judge asking any questions they have of the claimant. The judge will normally then question any experts (more on them later) and after they ask their questions, they will then tell the claimant they may ask questions if they have any.

After this, the judge will ask the claimant if they have any evidence to present. At this point any witnesses can be called to testify, the claimant can make an oral statement themselves, and offer or point out any other evidence they have placed into the record.

After the claimant completes their presentation, if they have any, the judge will normally thank the claimant for attending and adjourn the proceeding. Then, at some point in the future, the SSA will send the decision of the judge to the clamant.

Another possibility, one which used to be very common and particularly in cases where the claimant was still being actively treated by medical providers, is that the hearing will be conducted and then "continued" or postponed until a later date. This is usually done when testimony during the hearing reveals there is additional evidence which is not a part of the record and needs to be obtained. The ALJ may also look at the new evidence which was filed just before the hearing and request further examinations or review by the SSA experts. The ALJ may choose to direct someone to gather the information and evidence or may offer the claimant the opportunity to do it themselves since this is usually faster. The ALJ may set the date for the hearing to continue before the hearing is adjourned or may wait until the evidence is provided to the SSA and then set the hearing date.

Handling the Hearing

While everything in this book, the appendices, and the website links we've provided are important, this section dealing with the hearing before the Administrative Law Judge is probably the most important and the hardest on which to find information which actually helps in the hearing room so this section needs to be read and reread along with the links and the appendices referenced. In addition, a claimant who has made the decision to represent themselves in this matter may want to consider investing in other books which deal with handling yourself in a courtroom, such as another of our e-books, The Guerrilla Guide to Small Claims Court, as the ALJ hearing is closer to a small claims court setting than any other type of civil court hearing or trial. While most of *that* book won't apply, the chapters on ***Getting Ready for Small Claims Court*** and on ***The Trial*** cover how to prepare for court, how to present evidence, and the behavior expected while in court and is applicable to any judicial setting and may make the difference between winning or losing.

The first and most important rule regarding preparing for hearings is to prepare. It is impossible to spend too much time preparing for a hearing. When good lawyers have a trial coming up they often spend five to ten hours outside of court for every one they intend to spend in trial. That isn't including the time preparing pleadings and doing the normal work associated with getting a lawsuit filed and ready, this is just the time spent in making copies for use in trial, going over documents, preparing lists of questions to be asked of witnesses, etc.

The claimant should have a complete copy of the file, usually provided on CD upon request by the SSA or viewable online. As we mention elsewhere, using a CD copy is better since various software products, many of them free, can be used to make notes on any relevant documents.

The SSA may require experts to be present and may not. The claimant can make a written request that the experts be available in person or by video or telephone. Usually, a copy of their report will be in the file but sometimes it is not and those experts are almost always called to offer testimony at the hearing by one method or another. If the report is not contained in the file then the claimant can ask that the hearing be "continued" or postponed after the expert testifies and that a copy of the audio of their testimony be available so they may be able to cross-examine the expert effectively. However, this means further delays in the processing of the claim, but this delay is well worth the additional time since it is unlikely a layman such as the claimant can "wing it" on the questioning and rely on being able to be effective without adequate preparation.

The judge will always ask the first set of questions to the experts hired by the SSA. However, the questions they will ask are fairly predictable since there are certain findings which are supposed to be addressed in the decision. If the claimant knows what questions the judge will ask then they can predict what questions they should ask when it is their turn. The most common expert called to testify at an ALJ hearing is a Vocational Expert. The SSA handbook for Vocational Experts can be found at https://www.ssa.gov/appeals/public_experts/Vocational_Experts_(VE)_Handbook-508.pdf.

These questions can be found in Appendix N of this book.

There are also a couple of good articles on questioning written by attorneys involved in representing people with disability claims. The links to those articles are:

https://parmelelawfirm.com/vocational-expert-3/

https://www.illinoislegalaid.org/sites/default/files/attachments/Cross-examination%20of%20experts.pdf

The other type of expert which is seen occasionally at ALJ hearings is a medical expert, usually an M.D. However, the SSA is not known for paying their experts particularly well. They pay a flat fee which means most doctors who testify spend as little time as possible on the file and most physicians can make more doing any type of medical work instead of SSA work. This means most physicians who appear at ALJ hearings will be retired and are no longer actively practicing. A knowledge of these realities provide some lines of questioning, particularly as to what else the expert does now (if anything), how much time they spent reviewing the file, and then specific questions as to the contents of the medical records. It's not unusual to find a medical expert testifying who cannot answer specific questions on the file other than the questions asked by the judge.

In addition, the claimant can be expected to be questioned by the judge although it doesn't always happen. As with the experts, the questions are fairly uniform and therefore predictable. The claimant should review these questions in Appendix N and be prepared with their answers. If the judge fails to ask something which would provide important information, the claimant should be prepared to offer the information in their testimony. In regular court, a party representing themselves must provide their testimony in a question and answer format, if required, but the ALJ will usually just let the applicant for benefits tell them their story and the facts without following a specific format. However, the tendency in these types of situations is for the person seeking benefits to say too much and "babble" instead of being very specific in the information they want to convey. The way lawyers usually phrase this is to tell the client, "If the topic is the time of the day, don't explain how to build a clock."

Notice of the Decision

The decision will usually be issued in a manner which is very comprehensive. The judge should set forth the evidence which was considered, the evidence relied on (if different), and the actual decision which can be Unfavorable, Partially Favorable, or Fully Favorable.

An Unfavorable decision means, simply, the claimant loses.

A Favorable decision means the claimant wins completely.

The decision which is Partially Favorable can mean the claimant wins a part of their case. This can mean almost anything but the most common finding is the claimant isn't entitled to everything they asked for, but is disabled for a part of the time but not the remainder. It could mean the judge doesn't believe the disability started at the time the claimant alleges, that they were disabled in the past but aren't any longer, or some combination along those lines.

Of all of these, the ones we have seen the most is that the claimant's disability began later than they claim and therefore their "back pay" is not for the full time, but the claimant is now disabled. While many think this is a contradiction, it really is not when you consider a finding of disability does not have to be based on a single condition alone. Disability can be based on a combination of multiple conditions as well as the medications given to treat the ailments. For instance, a back injury, the most common reason for disability, will often not be considered disabling since a significant amount of jobs exist in the workplace which are sedentary in nature (remember, this uses theoretical jobs and numbers in a very wide portion of the economy and geographic location). However, with the back injuries can come surgeries which do not decrease and may actually increase the pain, thus necessitating varying medications such as muscle relaxers and pain medications which cause drowsiness and an inability to function. Thus, it is the back injury ***combined*** with the effects of the medication which result in the condition being disabling if the claimant does a good job of documenting these issues and presenting the documents to the SSA. Since it was the **increase** in pain which caused the need for the medications, the disabling condition may have come about at a later point than the injury itself.

Appealing the Decision of the ALJ

Obviously, if the ALJ issues a fully Unfavorable decision as to the disability benefits, then the claimant will want to appeal that decision to the Appeals Council.

If the decision is Partially Favorable and Partially Unfavorable then the claimant has a tough choice to make since the Appeals Council can choose to reverse all or a part of the decision made by the ALJ. So, appealing the decision trying to get a fully favorable finding gives the Appeals Council the opportunity to reverse just the part that was favorable, meaning the claimant doesn't get anything.

The Appeals Council can also choose to review any decision of the ALJ courts, even if the claimant does not appeal. It's not common, but it can happen.

To appeal the decision of the ALJ, the claimant must fill out and return Form HA-520-U5 Request for Review of Hearing Decision/Order. The web page explaining this particular form is at https://www.ssa.gov/forms/ha-520.html and there is a link there to the form itself.

This form is also extremely easy to complete as it is one page and only the top half is completed by the claimant. The form can be seen at the webpage above or in Appendix M of this book.

The only part of the appeal form which is the least bit difficult is number 4 where the claimant sets forth the reason they feel the ALJ should be reversed. If the claimant feels the ALJ did not give them time to present their side of the case, did not allow them to properly question the expert, or in any way did not give them a fair hearing then it can be set forth here as can the general reason they felt the judge's decision was incorrect.

There is a section which is titled ADDITIONAL EVIDENCE and which instructs the claimant as to how to present additional evidence or any legal arguments. The claimant can consider hiring an attorney to review the record and prepare a legal brief for them to submit to the Appeals Council but if additional time is required it must be requested.

While number 4 is the area in which a claimant should enter the reasons for asking the Appeals Council to reverse the decision of the ALJ, it is actually better to use general reasons in that section and to set forth the more specific arguments in a legal brief submitted under the ADDITIONAL EVIDENCE section.

Unfortunately, there is no way for a book designed for non-lawyers to present every possible scenario in which the ALJ may make a mistake in their decision. However, there are certain areas which seem to be the source of more mistakes which can be used to request a reversal. While this strategy wouldn't work in a normal court case, because of the unique requirements imposed on the ALJ, this method can be effective in this setting. There are no specific requirements as to the form a "legal brief" must take when submitted under the ADDITIONAL EVIDENCE section, so we can present the most common mistakes and then the claimant can determine if these apply to their case and submit them in a written form with the title *Brief of ALJ Errors*.

Insufficient Weight Given to Opinion of Treating Physician

One issue which we have mentioned earlier is the opinion of the treating physicians should be given greater weight than any doctor hired by SSA just to perform an examination. If the records of the treating physician are in opposition to the opinion of the hired expert and the judge relies on the expert's opinion rather than the treating physician or if the ALJ simply does not explain what weight was given to the opinions of the expert versus the opinions of the treating physician then that may be reason to reverse the ALJ. This is particularly so if the treating physician provided a Medical Source Statement or a Residual Functional Capacity (RFC) form indicating the claimant had substantial work-related limitations and the expert also provided the forms or simply disagreed with the treating physician's assessment.

ALJ Did Not Develop the Medical Record of the Claimant

This is an area in which the duties of the ALJ differ significantly from the judge in a normal court case. In a case in a regular court, each side is responsible for developing and presenting their own evidence. However in an ALJ hearing, the U.S. Supreme Court has specifically found Social Security proceedings are "inquisitorial" instead of "adversarial". The effect of this ruling is that Administrative Law Judges are under an affirmative duty to develop the case both for and against the claimant as well as to investigate the facts. This means that if the medical evidence in the case is insufficient for them to make a decision which is fully informed, then the ALJ must further develop it by either contacting the medical providers or calling one of the SSA experts for a consultative examination. Also, if there is any evidence of some type of mental deficiency which could affect the ability of the claimant to effectively handle their case or in the area of being qualified for employment then the ALJ must provide for testing in that area, even if the claimant didn't raise the issue.

Incorrect RFC (Residual Functional Capacity) used by Vocational Expert

During the hearing, the Vocational Expert normally replies to hypothetical questions asked by the judge. Many times the judge fails to ask questions which include all of the limitations which the claimant is experiencing.

A typical hypothetical question asked by the ALJ might be something along the lines of: "What jobs, if any, could a person of the same age, education, and with the same work history as the claimant be able to do if they could lift no more than 10 pounds on a regular basis, could stand no more than two hours per day, and could not have contact with the general public?"

While that hypothetical, or one very close to that wording, is typical, if the RFC actually had a limitation of being able to lift no more than 5 pounds on a regular basis, could stand no more than an hour a day, or the claimant had a condition which prevented them from having contact with the general public, then the hypothetical would not indicate jobs **the claimant** could do.

This is the type of question the claimant might not catch as an error during the hearing but if they requested a copy of the audio, which they are entitled to, and compared the hypothetical question to the RFC in their file (on the CD which was requested before the hearing) then this would provide a point for reversal.

RFC Not Supported By Substantial Evidence

An assessment of the RFC of the claimant should be in the decision made by every ALJ, whether the decision is Favorable or

Unfavorable. This assessment should be a description of the most that can be done by the claimant, taking into account all of their impairments.

The assessment of the RFC is incredibly important since it is what provides the basis for the determination as to whether there are any jobs that exist in significant numbers in the US economy which the claimant can perform. Going back to the role of the ALJ as defined by the SSA, they cannot ignore or disregard limitations contained in the medical file and take the position the claimant is capable of doing more or different work than that indicated by the medical records. If the ALJ does that, then it should be an issue raised to the Appeals Council and could/should reverse the decision.

Both Severe and Non-Severe Impairments as well as the Prescription Side Effects Were Not Considered by the ALJ

All of the claimant's impairments are supposed to be considered, even those labeled as non-severe. The impairments can play a part in the claimant's ability to work since, potentially, one or more non-severe conditions can add to each other and end up being disabling or limiting the types of jobs that could be done. The side effects of the various prescription medications and how this would affect the claimant should also be discussed.

If the ALJ fails to address all of the impairments it should be an issue raised on any appeal which is filed.

ALJ Found Claimant/Witnesses not Believable Without Providing Reasons

The SSA gives the Administrative Law Judge wide latitude in making determinations as to the credibility of the claimant or any other witnesses. However, the ALJ is required to specify any reasons they used to make this finding. They are not allowed to just make a conclusory statement as to credibility. The reason can be simple, such as "the claimant made inconsistent statements during the hearing" or "the claimant's statements to the court were contradicted by statements made in the medical records".

A failure to provide the reasoning for discounting testimony can provide a reason for the Appeals Council to reverse the decision of the ALJ.

Claimant's Testimony was Mischaracterized by ALJ

Another common error made by the ALJs regards the testimony given during the hearing. In the decision, the ALJ will likely summarize the testimony of any witnesses, including the claimant. This summarization must be accurate. One common example is where the claimant states they go grocery shopping with a friend or a family member periodically, but while shopping they have to be dropped off at the front of the store and then must use a motorized cart to navigate the store. The ALJ would not be allowed to simply summarize this testimony in their decision as, "the applicant testified they go grocery shopping every week" since that mischaracterizes both the reality and the spirit of what was actually said. This is another reason why it is important for the claimant to request the audio of the hearing and carefully go through it while looking at the various parts of the written decision.

Non-Physician Medical Professional Opinions Not Properly Considered

As discussed earlier in the book, the Social Security Administration has two different classifications for medical professionals. "Acceptable" medical sources which include physicians, psychiatrists, licensed psychologists and what they term "other" medical sources, which essentially includes therapists, counselors, chiropractors, nurses, etc. It is well settled that these “other” sources cannot provide a diagnosis of the condition which is causing the claimant's issues. These other sources are allowed and can provide information and opinions about the severity of the impairment. Again, the opinions of these professionals must be addressed and the ALJ must explain the weight given to them as well as any reasons they would have for discounting their findings or opinions.

Of course, there are many other reasons which might lead to a Reversal and Rendering (the decision is changed for all purposes) or a Reversal and Remand (the Appeals Council sends the case back to the ALJ for some type of correction). However, the examples given above will show the claimant how the system is supposed to work and thus allow them to potentially spot other problems in a decision in which the ALJ issued a finding which was unfavorable.

Again, the **Form HA-520-U5 Request for Review of Hearing Decision/Order** must be completed online or completed and returned to the local SSA office within 60 days of the date of the hearing decision, which is on the decision or the letter which accompanied the decision. The completed form can also be sent to the Appeals Council office, which is shown on the web page but which is currently Appeals Council, 5107 Leesburg Pike, Falls Church, VA 22041-3255.

Just as with anything else to do with the SSA, if the form is mailed, it should be sent by U.S. Mail, Certified Mail Return Receipt Requested and the claimant should check the website or call the toll free number at 1-800-772-1213 to be sure the address is the correct one at the time the appeal is filed.

Filing a Federal Lawsuit

If the appeal to the Appeals Council doesn't result in a favorable finding then the last possible step to take is to file a federal lawsuit in the local federal district court asking the judge to reverse the findings of the SSA. While the federal judge is supposed to be limiting their review to only legal errors, many judges rule on factual issues as well.

The odds are pretty good for claimants who appeal to federal court as well, the latest statistics show the federal judges reverse around a third of all Social Security cases, with the chief reasons being the SSA failed to give the proper weight to the treating physician's opinion, failed to consider all of the symptoms including pain, or failed to require the proper assessments be performed.

There is the same requirement that the lawsuit be filed within 60 days after the date of the decision of the Appeals Council

While a claimant is allowed to file the lawsuit themselves and not use an attorney, federal courts are incredibly difficult to work in and federal judges are less "forgiving" than state judges.

However, in Social Security lawsuits the case is one which will be reviewed by the judge based on the briefs of the parties so there is not a jury or extensive discovery with which to deal. Unfortunately, since the case will be decided based on the briefs, the claimant must be prepared to do a great deal of legal research.

We'll do a little self-promotion here and recommend the claimant consider purchasing The Guerrilla Guide to Legal Research: Finding the Law for Non-Lawyers. It not only explains the basic concepts of legal research and how to craft a query likely to return helpful results but it also explains how these results can be used and provide a link to a "hidden" section of Google which contains all of the case law needed and which can be accessed at no charge. Although very few people actually do research in the printed copies of the various legal publications now, it also explains how they can be used. When doing their research the claimant must be very careful to use cases from their own Circuit of Courts since that is the only ones which are binding. The book sets forth which geographical areas are covered by which Circuits.

Despite the fact that the claimant has resources including books and a free website to do the legal research, almost everyone in the system will agree that a lawyer should be used for the ALJ process if possible and, if not, then certainly for the federal lawsuit. Many lawyers don't practice in federal court due to the complexities involved, the judge's strict adherence to deadlines, and the court rules so a non-lawyer is at a distinct disadvantage in trying to do this themselves and there is no way to explain how to handle these cases which will apply to each case.

The SSA website has a page on the Federal Court Review Process at https://www.ssa.gov/appeals/court_process.html.

The federal courts also provide a sample complaint for this type of lawsuit at http://www.uscourts.gov/sites/default/files/complaint_for_review_of_social_security.pdf . That complaint can actually be filled out at that web page and then submitted to the courts. The same form can be found in other formats at http://www.uscourts.gov/forms/pro-se-forms/complaint-review-social-security-decision .

The claimant will be expected to know and abide by the Federal Rules of Civil Procedure, which has a webpage and a link to the actual rules at the federal courts' website: http://www.uscourts.gov/rules-policies/current-rules-practice-procedure/federal-rules-civil-procedure

However, the claimant should be aware that the federal court personnel does not provide assistance in filing the claim, answer questions, or take any steps to advise anyone representing themselves and no attempt to get assistance from the personnel of the courts should even be asked.

After the complaint is prepared it must be filed with the court. The federal courts now require the documents to be filed electronically through the PACER system. Information on that as well as other federal court topics can be found at https://www.uscfc.uscourts.gov/pro-se-information . That page also explains how to pay the filing fee, how to serve the SSA, instructions on the cover sheet which is to be filed with the complaint, etc. This web page is the most complete location for information on filing this type of lawsuit.

What Happens if the Claimant Loses the Federal Court Lawsuit

While, in theory, the decision of the federal district court could proceed on through the lawsuit appeal process all the way to the Supreme Court of the United States, it doesn't really happen. The primary reason is that at each step more expenses are incurred and much more time is taken.

Instead, if the case is lost at the federal district court level, then the claimant should start over and reapply for benefits. The date of onset of disability will change since the court has ruled on the original date and the claimant should allege new symptoms, a worsening of the condition, and anything else which will serve to make the "new" claim distinguishable from the "old" claim. The new claim can actually be filed while the case is pending and the SSA will process the claim so long as the date of onset is after the last administrative action, which is usually the date of the decision by the Appeals Council.

At this point, the claimant may also want to reconsider their decision not to retain an attorney since obviously there was something in the original presentation which caused the claim for benefits to be rejected. A lawyer may be able to spot the problem(s) and increase the chances of a positive outcome this time.

You Are Approved!

Congratulations, you have been approved for Social Security Disability. Now what?

Once the claimant is approved for Social Security Disability benefits the claimant will receive an approval letter stating the amount of monthly benefits, the date the benefits will start and the amount of back pay the claimant will receive. It can take one to three months after the approval date before a benefit check will be issued.

It can take longer for recipients to receive the eligible back pay. Any time that has passed between approval and the first benefit payment should be added to the claimant's back pay.

If the funds have not been received within 90 days after approval, then contact your local Social Security Office.

Social Security Disability payments are not sent using a paper check. The majority of recipients receive their monthly benefits through Direct Deposit into their bank account. For those who do not have a bank account, the SSA offers debit cards.

Monthly benefits will be deposited to the debit card which can be used for purchases.

When you are approved for benefits the SSA will ask the claimant how they would like to receive their funds.

Social Security Benefit payments are issued three times each month. The benefit monthly payment date is based on the claimant's date of birth.

Recipients with birthdays on the 1st through the 10th of any month will receive their monthly benefit funds on the second Wednesday of each month.

Recipients with birthdays on the 11th through the 20th of any month will receive their monthly benefit funds on the third Wednesday of each month.

Recipients with birthdays on the 21st through the 31st of any month will receive their monthly benefit funds on the fourth Wednesday of each month.

Recipients who were approved prior to May 1997 or who are receiving both Social Security Disability and SSI are paid on the third day of each month. If the 3rd falls on a weekend or holiday, then the funds will be issued on the previous business work day.

Recipients who are approved for SSI only, funds will be issued on the 1st day of each month. If the first falls on a weekend or holiday, then the funds will be issued on the previous business work day.

FRAUD

When people apply for Social Security Benefits, they state that all information they provide on the forms are true and correct to the best of their knowledge. If an applicant knowingly lied or misrepresents any information related to the claim or eligibility for disability benefits, then it may be a crime and that person may face criminal charges for fraud.

The office of the Inspector General investigates all suspected situations of fraud perpetrated upon Social Security benefits. Fraud can consist of:

- Concealed work activity while receiving disability benefits
- Receiving disability benefits for a child not under their care
- Failure to notify SSA of the death of a beneficiary and continues to receive and cash the checks of the deceased.

- Conceals the marriage or assets from the Social Security Administration while receiving Supplemental Security Income payments
- Resides overseas and is receiving Supplemental Security Income payments
- Misuses benefits when acting as a Representative Payee
- Making false statements or claims on the Social Security Disability application
- Concealing facts or events which may affect eligibility for Social Security Benefits
- Not reporting income or Worker's Compensation to SSA

CONTINUING DISABILITY REVIEW

The Social Security Administration is required to periodically of all persons receiving Social Security Disability benefits. The process is to identify people who might no longer be eligible for benefits. If during the review, If the Social Security Administration finds that your medical condition has improved enough so that you can work, then your Social Security Disability benefits will end.

Generally, it is much easier to pass a continuing disability review than it is to be granted benefits in the first place.

A Continuing Disability Review (CDR) is different for each recipient. Most cases are set for review every three to seven years depending on the likelihood of the condition to improve.

The Certificate of Award you received from the Social Security Administration should indicate when you can expect your first review.

If your case was labeled as Medical Improvement Possible (MIP), then you can expect a review at least once every three years.

If your case was labeled as Medical Improvement Expected (MIE), then you can expect a review within six to eighteen months after first confirmed for having a disability.

If your case was labeled as Medical Improvement Not Expected (MINE), then you can expect a review at least once every seven years. In addition, those over the age of 55 are often assigned a seven-year review.

SSI recipients who are children will be assigned a review every three years and when they turn 18 years of age.

APPENDIX A

Social Security Disability Insurance Application - Form SSA-16-BK

Form **SSA-16** (06-2018) UF
Discontinue prior editions
Social Security Administration

Page 1 of 7
OMB No. 0960-0618

(Do not write in this space)

APPLICATION FOR DISABILITY INSURANCE BENEFITS

I apply for a period of disability and/or all insurance benefits for which I am eligible under Title II and Part A of Title XVIII of the Social Security Act, as presently amended.

1.	**PRINT your name**	FIRST NAME, MIDDLE INITIAL, LAST NAME
2.	Enter your Social Security Number	
3.	Check (X) whether you are	☐ Female ☐ Male
	Answer question 4 if English is not your preferred language. Otherwise, go to item 5.	
4.	Enter the language you prefer to: speak	write
5.	(a) Enter your date of birth	
	(b) Enter name of city and state or foreign country where you were born.	
	(c) Was a public record of your birth made before you were age 5?	☐ Yes ☐ No ☐ Unknown
	(d) Was a religious record of your birth made before you were age 5?	☐ Yes ☐ No ☐ Unknown
6.	(a) Are you a U.S. citizen?	☐ Yes (If "Yes," go to item 7) ☐ No (If "No," answer (b))
	(b) Are you an alien lawfully present in the U.S.?	☐ Yes (If "Yes," answer (c)) ☐ No (If "No," go to item 7)
	(c) When were you lawfully admitted to the U.S.?	
7.	(a) Enter your name at birth if different from item (1)	
	(b) Have you used any other names?	☐ Yes (If "Yes," answer (c)) ☐ No (If "No," go to item 8)
	(c) Other name(s) used.	
8.	(a) Have you used any other Social Security number(s)?	☐ Yes (If "Yes," answer (b)) ☐ No (If "No" go to item 9)
	(b) Enter Social Security number(s) used.	
9.	When do you believe your condition(s) became severe enough to keep you from working (even if you have never worked)?	
10.	(a) Have you (or has someone on your behalf) ever filed an application for Social Security benefits, a period of disability under Social Security, Supplemental Security Income, or hospital or medical insurance under Medicare?	☐ Yes (If "Yes," answer (b) and (c)) ☐ No ☐ Unknown (If "No," or "Unknown," go to item 11)
	(b) Enter name of person on whose Social Security record you filed the other application.	
	(c) Enter Social Security Number of person named in (b). *If unknown, check this block.* ☐ Unknown	

11.	(a) Were you in the active military or naval service (including Reserve or National Guard active duty or active duty for training) after September 7, 1939 and before 1968?	☐ Yes (If "Yes," answer (b) and (c))	☐ No (If "No," go to item 12)
	(b) Enter dates of service	FROM: (Month, Year)	TO: (Month, Year)
	(c) Have you ever been (or will you be) eligible for a monthly benefit from a military or civilian Federal agency? (Include Veteran's Administration benefits only if you waived military retirement pay.)	☐ Yes	☐ No
12.	Did you or your spouse (or prior spouse) work in the railroad industry for 5 years or more?	☐ Yes	☐ No
13.	(a) Do you have Social Security credits (for example, based on work or residence) under another country's Social Security System?	☐ Yes (If "Yes," answer (b))	☐ No (If "No," go to item 14)
	(b) List the country(ies):		
14.	(a) Are you entitled to, or do you expect to be entitled to, a pension or annuity (or a lump sum in place of a pension or annuity) based on your work after 1956 not covered by Social Security?	☐ Yes (If "Yes," answer (b) and (c))	☐ No (If "No," go to item 15)
	(b) ☐ I became entitled, or expect to become entitled, beginning	MONTH	YEAR
	(c) ☐ I became eligible, or expect to become eligible, beginning	MONTH	YEAR
	I AGREE TO PROMPTLY NOTIFY the Social Security Administration if I become entitled to a pension or annuity based on my employment not covered by Social Security, or if such pension or annuity stops.		
15.	(a) Have you ever been married?	☐ Yes (If "Yes," answer (b))	☐ No (If "No," go to item 16)

(b) Give the following information about your current marriage. If not currently married, write "None." __________ (If "None," go on to item 15(c))

Spouse's name (including maiden name)	When (Month, day, year)	Where (Name of City and State)

Marriage performed by:	Spouse's date of birth (or age)	Spouse's Social Security Number (If none or unknown, so indicate)
☐ Clergyman or public official ☐ Other (Explain in Remarks)		

(c) Enter information about any other marriage if you:

- Had a marriage that lasted at least 10 years; or
- Had a marriage that ended due to the death of your spouse, regardless of duration; or
- Were divorced, remarried the same individual within the year immediately following the year of the divorce, and the combined period of marriage totaled 10 years or more. If none, write "None." __________ Go on to item 15 (d) if you have a child(ren) who is under age 16 or disabled or handicapped (age 16 or over and disability began before age 22) and you are divorced from the child's other parent who is now deceased and the marriage lasted less than 10 years.

Spouse's name (including maiden name)	When (Month, day, year)	Where (Name of City and State)
How marriage ended	**When (Month, day, year)**	**Where (Name of City and State)**

Marriage performed by:	Spouse's date of birth (or age)	Date of spouse's death	Spouse's Social Security Number (If none or unknown, so indicate)
☐ Clergyman or public official ☐ Other (Explain in Remarks)			

15. (d) Enter information about any marriage if you:

- Have a child(ren) who is under age 16 or disabled or handicapped (age 16 or over and disability began before age 22); and
- Were married for less than 10 years to the child's mother or father, who is now deceased; and
- The marriage ended in divorce

If none, write "None." ______________

Spouse's name (including maiden name)		When (Month, day, year)	Where (Name of City and State)
Date of divorce (Month, day, year)		Where (Name of City and State)	
Marriage performed by: ☐ Clergyman or public official ☐ Other (Explain in Remarks)	Spouse's date of birth (or age)	Date of spouse's death	Spouse's Social Security Number (If none or unknown, so indicate)

Use the "REMARKS" space on page 5 for marriage continuation or explanation.

16. If your claim for disability benefits is approved, your children (including adopted children, and stepchildren) or dependent grandchildren (including stepgrandchildren) may be eligible for benefits based on your earnings record.

List below: FULL NAME OF ALL such children who are now or were in the past 12 months UNMARRIED and:

- UNDER AGE 18
- AGE 18 TO 19 AND ATTENDING ELEMENTARY OR SECONDARY SCHOOL FULL-TIME
- DISABLED OR HANDICAPPED (age 18 or over and disability began before age 22)

17.

(a) Did you have wages or self-employment income covered under Social Security in all years from 1978 through last year?	☐ Yes (If "Yes," go to item 18) ☐ No (If "No," answer (b))
(b) List the years from 1978 through last year in which you did not have wages or self-employment income covered under Social Security.	

18. Enter below the names and addresses of all the persons, companies, or Government agencies for whom you have worked this year and last year. IF NONE, WRITE "NONE" BELOW AND GO TO ITEM 19.

NAME AND ADDRESS OF EMPLOYER (If you had more than one employer, please list them in order beginning with your last (most recent) employer)	Work Began		Work Ended (If still working show "Not Ended")	
	MONTH	YEAR	MONTH	YEAR

(If you need more space, use "Remarks".)

19.	Complete item 19 even if you were an employee.		
	(a) Were you self-employed this year or last year?		☐ Yes (If "Yes," answer (b)) ☐ No (If "No," go to item 20)
	(b) Check the year (or years) you were self-employed	In what type of trade/business were you self-employed? (For example, storekeeper, farmer, physician)	Were your net earnings from the trade or business $400 or more? (Check "Yes" or "No")
	☐ This year		
	☐ Last year		☐ Yes ☐ No
20.	(a) How much were your total earnings last year? Count both wage and self-employment income. (If none, write "None.") ________		Amount $ ________
	(b) How much have you earned so far this year? (If none, write "None.") ________		Amount $ ________
21.	(a) Are you still unable to work because of your illnesses, injuries, or conditions?		☐ Yes (If "Yes," go to item 22) ☐ No (If "No," answer (b))
	(b) Enter the date you became able to work.		MONTH, DAY, YEAR
22.	Are your illnesses, injuries, or conditions related to your work in any way?		☐ Yes ☐ No
23.	Are you blind or do you have low vision even with glasses or contacts?		☐ Yes ☐ No
24.	(a) Have you filed, or do you intend to file, for any other public disability benefits (including workers' compensation, Black Lung benefits and SSI)?		☐ Yes (If "Yes," answer (b)) ☐ No (If "No," to item 25)
	(b) The other public disability benefit(s) you have filed (or intend to file) for is (Check as many as apply): ☐ Veterans Administration Benefits ☐ Welfare ☐ Supplemental Security Income ☐ Other (If "Other," complete a Workers' Compensation/Public Disability Benefit Questionnaire)		
25.	(a) Did you receive any money from an employer(s) on or after the date in item 9 when you became unable to work because of your illnesses, injuries, or conditions? If "Yes", give the amounts and explain in "Remarks".		☐ Yes ☐ No Amount $ ________
	(b) Do you expect to receive any additional money from an employer, such as sick pay, vacation pay, other special pay? If "Yes," please give amounts and explain in "Remarks".		☐ Yes ☐ No Amount $ ________
26.	Do you, or did you, have a child under age 3 (your own or your spouse's) living with you in one or more calendar years when you had no earnings?		☐ Yes ☐ No
27.	Do you have a dependent parent who was receiving at least one-half support from you when you became unable to work because of your disability? If "Yes," enter the parent's name and address and Social Security number, if known, in "Remarks".		☐ Yes ☐ No
28.	If you were unable to work before age 22 because of an illness, injury or condition, do you have a parent (including adoptive or stepparent) or grandparent who is receiving social security retirement or disability benefits or who is deceased? If yes, enter the name(s) and Social Security number, if known, in "Remarks" (if unknown, check "Unknown").		☐ Yes ☐ No ☐ Unknown

REMARKS (You may use this space for any explanation. If you need more space, attach a separate sheet.)

I declare under penalty of perjury that I have examined all the information on this form, and on any accompanying statements or forms, and it is true and correct to the best of my knowledge. I understand that anyone who knowingly gives a false statement about a material fact in this information, or causes someone else to do so, commits a crime and may be subject to a fine or imprisonment.

SIGNATURE OF APPLICANT	Date (Month, Day, Year)
Signature (First name, middle initial, last name) (Write in ink)	Telephone Number(s) at which you may be contacted during the day. (Include the area code)

DIRECT DEPOSIT PAYMENT INFORMATION (FINANCIAL INSTITUTION)

Routing Transit Number	Account Number	☐ Checking	☐ Enroll in Direct Express
		☐ Savings	☐ Direct Deposit Refused

Applicant's Mailing Address *(Number and street, Apt No., P.O. Box, or Rural Route) (Enter Residence Address in "Remarks," if different.)*

City and State	ZIP Code	County *(if any)* in which you now live

Witnesses are required ONLY if this application has been signed by mark (X) above. If signed by mark (X), two witnesses to the signing who know the applicant must sign below, giving their full addresses. Also, print the applicant's name in Signature block.

1. Signature of Witness	2. Signature of Witness
Address *(Number and street, City, State and ZIP Code)*	Address *(Number and street, City, State and ZIP Code)*

FOR YOUR INFORMATION

An agency in your State that works with us in administering the Social Security disability program is responsible for making the disability decision on your claim. In some cases, it is necessary for them to get additional information about your condition or to arrange for you to have a medical examination at Government expense.

Privacy Act Statement
Collection and Use of Information

Sections 202, 205, and 223 of the Social Security Act, as amended, allow us to collect this information. Furnishing us this information is voluntary. However, failing to provide all or part of the information may prevent us from making an accurate and timely decision concerning your or a dependent's eligibility to benefit payments.

We will use the information you provide to help us determine your or a dependent's eligibility for benefit payments. We may also share the information for the following purposes, called routine uses:

1. To State audit agencies for auditing State supplementation payments and Medicaid eligibility considerations.

2. To contractors and other Federal agencies, as necessary, for the purpose of assisting the Social Security Administration in the efficient administration of its programs.

In addition, we may share this information in accordance with the Privacy Act and other Federal laws. For example, where authorized, we may use and disclose this information in computer matching programs, in which our records are compared with other records to establish or verify a person's eligibility for Federal benefit programs and for repayment of incorrect or delinquent debts under these programs.

A list of additional routine uses is available in our Privacy Act System of Records Notices (SORN) 60-0059, entitled Earnings Recording and Self-Employment Income System and 60-0089, entitled Claims Folders System. Additional information and a full listing of all our SORNs are available on our website at www.socialsecurity.gov/foia/bluebook.

Paperwork Reduction Act Statement

This information collection meets the requirements of 44 U.S.C. § 3507, as amended by section 2 of the Paperwork Reduction Act of 1995 . You do not need to answer these questions unless we display a valid Office of Management and Budget control number. We estimate that it will take about 20 minutes to read the instructions, gather the facts, and answer the questions. **SEND OR BRING THE COMPLETED FORM TO YOUR LOCAL SOCIAL SECURITY OFFICE. You can find your local Social Security office through SSA's website at www.socialsecurity.gov. Offices are also listed under U. S. Government agencies in your telephone directory or you may call Social Security at 1-800-772-1213 (TTY 1-800-325-0778).** *You may send comments on our time estimate above to: SSA, 6401 Security Blvd, Baltimore, MD 21235-6401 .* ***Send only comments relating to our time estimate to this address, not the completed form.***

RECEIPT FOR YOUR CLAIM FOR SOCIAL SECURITY DISABILITY INSURANCE BENEFITS

Person to Contact About Your Claim	SSA OFFICE	Date Claim Received
Telephone Number (Include Area Code)		

Your application for Social Security disability benefits has been received and will be processed as quickly as possible.

You should hear from us within ________ days after you have given us all the information we requested. Some claims may take longer if additional information is needed.

In the meantime, if you change your address, or if there is some other change that may affect your claim, you - or someone for you - should report the change. The changes to be reported are listed below.

Always give us your claim number when writing or telephoning about your claim.

If you have any questions about your claim, we will be glad to help you.

CLAIMANT	SOCIAL SECURITY CLAIM NUMBER

CHANGES TO BE REPORTED AND HOW TO REPORT

FAILURE TO REPORT MAY RESULT IN OVERPAYMENTS THAT MUST BE REPAID

- You change your mailing address for checks or residence. To avoid delay in receipt of checks you should ALSO file a regular change of address notice with your post office.
- Your citizenship or immigration status changes.
- You go outside the U.S.A. for 30 consecutive days or longer.
- Any beneficiary dies or becomes unable to handle benefits.
- Custody Change - Report if a person for whom you are filing or who is in your care dies, leaves your care or custody, or changes address.
- You are confined to a jail, prison, penal institution or correctional facility for more than 30 continuous days for conviction of a crime, or you are confined for more than 30 continuous days to a public institution by a court order in connection with a crime.
- You become entitled to a pension, an annuity, or a lump sum payment based on your employment not covered by Social Security, or if such pension or annuity stops.
- Your stepchild is entitled to benefits on your record and you and the stepchild's parent divorce. Stepchild benefits are not payable beginning with the month after the month the divorce becomes final.
- You have an unsatisfied warrant for more than 30 continuous days for your arrest for a crime or attempted crime that is a felony of flight to avoid prosecution or confinement, escape from custody and flight-escape. In most jurisdictions that do not classify crimes as felonies, this applies to a crime that is punishable by death or imprisonment for a term exceeding one year (regardless of the actual sentence imposed).
- You have an unsatisfied warrant for more than 30 continuous days for a violation of probation or parole under Federal or State law.
- Change of Marital Status - Marriage, divorce, annulment of marriage.
- If you become the parent of a child (including an adopted child) after you have filed your claim, let us know about the child so we can decide if the child is eligible for benefits. Failure to report the existence of these children may result in the loss of possible benefits to the child(ren).
- You return to work (as an employee or self-employed) regardless of amount of earnings.
- Your condition improves.
- You are under age 65 and you apply for or begin to receive workers' compensation (including black lung benefits) or another public disability benefit, or the amount of your present workers' compensation or public disability benefit changes or stops, or you receive a lump-sum settlement.

HOW TO REPORT

You can make your reports online, by telephone, mail, or in person, whichever you prefer. If you are awarded benefits, and one or more of the above change(s) occur, you should report by:

- Visiting the section "my Social Security" at our web site at www.socialsecurity.gov;
- Calling us TOLL FREE at 1-800-772-1213;
- If you are deaf or hearing impaired, calling us TOLL FREE at TTY 1-800-325-0778; or
- Calling, visiting or writing your local Social Security office at the phone number and address shown on your claim receipt.

For general information about Social Security, visit our web site at www.socialsecurity.gov.

SSI APPLICATION - FORM - SSA-8000-BK

SOCIAL SECURITY ADMINISTRATION ☐ TEL

Form Approved
OMB No. 0960-0229

APPLICATION FOR SUPPLEMENTAL SECURITY INCOME (SSI)

Note: Social Security Administration staff or others who help people apply for SSI will fill out this form for you.

Do Not Write in This Space
DATE STAMP

I am/We are applying for Supplemental Security Income and any federally administered state supplementation under Title XVI of the Social Security Act, for benefits under the other programs administered by the Social Security Administration, and where applicable, for medical assistance under Title XIX of the Social Security Act.

Filing Date (month, day, year)

☐ Receipt ☐ Protective

☐ FS-SSA/APP ☐ FS-REFERRED

Preferred Language
Written: Spoken:

TYPE OF CLAIM ☐ Individual ☐ Individual with Ineligible Spouse ☐ Couple ☐ Child ☐ Child with Parents

PART I--BASIC ELIGIBILITY-- Answer the questions below beginning with the first moment of the filing date month.

1. (a) First Name, Middle Initial, Last Name | Sex ☐ Male ☐ Female | Birthdate (month, day, year) | Social Security Number

(b) Did you ever use any other names (including maiden name) or any other Social Security Numbers? ☐ YES Go to (c) ☐ NO Go to (d)

(c) Other Name(s) | Other Social Security Number(s) used

(d) If you are also filing for Social Security Benefits, go to #2; otherwise complete the following:

Mother's Maiden Name: Father's Name: Go to #2

2. Applicant's Mailing Address (Number & Street, Apt. No. P.O. Box, Rural Route)

City and State | ZIP Code | County

3. Claimant's Residence Address (If different from applicant's mailing address)

City and State | ZIP Code | County

4. DIRECT DEPOSIT PAYMENT ADDRESS (FINANCIAL INSTITUTION)

Routing Transit Number | Account Number | ☐ Checking ☐ Savings | ☐ Enroll in Direct Express ☐ Direct Deposit Refused

Form SSA-8000-BK (01 2012)
Destroy Prior Editions

Page 1

5.	(a) Are you married?	☐ YES Go to (b) ☐ NO Go to #6
	(b) Date of marriage: (month, day, year)	
	(c) Spouse's Name (First, middle initial, last)	Birthdate (month, day, year) / Social Security Number
	(d) Did your spouse ever use any other names (including maiden name) or Social Security Numbers?	☐ YES Go to (e) ☐ NO Go to (f)
	(e) Other Name(s)	Other Social Security Number(s) Used
	(f) Are you and your spouse living together?	☐ YES Go to #6 ☐ NO Go to (g)
	(g) Date you began living apart : (month, day, year)	
	(h) Address of spouse or name of someone who knows where spouse is. (Complete only if spouse is age 65, blind or disabled.)	

		You	Your Spouse, if filing
6.	(a) Have you had any other marriages? If never married, check this box ☐	☐ YES Go to (b) ☐ NO Go to #7	☐ YES Go to (b) ☐ NO Go to #7

(b) Give the following information about your former spouse. If there was more than one former marriage, show the remaining information in Remarks and go to #4.

	YOU	YOUR SPOUSE
FORMER SPOUSE'S NAME (including maiden name)		
BIRTHDATE (month, day, year)		
SOCIAL SECURITY NUMBER		
DATE OF MARRIAGE (month, day, year)		
DATE MARRIAGE ENDED (month, day, year)		
HOW MARRIAGE ENDED		

7. If you are filing for yourself, go to (a); if you are filing for a child, go to (e).

	You	Your Spouse
(a) Are you unable to work because of illnesses, injuries or conditions?	☐ YES Go to (b) ☐ NO Go to #8	☐ YES Go to (b) ☐ NO Go to #7
(b) Enter the date you became unable to work.	(month, day, year)	(month, day, year)

(c) What are your illnesses, injuries or conditions?

You	Your Spouse
Go to (d)	Go to (d)

7. (d) If you were unable to work because of illnesses, injuries, or conditions before you were age 22, do you have a parent who is age 62 or older, unable to work because of illnesses, injuries or conditions, or deceased?

☐ YES Parent's Name: ____________________

Social Security Number: ____________________

Address: ____________________

____

☐ NO Go to #8

(e) When did the child become disabled? ____________ (month, day, year) Go to (f)

(f) What are the child's disabling illnesses, injuries or conditions?

Go to (g)

(g) Does the child have a parent(s) who is age 62 or older, unable to work because of illness, injuries, or conditions, or deceased?

☐ YES Parent's Name: ____________________

Social Security Number: ____________________

Address: ____________________

____

☐ NO Go to #8

8.	Birthplace	City	State	Country (if other than the U.S.)
	You			
	Your Spouse, if filing			Go to #9

		You		Your Spouse, if filing	
9.	Are you a United States citizen by birth?	☐ YES Go to #15	☐ NO Go to #10	☐ YES Go to #15	☐ NO Go to #10
10.	Are you a naturalized United States citizen?	☐ YES Go to #15	☐ NO Go to #11	☐ YES Go to #15	☐ NO Go to #11
11.	(a) Are you an American Indian born outside the United States?	☐ YES Go to (b)	☐ NO Go to (c)	☐ YES Go to (b)	☐ NO Go to (c)

(b) Check the block that shows your American Indian status.

You	Your Spouse, if filing
☐ American Indian born in Canada Go to #15	☐ American Indian born in Canada Go to #15
☐ Member of a Federally recognized Indian Tribe; Name of Tribe Go to #15	☐ Member of a Federally recognized Indian Tribe; Name of Tribe Go to #15
☐ Other American Indian Explain in Remarks, then Go to (c)	☐ Other American Indian Explain in Remarks, then Go to (c)

11.	(c) Check the block below that shows your current immigration status	
	You	Your Spouse, if filing
	☐ Amerasian Immigrant Go to #12	☐ Amerasian Immigrant Go to #12
	☐ Lawful Permanent Resident Go to #12	☐ Lawful Permanent Resident Go to #12
	☐ Refugee Date of entry: Go to #14	☐ Refugee Date of entry: Go to #14
	☐ Asylee Date status granted: Go to #14	☐ Asylee Date status granted: Go to #14
	☐ Conditional Entrant Date status granted: Go to #14	☐ Conditional Entrant Date status granted: Go to #14
	☐ Parolee for One Year Go to #14	☐ Parolee for One Year Go to #14
	☐ Cuban/Haitian Entrant Go to #14	☐ Cuban/Haitian Entrant Go to #14
	☐ Deportation/Removal Withheld Date: Go to #14	☐ Deportation/Removal Withheld Date: Go to #14
	☐ Other Explain in Remarks, then Go to (d)	☐ Other Explain in Remarks, then Go to (d)
	(d) If you have status, or have applied for status as the spouse, child, or parent of a child of a US citizen, or lawfully admitted permanent resident alien, Go to #13; otherwise Go to #15.	

12. If you are lawfully admitted for permanent residence:

	You	Your Spouse
(a) Date of Admission	(month, day, year)	(month, day, year)
(b) Was your entry into the United States sponsored by any person or promoted by an institution or group?	☐ YES Go to (c) ☐ NO Go to (d)	☐ YES Go to (c) ☐ NO Go to (d)

(c) Give the following information about the person, institution, or group, then Go to (d):

Name	Address	Telephone Number
		( ) -

	You	Your Spouse, if filing
(d) What was your immigration status, if any, before adjustment to lawful permanent resident?	Status:	Status:
	(month, day, year) From: To:	(month, day, year) From: To: Go to (e)
(e) If filing as an adult, did your parents ever work in the United States before you were age 18?	☐ YES Go to (f) ☐ NO Go to #14	☐ YES Go to (f) ☐ NO Go to #14

(f) Name and Social Security Number of parent(s) who worked.

Name	Social Security Number
Name	Social Security Number

		You		Your Spouse, if filing	
13.	(a) Have you, your child or your parent, been subjected to battery or extreme cruelty while in the United States?	☐ YES Go to (b)	☐ NO Go to #15	☐ YES Go to (b)	☐ NO Go to #15
	(b) Have you, your child, or your parent filed a petition with the Department of Homeland Security for a change in immigration status because of being subjected to battery or extreme cruelty?	☐ YES Go to #14	☐ NO Go to #15	☐ YES Go to #14	☐ NO Go to #15
14.	Are you, your spouse, or parent an active duty member or a veteran of the armed forces of the United States?	☐ YES Explain in #60(b), then Go to #15	☐ NO Go to #15	☐ YES Explain in #60(b), then Go to #15	☐ NO Go to #15
15.	(a) When did you first make your home in the United States?	(month, day, year)		(month, day, year)	
	(b) Have you lived outside of the United States since then?	☐ YES Go to (c)	☐ NO Go to #16	☐ YES Go to (c)	☐ NO Go to #16
	(c) Give the dates of residence outside the United States.	(month, day, year) From: To:		(month, day, year) From: To:	
16.	(a) Have you been outside the United States (the 50 states, District of Columbia and Northern Mariana Islands) 30 consecutive days prior to the filing date?	☐ YES Go to (b)	☐ NO Go to #17	☐ YES Go to (b)	☐ NO Go to #17
	(b) Give the date (month, day, year) you left the United States and the date you returned to the United States.	Date Left: Date Returned:		Date Left: Date Returned:	

IF YOU ARE FILING ON BEHALF OF YOUR CHILD, GO TO #17.
IF YOU ARE MARRIED AND YOUR SPOUSE IS NOT FILING FOR SUPPLEMENTAL SECURITY INCOME AND YOU LIVED TOGETHER AT ANY TIME SINCE THE FIRST MOMENT OF THE FILING DATE MONTH, GO TO #17; OTHERWISE GO TO #18.

17.	(a) Is your spouse/parent the sponsor of an alien who is eligible for supplemental security income?	☐ YES Go to (b) ☐ No Go to #18
	(b) Eligible Alien's Name	Eligible Alien's Social Security Number Go to #18

		You		Your Spouse, if filing	
18.	(a) Do you have any unsatisfied felony warrants for your arrest?	☐ YES Go to (b)	☐ NO Go to #19	☐ YES Go to (b)	☐ NO Go to #19
	(b) In which state or country was this warrant issued?	Name of State/Country Go to (c)		Name of State/Country Go to (c)	
	(c) Was the warrant satisfied?	☐ YES Go to (d)	☐ NO Go to #19	☐ YES Go to (d)	☐ NO Go to #19
	(d) Date warrant satisfied	(month, day, year)		(month, day, year)	
19.	(a) Do you have any unsatisfied Federal or State warrants for violating the conditions of probation or parole?	☐ YES Go to (b)	☐ NO Go to #20	☐ YES Go to (b)	☐ NO Go to #20

19.			
	(b) In which state or country was the warrant issued?	Name of State/Country Go to (c)	Name of State/Country Go to (c)
	(c) Was the warrant satisfied?	☐ YES Go to (d) ☐ NO Go to #20	☐ YES Go to (d) ☐ NO Go to #20
	(d) Date warrant satisfied	(month, day, year)	(month, day, year)

PART II - LIVING ARRANGEMENTS - The questions in this section refer to the signature date.

20.	Check the block which best describes your present living situation:	
	☐ Household	Since (month, day, year) Go to #25
	☐ Non Institutional Care	Since (month, day, year) Go to #23
	☐ Institution	Since (month, day, year) Go to #21
	☐ Transient or homeless	Since (month, day, year) Go to #38

INSTITUTION

21.	Check the block that identifies the type of institution where you currently reside, then Go to #22:	
	☐ School	☐ Rehabilitation Center
	☐ Hospital	☐ Jail
	☐ Rest or Retirement Home	☐ Other (Specify)
	☐ Nursing Home	

22.	Give the following information about the INSTITUTION:
	(a) Name of institution:
	(b) Date of admission:
	(c) Date you expect to be released from this institution: Go to #38

NON-INSTITUTIONAL CARE

23.	Check the block that best describes your current residence, then Go to #24:		
	☐ Foster Home	☐ Group Home	☐ Other (Specify)

24.	Give the following information about your Noninstitutional Care:
	(a) Name of facility where you live:

24.	(b) Name of placing agency	Address	Telephone Number
			( ) -

(c) Does this agency pay for your room and board?

☐ YES Go to #38 ☐ NO If NO, who pays? Go to #38

HOUSEHOLD ARRANGEMENTS

25. Check the block that describes your current residence, then Go to #26:

☐ House	☐ Mobile Home
☐ Apartment	☐ Houseboat
☐ Room (private home)	☐ Other (Specify)
☐ Room (commercial establishment)	

26. Do you live alone or only with your spouse? ☐ YES Go to #28 ☐ NO Go to #27

27. (a) Give the following information about everyone who lives with you:

Name	Relationship	Public Assistance		Sex		Birthdate	Blind or Disabled		If Under 22				Social Security Number
									Married		Student		
		YES	NO	M	F	mm/dd/yy	YES	NO	YES	NO	YES	NO	

If anyone listed is under age 22 and not married, Go to (b); otherwise, Go to #28.

27.	(b) Does anyone listed in 27(a) who is under age 18, OR between ages 18 22 and a student, receive income?	☐ YES Go to (c)	☐ NO Go to #28

(c) Child Receiving Income	Source and Type	Monthly Amount
		$
		$
		$
		$
		$
		$

28.	(a) Do you (or does anyone who lives with you) own or rent the place where you live?	☐ YES Go to #29	☐ No Go to (b)

(b) Name of person who owns or rents the place where you live	Address	Telephone Number
		( ) -

(c) If you live alone or only with your spouse, and do not own or rent, Go to #38; otherwise, Go to #32.

29.	(a) Are you (or your living with spouse) buying or do you own the place where you live?	☐ YES Go to (c)	☐ No If you are a child living with your parent(s) Go to (b); otherwise Go to #30
	(b) Are your parent(s) buying or do they own the place where you live?	☐ YES Go to (c)	☐ NO Go to #30

(c) What is the amount and frequency of the mortgage payment?

Amount: $ Frequency of Payment: Go to (d)

(d) If you are a child living only with your parents, or only with your parents and their other children who are subject to deeming, or with others in a public assistance household, or living alone or with your spouse, Go to #38; otherwise Go to #32.

30.	(a) Do you (or your living with spouse) have rental liability for the place where you live?	☐ YES Go to (d)	☐ NO If you are a child living with your parent(s) Go to (b); otherwise Go to (c)
	(b) Does your parent(s) have rental liability?	☐ YES Go to (d)	☐ NO Go to (c)

30. (c) Does anyone who lives with you have rental liability for the place where you live?

☐ YES Give name of person with rental liability: ____________ Go to #31

☐ NO Give name of person with home ownership: ____________ Go to #32

(d) What is the amount and frequency of the rent payment?

Amount: $ Frequency of Payment:

Go to #31

31. (a) Are you (or anyone who lives with you) the parent or child of the landlord or the landlord's spouse? ☐ YES Go to (b) ☐ NO Go to (c)

(b) Name of person related to landlord or landlord's spouse	Relationship	Name and address of landlord (include telephone number and area code, if known):

(c) If you are a child living only with your parents, or only with your parents and their other children who are subject to deeming, or with others in a public assistance household, or living alone or with your spouse, Go to #38.

32. (a) Does anyone living with you contribute to the household expenses? (NOTE: See list of household expenses in #37) ☐ YES Go to (b) ☐ NO Go to #33

(b) Amount others contribute: $

Go to #33

33. (a) Do you eat all your meals out? ☐ YES Go to #34 ☐ NO Go to (b)

(b) Do you buy all your food separately from other household members: ☐ YES Go to #34 ☐ NO Go to #34

34. Do you contribute to household expenses?

☐ YES Average Monthly Amount: $ ____________ Go to #35

☐ NO Go to #35

35 (a) Do you have a loan agreement with anyone to repay the value of your share of the household expenses? ☐ YES Go to (b) ☐ NO Go to #35(d)

(b) Give the name, address and telephone number of the person with whom you have a loan agreement :

(c) Will the amount of this loan cover your share of the household expenses? ☐ YES Go to #38 ☐ NO Go to (d)

(d) If you contribute toward household expenses and you answered "NO" to both 33(a) & (b), Go To #36. If you answered "YES" to either 33(a) or 33(b), Go to #37.
If you do not contribute toward household expenses, go to #38.

36. (a) Is part or all of the amount in #34 just for food?

☐ YES Give Amount: $ ____________ Go to (b) ☐ NO Go to (b)

(b) Is part or all of the amount in #34 just for shelter?

☐ YES Give Amount: $ ____________ Go to #37 ☐ NO Go to #37

37. What is the average monthly amount of the following household expenses:
(Show average over the past 12 months unless you have been residing at your present address less than 12 months. If so, show average for the months you have resided at your present address.)

CASH EXPENSES	AVERAGE MONTHLY AMOUNT
Food (complete only if #33(a) & (b) are answered NO)	$
Mortgage or Rent	$
Property Insurance (if required by mortgage lender)	$
Real Property Taxes	$
Electricity	$
Heating Fuel	$
Gas	$
Sewer	$
Garbage Removal	$
Water	$
TOTAL	$ Go to #38

38. (a) Does anyone who does NOT LIVE with you pay for, or provide you or your household (if applicable), any of your food or shelter items?

☐ YES Name of Provider (Person or Agency) ____________

List of Items ____________

Monthly Value: $ ____________

☐ NO — Go to (b)

(b) Does anyone who does NOT LIVE with you give you, or your household (if applicable), money to pay for any of your or your household's food or shelter items?

☐ YES Name of Provider (Person or Agency) ____________

List of Items ____________

Monthly Value: $ ____________

☐ NO — Go to #39

39.		
(a) Has the information given in #20-38 been the same since the first moment of the filing date month?	☐ YES Go to (b)	☐ NO Explain in Remarks, then Go to (b)
(b) Do you expect any of this information to change?	☐ YES Explain in Remarks, then Go to #40	☐ NO Go to #40

PART III - RESOURCES - The questions in this section pertain to the first moment of the filing date month.

40.	You		Your Spouse	
(a) Do you own, or does your name appear (alone or with any other person's name) on the title of any vehicles (auto, truck, motorcycle, camper, boat, etc.)?	☐ YES Go to (b)	☐ NO Go to #41	☐ YES Go to (b)	☐ NO Go to #41

40.	(b) Owner's Name	Description (Year, Make & Model)	Used For	Current Market Value	Amount Owed
				$	$
				$	$
				$	$
				$	$

41. (a) Do you own or are you buying any life insurance policies?

	You		Your Spouse	
	☐ YES	☐ NO	☐ YES	☐ NO
	Go to (b)	Go to #42	Go to (b)	Go to #42

(b)	Owner's Name	Name of Insured	Name & Address of Insurance Company	Policy Number
Policy (#1)				
Policy (#2)				
Policy (#3)				

	Face Value	Cash Surrender Value	Date of Purchase	Dividends		Accumulations	
				YES	NO	YES	NO
Policy (#1)	$	$					
Policy (#2)	$	$					
Policy (#3)	$	$					

(c) Loans Against Policy? ☐ YES ☐ NO

Policy Number: ______________________________

Amount: $________________ Go to #42

42. (a) Do you (either alone or jointly with any other person) own any:	You		Your Spouse	
	YES	NO	YES	NO
Life estates or ownership interest in an unprobated estate?				
Items acquired or held for their value as an investment?	☐	☐	☐	☐

42. (b) Give the following information for any "Yes" answer in #42(a); otherwise, Go to #43.

Owner's Name	Name of Item	Value	Amount Owed	Give Name & Address of Bank or Other Organization
		$	$	
		$	$	
		$	$	
		$	$	

43. (a) Do you own, or does your name appear on (either alone or with any other person's name) any of the following items?

	You		Your Spouse	
	YES	NO	YES	NO
Cash at home, with you, or anywhere else				
Financial Institution Accounts				
Checking				
Savings				
Credit Union				
Christmas Club				
Time Deposits/Certificates of Deposit				
Individual Indian Money Account				
Other (Including IRAs and Keough Accounts)				

(b) If all the items in #43(a) are answered "NO", Go to #44. For any "YES" answer, give the following information:

Owner's/Trustee's Name	Name of Item	Value	Name & Address of Bank or Other Organization	Identifying Number
		$		
		$		
		$		

44.		You		Your Spouse, if filing	
	(a) Do you give us permission to obtain any financial records from any financial institution?	☐ YES Go to (b)	☐ NO Go to (b)	☐ YES Go to (b)	☐ NO Go to (b)
	(b) Do you own or does your name appear on any of the following items:	You		Your Spouse	
		YES	NO	YES	NO
	Stocks or Mutual Funds				
	Bonds (Including U.S. Savings Bonds)				
	Promissory Notes				
	Trusts				
	Other items that can be turned into cash				

(c) If all the items in #44(b) are answered "NO", Go to #45. For any "YES" answer, give the following information:

Owner's/Trustee's Name	Name of Item	Value	Name & Address of Bank or Other Organization	Identifying Number
		$		
		$		
		$		
		$		

45.		You		Your Spouse	
	(a) Do you own, or does your name appear (alone or with any other person's name) on any land, houses, buildings, real property, property in foreign country, equipment, mineral rights, items in a safe deposit box, assets set aside for emergencies or heirs, or any other property of any kind that has not been shown anywhere else on the application	☐ YES Go to (b)	☐ NO Go to #46	☐ YES Go to (b)	☐ NO Go to #46

(b) Describe the property (including size, location, and how it is used. If the property is not used now, when was it last used? Do you plan to use the property in the future?

Item #1

Item #2

45.	Owner's Name	Estimated Current Market Value	Tax Assessed Value	Mortgage	Owed on Item
		$	$	$	$
		$	$	$	$
		$	$	$	$

46.	(a) Have you or your spouse acquired any assets since the first moment of the filing date month?	☐ YES Go to (b) ☐ NO Go to (c)
	(b) Explain:	
	(c) Has there been any increase or decrease in the value of you or your spouse's resources since the first moment of the filing date month?	☐ YES Go to (d) ☐ NO Go to #47
	(d) Explain:	

		You	Your Spouse
47.	(a) Have you or your spouse sold, transferred title, disposed of or given away, any money or other property, (including money or property in foreign countries), since the first moment of the filing date month or within the 36 months prior to the filing date month?	☐ YES ☐ NO Go to (b)	☐ YES ☐ NO Go to (b)
	(b) If you co owned any money or property with another person(s), did you or any co owner sell, transfer, or give away any co owned money or property within the 36 months prior to the filing date month?	☐ YES ☐ NO	☐ YES ☐ NO

IF YOU ANSWERED "YES" TO (a) OR (b), GO TO (c). IF "NO" TO BOTH, GO TO #48.

(c)	OWNER'S/CO-OWNERS NAME	DESCRIPTION OF PROPERTY	DATE OF DISPOSAL
ITEM #1			
ITEM #2			
ITEM #3			
	NAME AND ADDRESS OR PURCHASER OR RECIPIENT	**RELATIONSHIP TO OWNER**	**VALUE OF PROPERTY AND/OR AMOUNT OF CASH GIFT**
ITEM #1			$

47.				
	ITEM #2			$
	ITEM #3			$
		SALES PRICE OR OTHER CONSIDERATION	ARE OTHER CONSIDERATION OR PROCEEDS EXPECTED? EXPLAIN.	DO YOU STILL OWN PART OF THE PROPERTY?
	ITEM #1			
	ITEM #2			
	ITEM #3			
		SOLD ON OPEN MARKET?	GIVEN AWAY?	TRADED FOR GOODS/SERVICES?
	ITEM #1	☐ YES ☐ NO	☐ YES ☐ NO	☐ YES ☐ NO
	ITEM #2	☐ YES ☐ NO	☐ YES ☐ NO	☐ YES ☐ NO
	ITEM #3	☐ YES ☐ NO	☐ YES ☐ NO	☐ YES ☐ NO

48. (a) Do you have any assets set aside for burial expenses such as burial contracts, trusts, agreements, or anything else you intend for your burial expenses? Include any items mentioned in #41 and #43 47.

You		Your Spouse	
☐ YES Go to (b)	☐ NO Go to #49	☐ YES Go to (b)	☐ NO Go to #49

(b) DESCRIPTION (Where appropriate, give name & address of organization and account/policy number.)	VALUE	WHEN SET ASIDE (month, day, year)	OWNER'S NAME
Item 1	$		
Item 2	$		

FOR WHOSE BURIAL	IS ITEM IRREVOCABLE?	WILL INTEREST EARNED OR APPRECIATION IN VALUE REMAIN IN THE BURIAL FUND?
Item 1	☐ YES ☐ NO	☐ YES Go to #49 ☐ NO Explain in (c)
Item 1	☐ YES ☐ NO	☐ YES Go to #49 ☐ NO Explain in (c)

(c) EXPLANATION

		You		Your Spouse	
49.	(a) Do you own any cemetery lots, crypts, caskets, vaults, urns, mausoleums, or other repositories for burial or any headstones or markers?	☐ YES Go to (b)	☐ NO Go to #50	☐ YES Go to (b)	☐ NO Go to #50

(b) Owner's Name	Description	For Whose Burial	Relationship to You or Your Spouse	Current Market Value
				$
				$
				$

Go to #50

PART IV -- INCOME

50. (a) Since the first moment of the filing date month, have you (or your spouse) received or do you (or your spouse) expect to receive income in the next 14 months from any of the following sources?	You		Your Spouse	
	YES	NO	YES	NO
State or Local Assistance Based on Need				
Refugee Cash Assistance				
Temporary Assistance for Needy Families				
General Assistance from the Bureau of Indian Affairs				
Disaster Relief				
Veteran Benefits Based on Need (Paid Directly or Indirectly as a Dependent)				
Veteran Payments Not Based on Need (Paid Directly or Indirectly as a Dependent)				
Other Income Based on Need				
Social Security				
Black Lung				
Railroad Retirement Board Benefits				
Office of Personnel Management (Civil Service)				
Pension (Foreign Military, State, Local, Private, Union, Retirement or Disability)				
Military Special Pay or Allowance				
Unemployment Compensation				

50.	Workers' Compensation				
	State Disability				
	Insurance or Annuity Payments				
	Dividends/Royalties				
	Rental/Lease Income Not from a Trade or Business				
	Alimony				
	Child Support				
	Other Bureau of Indian Affairs Income				
	Gambling/Lottery Winnings				
	Other Income or Support				

(b) Give the following information for any block checked YES in #50(a); otherwise, Go to #51

Person Receiving Income	Type of Income	Amount Received	Frequency of Payment	Date Expected or Received	Source (Name, Address of Person, Bank, Organization or Company)	Identifying Number
		$				
		$				
		$				

IF YOU EVER RECEIVED SSI BEFORE, GO TO #51; OTHERWISE GO TO #52

		You		Your Spouse	
51.	Are any overpayments being collected from benefits you receive from the Social Security Administration, Railroad Retirement Board, Office of Personnel Management, Veterans' Affairs, Military Pensions, Military Special Pay Allowances, Black Lung, Workers' Compensation, or State Disability or Unemployment Benefits?	☐ YES Explain in Remarks, then Go to #52	☐ NO Go to #52	☐ YES Explain in Remarks, then Go to #52	☐ NO Go to #52
52.	Since the first moment of the filing date month, have you received or do you expect to receive any meals or other gifts which are not cash?	☐ YES Explain in Remarks, then Go to #53	☐ NO Go to #53	☐ YES Explain in Remarks, then Go to #53	☐ NO Go to #53
53.	(a) Have you (or your spouse) received wages or sick pay since the first moment of the filing date month through the current month?	☐ YES Go to (b)	☐ NO Go to (e)	☐ YES Go to (b)	☐ NO Go to (e)

(b) Name and Address of Employer (include telephone number and area code, if known)

You	Your Spouse
Go to (c)	Go to (c)

53. (c)	Date last worked (month, day, year)	Date last paid (month, day, year)	Date next paid (month, day, year)
You			
Your Spouse			

(d) Total monthly wages received (before any deductions)	Your Amount $	Your Spouse's Amount $
(e) Do you (or your spouse) expect to receive any wages in the next 14 months?	You: ☐ YES Go to (f) ☐ NO Go to #54	Your Spouse: ☐ YES Go to (f) ☐ NO Go to #54

(f) Name and address of employer if different from #53(b) (include telephone number, if known)

You	Your Spouse

(g) Give the following information:

	RATE OF PAY	AMOUNT WORKED PER PAY PERIOD	HOW OFTEN PAID	PAY DAY OR DATE PAID	DATE LAST PAID (month, day, year)
You	$				
Your Spouse	$				

(h) Do you expect any change in wage information provided in #53(g)	You: ☐ YES Go to (i) ☐ NO Go to #54	Your Spouse: ☐ YES Go to (i) ☐ NO Go to #54

(i) Explain Change:

You	Your Spouse

54. (a) Have you been self employed at any time since the beginning of the taxable year in which the filing date month occurs or do you expect to be self employed in the current taxable year?	You: ☐ YES Go to (b) ☐ NO Go to #55	Your Spouse: ☐ YES Go to (b) ☐ NO Go to #55

(b) Give the following information; then Go to #55

Date(s) Self-Employed	Type of Business	Last Year's: Gross Income	Last Year's: Net Profit	Last Year's: Net Loss
		$	$	$
Date(s) Self-Employed	**Type of Business**	**This Year's: Gross Income**	**This Year's: Net Profit**	**This Year's: Net Loss**
		$	$	$

		You		Your Spouse	
55.	If you or your spouse are blind or disabled, do you have any special expenses that you paid which are necessary for you to work?	☐ YES Explain in Remarks; then Go to #56	☐ NO Go to #56	☐ YES Explain in Remarks; then Go to #56	☐ NO Go to #56

56.	(a) Does your spouse/parent who lives with you have to pay court ordered support?	☐ YES Go to (b)	☐ NO Go to NOTE
	(b) Give amount and frequency of court ordered support payment.	Amount: $	Frequency: Go to (c)
	(c) Give the following information about the person who receives these payments:	Name:	Address:

NOTE: IF YOU ARE FILING AS A CHILD AND YOU ARE EMPLOYED OR AGE 18 - 22 (WHETHER EMPLOYED OR NOT), GO TO #57; OTHERWISE, GO TO #58.

57.	(a) Have you attended school regularly since the filing date month?	☐ YES Go to (d)	☐ NO Go to (b)
	(b) Have you been out of school for more than 4 calendar months?	☐ YES Go to (c)	☐ NO Go to (c)
	(c) Do you plan to attend school regularly during the next 4 months?	☐ YES Explain absence in Remarks and Go to (d)	☐ NO Go to #58

(d) Name of School	Name of School Contact	Dates of Attendance From	To	Course of Study
	Phone Number	Hours Attending or Planning to Attend		

PART V - POTENTIAL ELIGIBILITY FOR FOOD STAMPS/MEDICAL ASSISTANCE/OTHER BENEFITS - If a California resident, Skip to #59

		You		Your Spouse, if filing	
58.	(a) Are you currently receiving food stamps?	☐ YES Go to (b)	☐ NO Go to (c)	☐ YES Go to (b)	☐ NO Go to (c)
	(b) Have you received a recertification notice within the past 30 days?	☐ YES Go to (e)	☐ NO Go to #59	☐ YES Go to (e)	☐ NO Go to #59
	(c) Have you filed for food stamps in the last 60 days?	☐ YES Go to (d)	☐ NO Go to (e)	☐ YES Go to (d)	☐ NO Go to (e)
	(d) Have you received an unfavorable decision?	☐ YES Go to (e)	☐ NO Go to #59	☐ YES Go to (e)	☐ NO Go to #59
	(e) If everyone in the household receives or is applying for SSI, Go to (f); otherwise Go to #59.				
	(f) May I take your food stamp application today?	☐ YES Go to #59	☐ NO Explain in (g)	☐ YES Go to #59	☐ NO Explain in (g)
	(g) Explanation:				

59.	You may be eligible for Medicaid. However, you must help your State identify other sources that pay for medical care. Also, you must give information to help the State get medical support for any child(ren) who is your legal responsibility. This includes information to help the State determine who a child's father is. If you want Medicaid, you must agree to allow your State to seek payments from sources, such as insurance companies, that are available to pay for your medical care. This includes payments for medical care for you or any person who receives Medicaid and is your legal responsibility. The State cannot provide you Medicaid if you do not agree to this Medicaid requirement. If you need further information, you may contact your Medicaid Agency.				
	IN STATES WITH AUTOMATIC ASSIGNMENT OF RIGHTS LAWS. Go to (b).				
		You		Your Spouse, if filing	
	(a) Do you agree to assign your rights (or the rights of anyone for whom you can legally assign rights) to payments for medical support and other medical care to the State Medicaid agency?	☐ YES Go to (b)	☐ NO Go to #60	☐ YES Go to (b)	☐ NO Go to #60
	(b) Do you, your spouse, parent or stepparent have any private, group, or governmental health insurance that pays the cost of your medical care? (Do not include Medicare or Medicaid.)	☐ YES Go to (c)	☐ NO Go to (c)	☐ YES Go to (c)	☐ NO Go to (c)
	(c) Do you have any unpaid medical expenses for the 3 months prior to the filing date month?	☐ YES Go to #60	☐ NO Go to #60	☐ YES Go to #60	☐ NO Go to #60
60.	(a) Have you ever worked under the U.S. Social Security System?	☐ YES Go to (b)		☐ NO Go to (b)	

(b) Have you, your spouse, or a former spouse (or parent if you are filing as a child) ever:	You		Your Spouse/Parent		Filed for Benefits	
	Yes	No	Yes	No	Yes	No
Worked for a railroad						
Been in military service						
Worked for the Federal Government						
Worked for a State or Local Government						
Worked for an employer with a pension plan						
Belonged to union with a pension plan						
Worked under a Social Security system or pension plan of a country other than the United States?						

(c) Explain and include dates for any "Yes" answer given in #14 or #60(a); otherwise Go to #61.

You:	Your Spouse, if filing/Your Parent, if filing as a child:

PART VI -- MISCELLANEOUS (Answer #61 ONLY IF YOU ARE APPLYING ON BEHALF OF SOMEONE ELSE; OTHERWISE GO TO #62.

61.	(a) Name of Person/Agency Requesting Benefits.	Relationship to Claimant	Your Social Security Number (or EIN)
	(b) If SSA determines that the claimant needs help managing benefits, do you wish to be selected representative payee?	☐ YES	☐ NO (Explain in Remarks)

PART VII -- REMARKS--(You may use this space for any explanations. Enter the item number before each explanation. If you need more space, use a signed form SSA-795.)

PART VIII -- IMPORTANT INFORMATION AND SIGNATURES

62. IMPORTANT INFORMATION--PLEASE READ CAREFULLY

- ▶ Failure to report any change within 10 days after the end of the month in which the change occurs could result in a penalty deduction.
- ▶ The Social Security Administration will check your statements and compare its records with records from other State and Federal agencies, including the Internal Revenue Service, to make sure you are paid the correct amount.
- ▶ We have asked you for permission to obtain, from any financial institution, any financial record about you that is held by the institution. We will ask financial institutions for this information whenever we think it is needed to decide if you are eligible or if you continue to be eligible for SSI benefits. Once authorized, our permission to contact financial institutions remains in effect until one of the following occurs: (1) you or your spouse notify us in writing that you are canceling your permission, (2) your application for SSI is denied in a final decision, (3) your eligibility for SSI terminates, or (4) we no longer consider your spouse's income and resources to be available to you. If you or your spouse do not give or cancel your permission you may not be eligible for SSI and we may deny your claim or stop your payments.

63. I declare under penalty of perjury that I have examined all the information on this form, and on any accompanying statements or forms, and it is true and correct to the best of my knowledge. I understand that anyone who knowingly gives a false or misleading statement about a material fact in this information, or causes someone else to do so, commits a crime and may be sent to prison, or may face other penalties, or both.

Your Signature (First name, middle initial, last name) (Sign in ink.)	Date (month, day, year)
SIGN HERE ▶	Telephone Number(s) where we can contact you during the day: ( ) -

Spouse's Signature (Sign only if applying for payments.) (First name, middle initial, last name) (Sign in ink.)

SIGN HERE ▶

64. If you are blind or visually impaired, check the type of mail you want to receive from us.

☐ Standard notice First Class ☐ Standard notice First-Class with a follow-up phone call ☐ Standard notice & data CD by First-Class

☐ Standard notice Certified ☐ Standard & Braille notices by First-Class ☐ Standard & large print notices ☐ Standard notice & audio CD

65. WITNESS

Your application does not ordinarily have to be witnessed. If, however, you have signed by mark (X), two witnesses to the signing who know you, must sign below giving their full address.

1. Signature of Witness	2. Signature of Witness
Address (Number and Street, City, State, and ZIP Code)	Address (Number and Street, City, State, and ZIP Code)

RECEIPT FOR YOUR CLAIM FOR SUPPLEMENTAL SECURITY INCOME

Name	Social Security Number	Date
Name	Social Security Number	Date

If you have a question or something to report call: ( ) -	Social Security Office you may visit or mail your request to:

For general information about Social Security, visit our website at www.socialsecurity.gov on the Internet.

We will process your application for Supplemental Security Income as quickly as possible. If you have trouble getting any information or records we have asked for, please contact us and we will help you.

You should hear from us within _____ days after you have given us all the information we requested. Some claims may take longer if additional information is needed. If you do not get a check or notice of determination within that time, please get in touch with us.

Privacy Act Statement/ Paperwork Reduction Act Statement
Collection and Use of Personal Information

Section 1631(e) of the Social Security Act, as amended, authorizes us to collect this information. We will use this information to help us determine your entitlement to benefits. Furnishing us this information is voluntary. However, failing to provide us with all or part of the requested information may prevent us from making an accurate and timely decision on your claim, which may result in the loss of payments. We rarely use the information you supply for any purpose other than for determining problems in Social Security programs. However, we may use it for the administration and integrity of Social Security programs. We may also disclose information to another person or to another agency in accordance with approved routine uses, which include, but are not limited to the following:

1. To enable a third party or an agency to assist Social Security in establishing rights to Medicare benefits and/or coverage;
2. To comply with Federal laws requiring the release of information from Social Security records (e.g., to the Government Accountability Office and the Department of Veterans' Affairs);
3. To make determinations for eligibility in similar health and income maintenance programs at the Federal, State and local level; and,
4. To facilitate statistical research and audit activities necessary to assure the integrity and improvement of Social Security programs.

We may also use the information you provide in computer matching programs. Matching programs compare our records with records kept by other Federal, State, or local government agencies. Information from these matching programs can be used to establish or verify a person's eligibility for federally-funded or administered benefit programs and for repayment of payments or delinquent debts under these programs.

A complete use of routine uses for this information is available in System of Records Notices 60-0089, Claims Folder System and 60-0050, Completed Determination-Continuing Disability Determinations. These notices, additional information regarding this form, and information regarding our programs and systems, are available on-line at www.socialsecurity.gov or any local Social Security office.

Paperwork Reduction Act Statement - This information collection meets the requirements of 44 U.S.C. § 3507, as amended by section 2 of the Paperwork Reduction Act of 1995. You do not need to answer these questions unless we display a valid Office of Management and Budget control number. We estimate that it will take about 40 minutes to read the instructions, gather the facts, and answer the questions. **SEND OR BRING THE COMPLETED FORM TO YOUR LOCAL SOCIAL SECURITY OFFICE. The office is listed under U.S. Government agencies in your telephone directory or you may call Social Security at 1-800-772-1213 (TTY 1-800-325-0778).** You may send comments on our time estimate above to: SSA, 6401 Security Blvd., Baltimore, MD 21235-6401. **Send only comments relating to our time estimate to this address, not the completed form.**

REPORTING RESPONSIBILITIES

The amount of a Supplemental Security Income (SSI) check is based on the information told to us. You must tell Social Security every time there is a change-while we process your application AND if you start receiving SSI.

Remember, a change may make the SSI monthly payment bigger or smaller. Report changes in income of your ineligible husband/wife or child who lives with you or your sponsor or sponsor's spouse, if you are an alien. You must also report changes in the things of value that these people own. You must also report changes in income, school attendance and marital status of ineligible children who live with you.

You must tell us about any change within 10 days after the month it happens. If you do not report changes, we may have to take as much as $25, $50, or $100 out of future checks.

HOW TO REPORT

You may make your reports:

- **By telephone at the telephone number shown above or call us toll free at 1-800-772-1213 (TTY 1-800-325-0778) or**
- **In person or**
- **By mail at the address shown above.**

CHANGES TO REPORT

☐ **WHERE YOU LIVE** --You must report to Social Security if:

- You move.
- You (or your spouse) leave your household for a calendar month or longer. (For example, you enter a hospital or visit a relative.)
- You are admitted to (for a calendar month or longer), or released from, a hospital or nursing home, jail, prison, or other correctional facility or other institution.
- You leave the United States for 30 consecutive days.
- You are no longer a legal resident of the United States

☐ **HOW YOU LIVE** -You must report to Social Security:

- If anyone moves into or out of your household.
- If the amount of money you pay toward household expenses changes.
- Births and deaths of any people with whom you live.
- Your spouse or former spouse dies.
- Your marital status changes:
  You get married, separated, divorced, or your marriage is annulled.
  You begin living with someone as husband and wife.

☐ **INCOME**-You must report to Social Security if you, your spouse/your parent(s):

- Start to receive money (or checks or any other type of payment) from someone or someplace.
- Have a change in the amount of money you receive.
- Begin to receive child support payments or those payments go up or down.
- Win money from gambling or a lottery.
- Start work or stop work.
- Earn more or less money. (Keep all paystubs and provide them to SSA when requested.)
- Become eligible for benefits other than SSI.

☐ **HELP YOU GET FROM OTHERS** -You must report to Social Security if:

- The amount of help (money or food, or payment of household expenses) you receive goes up or down.
- Someone stops helping you.
- Someone starts helping you.

☐ **THINGS OF VALUE THAT YOU OWN** -You must report to Social Security if:

- The value of things that you own goes over $2000 when you add them all together ($3000 if you are married and live with your spouse).
- You sell or give any thing of value away.
- You buy or are given anything of value.

☐ **YOU ARE BLIND OR DISABLED**-You must report to Social Security if:

- Your condition improves or your doctor says you can return to work.
- You go to work.

☐ **IF YOU ARE THE PARENT, STEP PARENT, OR REPRESENTATIVE PAYEE FOR A CHILD UNDER 18** - A report to Social Security must be made if:

- There is a change in any income the child, his or her parent(s), step parent, or brother(s) or sister(s) receive.
- There is a change in the student status of the child's brother(s) or sister(s).
- There is a change in his or her parents' or step parents' marriage, a change in the value of anything they own, or a change in their residence.

☐ **YOU ARE UNMARRIED AND UNDER AGE 22** - A report to Social Security must be made if:

- You start or stop school
- You get married or divorced
- You start or stop working

☐ **YOUR IMMIGRATION STATUS CHANGES**-

- You must report any changes to Social Security.

☐ **YOU ARE SELECTED AS A REPRESENTATIVE PAYEE** -You must report to Social Security if:

- The person for whom you receive SSI checks has any changes listed above. (You may be held liable if you do not report changes that could affect the SSI recipient's payment amount, and he/she is overpaid.)
- You will no longer be able or no longer wish to act as that person's representative payee.

☐ **IF A WARRANT HAS BEEN ISSUED FOR YOUR ARREST** -You must report to Social Security if:

- Your warrant is for a crime or an attempted crime that is a felony (or, in jurisdictions that do not define crimes as felonies, a crime that is punishable by death or imprisonment for a term exceeding 1 year); or
- Your warrant is for a violation of probation or parole under Federal or State law.

APPENDIX B

ADULT DISABILITY REPORT- FORM - SSA-3368-BK

SOCIAL SECURITY ADMINISTRATION

Form Approved
OMB No. 0960-0579

DISABILITY REPORT ADULT	For SSA Use Only- Do not write in this box. Related SSN ______ Number Holder ______

Anyone who makes or causes to be made a false statement or representation of material fact for use in determining a payment under the Social Security Act, or knowingly conceals or fails to disclose an event with an intent to affect an initial or continued right to payment, commits a crime punishable under Federal law by fine, imprisonment, or both, and may be subject to administrative sanctions.

If you are filling out this report for someone else, please provide information about him or her. When a question refers to "you" or "your," it refers to the person who is applying for disability benefits.

SECTION 1 - INFORMATION ABOUT THE DISABLED PERSON

1.A. Name (First, Middle Initial, Last)	1.B. Social Security Number

1.C. Mailing Address (Street or PO Box) Include apartment number or unit if applicable.

City	State/Province	ZIP/Postal Code	Country (If not USA)

1.D. Email Address

1.E. Daytime Phone Number, including area code, and the IDD and country codes if you live outside the USA or Canada. Phone number ______

☐ Check this box if you do not have a phone or a number where we can leave a message .

1.F. Alternate Phone Number - another number where we may reach you, if any.

Alternate phone number ______

1.G. Can you speak and understand English? ☐ Yes ☐ No

If no, what language do you prefer? ______

If you cannot speak and understand English, we will provide an interpreter, free of charge.

1.H. Can you read and understand English? ☐ Yes ☐ No

1.I. Can you write more than your name in English? ☐ Yes ☐ No

1.J. Have you used any other names on your medical or educational records? Examples are maiden name, other married name, or nickname. ☐ Yes ☐ No

If yes, please list them here: ______

SECTION 2 - CONTACTS

Give the name of someone **(other than your doctors)** we can contact who knows about your medical conditions, and can help you with your claim.

2.A. Name (First, Middle Initial, Last)	2.B. Relationship to you

2.C. Daytime Phone Number (as described in 1.E. above)

______

2.D. Mailing Address (Street or PO Box) Include apartment number or unit if applicable.

City	State/Province	ZIP/Postal Code	Country (If not USA)

2.E. Can this person speak and understand English? ☐ Yes ☐ No

If no, what language is preferred? ______

Form **SSA-3368-BK** (10-2015) UF (10-2015)
Destroy Prior Editions

Page 1

SECTION 2 - CONTACTS (continued)

2.F. Who is completing this report?

- ☐ The person who is applying for disability. (Go to Section 3 - Medical Conditions)
- ☐ The person listed in 2.A. (Go to Section 3 - Medical Conditions)
- ☐ Someone else (Complete the rest of Section 2 below)

2.G. Name (First, Middle Initial, Last)	2.H. Relationship to Person Applying

2.I. Daytime Phone Number ______________________

2.J. Mailing Address (Street or PO Box) Include apartment number or unit if applicable.

City	State/Province	ZIP/Postal Code	Country (If not USA)

SECTION 3 - MEDICAL CONDITIONS

3.A. List all of the physical or mental conditions (including emotional or learning problems) that limit your ability to work. If you have cancer, please include the stage and type. List each condition separately.

1.
2.
3.
4.
5.

If you need more space, go to Section 11-Remarks on the last page

3.B. What is your height without shoes? ____ feet ____ inches OR ________ centimeters (if outside USA)

3.C. What is your weight without shoes? ________ pounds OR ________ kilograms (if outside USA)

3.D. Do your conditions cause you pain or other symptoms? ☐ Yes ☐ No

SECTION 4 - WORK ACTIVITY

4.A. Are you currently working?

- ☐ No, I have never worked (Go to question **4.B.** below)
- ☐ No, I have stopped working (Go to question **4.C.** below)
- ☐ Yes, I am currently working (Go to question **4.F.** on page 3)

IF YOU HAVE NEVER WORKED:

4.B. When do you believe your condition(s) became severe enough to keep you from working (even though you have never worked)? (month/day/year) ____________ (Go to Section 5 on page 3)

IF YOU HAVE STOPPED WORKING:

4.C. When did you stop working? (month/day/year) ____________

Why did you stop working?

- ☐ Because of my condition(s).
- ☐ Because of other reasons. Please explain why you stopped working (for example: laid off, early retirement, seasonal work ended, business closed)

____

Even though you stopped working for other reasons, when do you believe your condition(s) became severe enough to keep you from working? (month/day/year) ____________

4.D. Did your condition(s) cause you to make changes in your work activity? (for example: job duties, hours, or rate of pay)

- ☐ No (Go to Section 5 - Education and Training on page 3)
- ☐ Yes When did you make changes? (month/day/year) ____________

SECTION 4 - WORK ACTIVITY (continued)

4.E. Since the date in 4.D. above, have you had gross earnings greater than $1,090 in any month? Do not count sick leave, vacation, or disability pay. (We may contact you for more information.)

☐ No (Go to Section 5) ☐ Yes (Go to Section 5)

IF YOU ARE CURRENTLY WORKING:

4.F. Has your condition(s) caused you to make changes in your work activity? (for example: job duties or hours)

☐ No When did your condition(s) first start bothering you? (month/day/year) ____________

☐ Yes When did you make changes? (month/day/year) ____________

4.G. Since your condition(s) first bothered you, have you had gross earnings greater than $1,090 in any month? Do not count sick leave, vacation, or disability pay. (We may contact you for more information.)

☐ No ☐ Yes

SECTION 5 - EDUCATION AND TRAINING

5.A. Check the highest grade of school completed. College:

0	1	2	3	4	5	6	7	8	9	10	11	12	GED	1	2	3	4 or more
☐	☐	☐	☐	☐	☐	☐	☐	☐	☐	☐	☐	☐	☐	☐	☐	☐	☐

Date completed: ____________

5.B. Did you attend special education classes? ☐ Yes ☐ No (Go to 5.C.)

Name of School ____________

City ____________ State/Province ____________ Country (If not USA) ____________

Dates attended special education classes: from ____________ to ____________

5.C. Have you completed any type of specialized job training, trade, or vocational school?

☐ Yes ☐ No

If "Yes," what type? ____________ Date completed: ____________

If you need to list other education or training use Section 11 - Remarks on the last page.

SECTION 6 - JOB HISTORY

6.A. List the jobs (up to 5) that you have had in the 15 years before you became unable to work because of your physical or mental conditions. List your most recent job first.

☐ Check here and go to Section 7 on page 5 if you did not work at all in the 15 years before you became unable to work.

	Job Title	Type of Business	Dates Worked		Hours Per Day	Days Per Week	Rate of Pay	
			From MM/YY	To MM/YY			Amount	Frequency
1.								
2.								
3.								
4.								
5.								

SECTION 6 - JOB HISTORY (continued)

Check the box below that applies to you.

☐ I had **only one job** in the last 15 years before I became unable to work. Answer the questions below.

☐ I had **more than one job** in the last 15 years before I became unable to work. Do **not** answer the questions on this page; go to Section 7 on page 5. (We may contact you for more information.)

Do not complete this page if you had **more than one job** in the last 15 years before you became unable to work.

6.B. Describe this job. What did you do all day?

(If you need more space, use Section 11 - Remarks on the last page.)

6.C. In this job, did you:

Use machines, tools or equipment?	☐ Yes	☐ No
Use technical knowledge or skills?	☐ Yes	☐ No
Do any writing, complete reports, or perform any duties like this?	☐ Yes	☐ No

6.D. In this job, how many total hours each day did you do each of the tasks listed:

Task	Hours	Task	Hours	Task	Hours
Walk		Stoop *(Bend down & forward at waist.)*		Handle large objects	
Stand		Kneel *(Bend legs to rest on knees.)*		Write, type, or handle small objects	
Sit		Crouch *(Bend legs & back down & forward.)*		Reach	
Climb		Crawl *(Move on hands & knees.)*			

6.E. Lifting and carrying *(Explain in the box below, what you lifted, how far you carried it, and how often you did this in your job.)*

6.F. Check **heaviest** weight lifted:

☐ Less than 10 lbs. ☐ 10 lbs. ☐ 20 lbs. ☐ 50 lbs. ☐ 100 lbs. or more ☐ Other ________

6.G. Check weight **frequently** lifted: *(by frequently, we mean from 1/3 to 2/3 of the workday.)*

☐ Less than 10 lbs. ☐ 10 lbs. ☐ 25 lbs ☐ 50 lbs. or more ☐ Other ________

6.H. Did you supervise other people in this job? ☐ Yes (Complete items below.) ☐ No (If No, go to 6.I.)

How many people did you supervise? ____________

What part of your time did you spend supervising people? ____________

Did you hire and fire employees? ☐ Yes ☐ No

6.I. Were you a lead worker? ☐ Yes ☐ No

SECTION 7 - MEDICINES

7. Are you taking any medicines (prescription or non-prescription)?

☐ Yes (Give the information requested below. You may need to look at your medicine containers.)

☐ No (Go to Section 8-Medical Treatment.)

Name of Medicine	If prescribed, give name of doctor	Reason for medicine

If you need to list other medicines, go to Section 11 - Remarks on the last page.

SECTION 8 - MEDICAL TREATMENT

Have you seen a doctor or other health care professional or received treatment at a hospital or clinic, or **do you have a future appointment scheduled?**

8.A. For any **physical** condition(s)?

☐ Yes ☐ No

8.B. For any **mental** condition(s) **(including emotional or learning problems)**?

☐ Yes ☐ No

If you answered "No" to both 8.A. and 8.B., go to Section 9 - Other Medical Information on page 11.

SECTION 8 - MEDICAL TREATMENT (continued)

Tell us who may have medical records about any of your **physical and/or mental** condition(s) (including emotional or learning problems). This includes doctors' offices, hospitals (**including emergency room visits**), clinics, and other health care facilities. Tell us about your next appointment, if you have one scheduled.

8.C. Name of Facility or Office	Name of health care professional who treated you

ALL OF THE QUESTIONS ON THIS PAGE REFER TO THE HEALTH CARE PROVIDER ABOVE.

Phone Number	Patient ID# (if known)

Mailing Address

City	State/Province	ZIP/Postal Code	Country (If not USA)

Dates of Treatment

1. Office, Clinic or Outpatient visits	2. Emergency Room visits List the most recent date first	3. Overnight hospital stays List the most recent date first	
First Visit	A.	A. Date in	Date out
Last Visit	B.	B. Date in	Date out
Next scheduled appointment (if any)	C.	C. Date in	Date out

What medical conditions were treated or evaluated?

What treatment did you receive for the above conditions? (Do not describe medicines or tests in this box.)

Check the boxes below for any tests this provider performed or sent you to, or has scheduled you to take. Please give the dates for past and future tests. If you need to list more tests, use Section 11-Remarks on the last page.

☐ **Check this box if no tests by this provider or at this facility.**

Kind of Test	Dates of Tests	Kind of Test	Dates of Tests
☐ EKG (heart test)		☐ EEG (brain wave test)	
☐ Treadmill (exercise test)		☐ HIV Test	
☐ Cardiac Catheterization		☐ Blood Test (not HIV)	
☐ Biopsy (list body part)		☐ X-Ray (list body part)	
☐ Hearing Test		☐ MRI/CT Scan (list body part)	
☐ Speech/Language Test			
☐ Vision Test		☐ Other (please describe)	
☐ Breathing Test			

If you do not have any more doctors or hospitals to describe, go to Section 9 on page 11.

SECTION 8 - MEDICAL TREATMENT (continued)

Tell us who may have medical records about any of your **physical and/or mental** condition(s) (including emotional or learning problems). This includes doctors' offices, hospitals **(including emergency room visits)**, clinics, and other health care facilities. Tell us about your next appointment, if you have one scheduled.

8.D. Name of Facility or Office	Name of health care professional who treated you

ALL OF THE QUESTIONS ON THIS PAGE REFER TO THE HEALTH CARE PROVIDER ABOVE.

Phone Number	Patient ID# (if known)

Mailing Address

City	State/Province	ZIP/Postal Code	Country (If not USA)

Dates of Treatment

1. Office, Clinic or Outpatient visits	**2. Emergency Room visits** List the most recent date first	**3. Overnight hospital stays** List the most recent date first	
First Visit	A.	A. Date in	Date out
Last Visit	B.	B. Date in	Date out
Next scheduled appointment (if any)	C.	C. Date in	Date out

What medical conditions were treated or evaluated?

What treatment did you receive for the above conditions? (Do not describe medicines or tests in this box.)

Tell us about any tests this provider performed or sent you to, or has scheduled you to take. Please give the dates for past and future tests. If you need to list more tests, use Section 11 - Remarks on the last page.

☐ **Check this box if no tests by this provider or at this facility.**

Kind of Test	Dates of Tests	Kind of Test	Dates of Tests
☐ EKG (heart test)		☐ EEG (brain wave test)	
☐ Treadmill (exercise test)		☐ HIV Test	
☐ Cardiac Catheterization		☐ Blood Test (not HIV)	
☐ Biopsy (list body part)		☐ X-Ray (list body part)	
☐ Hearing Test		☐ MRI/CT Scan (list body part)	
☐ Speech/Language Test			
☐ Vision Test		☐ Other (please describe)	
☐ Breathing Test			

If you do not have any more doctors or hospitals to describe, go to Section 9 on page 11.

SECTION 8 - MEDICAL TREATMENT (continued)

Tell us who may have medical records about any of your **physical and/or mental** condition(s) (including emotional or learning problems). This includes doctors' offices, hospitals **(including emergency room visits)**, clinics, and other health care facilities. Tell us about your next appointment, if you have one scheduled.

8.E. Name of Facility or Office	Name of health care professional who treated you

ALL OF THE QUESTIONS ON THIS PAGE REFER TO THE HEALTH CARE PROVIDER ABOVE.

Phone Number	Patient ID# (if known)

Mailing Address

City	State/Province	ZIP/Postal Code	Country (If not USA)

Dates of Treatment

1. Office, Clinic or Outpatient visits	2. Emergency Room visits List the most recent date first	3. Overnight hospital stays List the most recent date first	
First Visit	A.	A. Date in	Date out
Last Visit	B.	B. Date in	Date out
Next scheduled appointment (if any)	C.	C. Date in	Date out

What medical conditions were treated or evaluated?

What treatment did you receive for the above conditions? (Do not describe medicines or tests in this box.)

Tell us about any tests this provider performed or sent you to, or has scheduled you to take. Please give the dates for past and future tests. If you need to list more tests, use Section 11 - Remarks on the last page.

☐ **Check this box if no tests by this provider or at this facility.**

Kind of Test	Dates of Tests	Kind of Test	Dates of Tests
☐ EKG (heart test)		☐ EEG (brain wave test)	
☐ Treadmill (exercise test)		☐ HIV Test	
☐ Cardiac Catheterization		☐ Blood Test (not HIV)	
☐ Biopsy (list body part)		☐ X-Ray (list body part)	
☐ Hearing Test		☐ MRI/CT Scan (list body part)	
☐ Speech/Language Test			
☐ Vision Test		☐ Other (please describe)	
☐ Breathing Test			

If you do not have any more doctors or hospitals to describe, go to Section 9 on page 11.

SECTION 8 - MEDICAL TREATMENT (continued)

Tell us who may have medical records about any of your **physical and/or mental** condition(s) (including emotional or learning problems). This includes doctors' offices, hospitals **(including emergency room visits)**, clinics, and other health care facilities. Tell us about your next appointment, if you have one scheduled.

8.F. Name of Facility or Office	Name of health care professional who treated you

ALL OF THE QUESTIONS ON THIS PAGE REFER TO THE HEALTH CARE PROVIDER ABOVE.

Phone Number	Patient ID# (if known)

Mailing Address

City	State/Province	ZIP/Postal Code	Country (If not USA)

Dates of Treatment

1. Office, Clinic or Outpatient visits	**2. Emergency Room visits** List the most recent date first	**3. Overnight hospital stays** List the most recent date first	
First Visit	A.	A. Date in	Date out
Last Visit	B.	B. Date in	Date out
Next scheduled appointment (if any)	C.	C. Date in	Date out

What medical conditions were treated or evaluated?

What treatment did you receive for the above conditions? (Do not describe medicines or tests in this box.)

Tell us about any tests this provider performed or sent you to, or has scheduled you to take. Please give the dates for past and future tests. If you need to list more tests, use Section 11 - Remarks on the last page.

☐ **Check this box if no tests by this provider or at this facility.**

Kind of Test	Dates of Tests	Kind of Test	Dates of Tests
☐ EKG (heart test)		☐ EEG (brain wave test)	
☐ Treadmill (exercise test)		☐ HIV Test	
☐ Cardiac Catheterization		☐ Blood Test (not HIV)	
☐ Biopsy (list body part)		☐ X-Ray (list body part)	
☐ Hearing Test		☐ MRI/CT Scan (list body part)	
☐ Speech/Language Test			
☐ Vision Test		☐ Other (please describe)	
☐ Breathing Test			

If you do not have any more doctors or hospitals to describe, go to Section 9 on page 11.

SECTION 8 - MEDICAL TREATMENT (continued)

Tell us who may have medical records about any of your **physical and/or mental** condition(s) (including emotional or learning problems). This includes doctors' offices, hospitals **(including emergency room visits)**, clinics, and other health care facilities. Tell us about your next appointment, if you have one scheduled.

8.G. Name of Facility or Office	Name of health care professional who treated you

ALL OF THE QUESTIONS ON THIS PAGE REFER TO THE HEALTH CARE PROVIDER ABOVE.

Phone Number	Patient ID# (if known)

Mailing Address

City	State/Province	ZIP/Postal Code	Country (If not USA)

Dates of Treatment

1. Office, Clinic or Outpatient visits	**2. Emergency Room visits** List the most recent date first	**3. Overnight hospital stays** List the most recent date first	
First Visit	A.	A. Date in	Date out
Last Visit	B.	B. Date in	Date out
Next scheduled appointment (if any)	C.	C. Date in	Date out

What medical conditions were treated or evaluated?

What treatment did you receive for the above conditions? (Do not describe medicines or tests in this box.)

Tell us about any tests this provider performed or sent you to, or has scheduled you to take. Please give the dates for past and future tests. If you need to list more tests, use Section 11 - Remarks on the last page.

☐ **Check this box if no tests by this provider or at this facility.**

Kind of Test	Dates of Tests	Kind of Test	Dates of Tests
☐ EKG (heart test)		☐ EEG (brain wave test)	
☐ Treadmill (exercise test)		☐ HIV Test	
☐ Cardiac Catheterization		☐ Blood Test (not HIV)	
☐ Biopsy (list body part)		☐ X-Ray (list body part)	
☐ Hearing Test		☐ MRI/CT Scan (list body part)	
☐ Speech/Language Test			
☐ Vision Test		☐ Other (please describe)	
☐ Breathing Test			

If you have been treated by more than five doctors or hospitals, use Section 11 - Remarks on the last page and give the same detailed information as above for each healthcare provider.

SECTION 9 - OTHER MEDICAL INFORMATION

9. Does **anyone else** have medical information about your physical and/or mental condition(s) (including emotional and learning problems), or are you scheduled to see anyone else? (This may include places such as workers' compensation, vocational rehabilitation, insurance companies who have paid you disability benefits, prisons, attorneys, social service agencies and welfare.)

☐ Yes (Please complete the information below.)

☐ No (If you are receiving Supplemental Security Income (SSI) and have been asked to complete this report, go to Section 10 - Vocational Rehabilitation; if not, go to Section 11 on the last page.)

Name of Organization			Phone Number
Mailing Address			
City	State/Province	ZIP/Postal Code	Country (If not USA)
Name of Contact Person			Claim or ID number (if any)
Date of First Contact	Date of Last Contact		Date of Next Contact (if any)
Reasons for Contacts			

If you need to list other people or organizations use Section 11 - Remarks on the last page and give the same detailed information as above for each one you list.

COMPLETE THIS SECTION ONLY IF YOU ARE ALREADY RECEIVING SSI.

SECTION 10 - VOCATIONAL REHABILITATION, EMPLOYMENT, OR OTHER SUPPORT SERVICES

10.A. Have you participated, or are you participating in:

- An individual work plan with an employment network under the Ticket to Work Program;
- An individualized plan for employment with a vocational rehabilitation agency or any other organization;
- A Plan to Achieve Self-Support (PASS);
- An Individualized Education Program (IEP) through a school (if a student age 18-21); or
- Any program providing vocational rehabilitation, employment services, or other support services to help you go to work?

☐ Yes (Complete the following information) ☐ No (Go to Section 11)

10.B. Name of Organization or School			
Name of Counselor, Instructor, or Job Coach			Phone Number
Mailing Address			
City	State/Province	ZIP/Postal Code	Country (If not USA)

10.C. **When did you start participating in the plan or program?**

SECTION 10 - VOCATIONAL REHABILITATION, EMPLOYMENT, OR OTHER SUPPORT SERVICES (continued)

10.D. Are you still participating in the plan or program?

☐ Yes, I am scheduled to complete the plan or program on: ____________

☐ No, I completed the plan or program on: ____________

☐ No, I stopped participating in the plan or program before completing it because:

10.E. List the types of services, tests, or evaluations that you received (for example: intelligence or psychological testing, vision or hearing test, physical exam, work evaluations, or classes).

If you need to list another plan or program use Section 11 - Remarks and give the same detailed information as above.

SECTION 11 - REMARKS

Please write any additional information you did not give in earlier parts of this report. If you did not have enough space in the sections of this report to write the requested information, please use this space to tell us the additional information requested in those sections. Be sure to show the section to which you are referring.

Date Report Completed ____________
month, day, year

APPENDIX C

MEDICAL VOCATIONAL GUIDELINES-TABLE 1

Table 1 - Residual functional capacity; Maximum sustained work capability limited to sedentary work as a result of severe medically determinable impairment(s).

Rule	**Age**	**Education**	**Previous Work Experience**	**Decision**
201.01	Advanced Age	Limited or Less	Unskilled or none	Disabled
201.02	Advanced Age	Limited or Less	Skilled or semiskilled-skills not transferable	Disabled
201.03	Advanced Age	Limited or Less	Skilled or semiskilled-skills transferable	Not disabled
201.04	Advanced Age	High school graduate or more - does not provide for direct entry into skilled work	Unskilled or none	Disabled
201.05	Advanced	High school	Unskilled or	Not

	Age	graduate or more - provides for direct entry into skilled work	none	disabled
201.06	Advanced Age	High school graduate or more - does not provide for direct entry into skilled work	Skilled or semiskilled-skills not transferable	Disabled
201.07	Advanced Age	High school graduate or more - does not provide for direct entry into skilled work	Skilled or semiskilled-skills transferable	Not disabled
201.08	Advanced Age	High school graduate or more - provides for direct entry into skilled	Skilled or semiskilled-skills not transferable	Not disabled

		work		
201.09	Closely approaching advanced age	Limited or less	Unskilled or none	Disabled
201.10	Closely approaching advanced age	Limited or less	Skilled or semiskilled-skills not transferable	Disabled
201.11	Closely approaching advanced age	Limited or less	Skilled or semiskilled-skills transferable	Not disabled
201.12	Closely approaching advanced age	High school graduate or more - does not provide for direct entry into skilled work	Unskilled or none	Disabled
201.13	Closely approaching advanced age	High school graduate or more - provides for direct entry	Unskilled or none	Not disabled

		into skilled work		
201.14	Closely approaching advanced age	High school graduate or more - does not provide for direct entry into skilled work	Skilled or semiskilled-skills not transferable	Disabled
201.15	Closely approaching advanced age	High school graduate or more - does not provide for direct entry into skilled work	Skilled or semiskilled-skills transferable	Not disabled
201.16	Closely approaching advanced age	High school graduate or more - provides for direct entry into skilled work	Skilled or semiskilled-skills not transferable	Not disabled
201.17	Younger individual	Illiterate or unable to communicate	Unskilled or none	Disabled

	age 45-59	in English		
201.18	Younger individual age 45-59	Limited or less - at least literate and able to communicate in English	Unskilled or none	Not disabled
201.19	Younger individual age 45-59	Limited or less	Skilled or semiskilled- skills not transferable	Not disabled
201.20	Younger individual age 45-59	Limited or less	Skilled or semiskilled- skills transferable	Not disabled
201.21	Younger individual age 45-59	High graduate or more	Skilled or semiskilled- skills not transferable	Not disabled
201.22	Younger individual age 45-59	High graduate or more	Skilled or semiskilled- skills transferable	Not disabled
201.23	Younger individual	Illiterate or unable to	Unskilled or	Not

	age 18-44	communicate in English	none	disabled
201.24	Younger individual age 18-44	Limited or less - at least literate and able to communicate in English	Unskilled or none	Not disabled
201.25	Younger individual age 18-44	Limited or less	Skilled or semiskilled-skills not transferable	Not disabled
201.26	Younger individual age 18-44	Limited or less	Skilled or semiskilled-skills transferable	Not disabled
201.27	Younger individual age 18-44	High graduate or more	Unskilled or none	Not disabled
201.28	Younger individual age 18-44	High graduate or more	Skilled or semiskilled-skills not transferable	Not disabled
201.29	Younger individual	High graduate or	Skilled or semiskilled-	Not

	age 18-44	more	skills transferable	disabled

Medical Vocational Guidelines-Table 2

Table 2 - Residual functional capacity; Maximum sustained work capability limited to light work as a result of severe medically determinable impairment(s).

Rule	**Age**	**Education**	**Previous Work Experience**	**Decision**
202.01	Advanced age	Limited or less	Unskilled or none	Disabled
202.02	Advanced age	Limited or less	Skilled or semiskilled-skills not transferable	Disabled
202.03	Advanced age	Limited or less	Skilled or semiskilled-skills transferable	Not disabled
202.04	Advanced age	High school graduate or more - does not provide for direct entry into skilled work	Unskilled or none	Disabled

202.05	Advanced age	High school graduate or more - provides for direct entry into skilled work	Unskilled or none	Not disabled
202.06	Advanced age	High school graduate or more - does not provide for direct entry into skilled work	Skilled or semiskilled-skills not transferable	Disabled
202.07	Advanced age	High school graduate or more - does not provide for direct entry into skilled work	Skilled or semiskilled-skills transferable	Not disabled
202.08	Advanced age	High school graduate or more - provides for direct entry	Skilled or semiskilled-skills not transferable	Not disabled

		into skilled work		
202.09	Closely approaching advanced age	Illiterate or unable to communicate in English	Unskilled or none	Disabled
202.10	Closely approaching advanced age	Limited or less - at least literate and able to communicate in English	Unskilled or none	Not disabled
202.11	Closely approaching advanced age	Limited or less	Skilled or semiskilled-skills not transferable	Not disabled
202.12	Closely approaching advanced age	Limited or less	Skilled or semiskilled-skills ransferable	Not disabled
202.13	Closely approaching advanced age	High school graduate or more	Unskilled or none	Not disabled

202.14	Closely approaching advanced age	High school graduate or more	Skilled or semiskilled-skills not transferable	Not disabled
202.15	Closely approaching advanced age	High school graduate or more	Skilled or semiskilled-skills transferable	Not disabled
202.16	Younger individual	Illiterate or unable to communicate in English	Unskilled or none	Not disabled
202.17	Younger individual	Limited or less - at least literate and able to communicate in English	Unskilled or none	Not disabled
202.18	Younger individual	Limited or less	Skilled or semiskilled-skills not transferable	Not disabled
202.19	Younger individual	Limited or less	Skilled or semiskilled-skills	Not disabled

			transferable	
202.20	Younger individual	High school graduate or more	Unskilled or none	Not disabled
202.21	Younger individual	High school graduate or more	Skilled or semiskilled-skills not transferable	Not disabled
202.22	Younger individual	High school graduate or more	Skilled or semiskilled-skills transferable	Not disabled

MEDICAL VOCATIONAL GUIDELINES-TABLE 3

Table 3 - Residual functional capacity; Maximum sustained work capability limited to medium work as a result of severe medically determinable impairment(s).

Rule	Age	Education	Previous Work Experience	Decision
203.01	Closely approaching advanced age	Marginal or none	Unskilled or none	Disabled
203.02	Closely approaching advanced age	Limited or less	None	Disabled
203.03	Closely approaching advanced age	Limited	Skilled	Not disabled
203.04	Closely approaching advanced age	Limited or less	Skilled or semiskilled - skills not transferable	Not disabled
203.05	Closely approaching	Limited or	Skilled or semiskilled	Not

	advanced age	less	- skills transferable	disabled
203.06	Closely approaching advanced age	High school graduate or	Unskilled or none	Not disabled
203.07	Closely approaching advanced age	High school graduate or more - does not provide for direct entry into skilled work	Skilled or semiskilled - skills not transferable	Not disabled
203.08	Closely approaching advanced age	High school graduate or more - does not provide for direct entry into skilled work	Skilled or semiskilled - skills transferable	Not disabled
203.09	Closely approaching advanced	High school graduate or more - provides for	Skilled or semiskilled - skills not	Not disabled

	age	direct entry into skilled work	transferable	
203.10	Advanced age	Limited or less	None	Disabled
203.11	Advanced age	Limited or less	Unskilled	Not disabled
203.12	Advanced age	Limited or less	Skilled or semiskilled - skills not transferable	Not disabled
203.13	Advanced age	Limited or less	Skilled or semiskilled - skills transferable	Not disabled
203.14	Advanced age	High school graduate or more	Unskilled or non	Not disabled
203.15	Advanced age	High school graduate or more - does not provide for direct entry into skilled	Skilled or semiskilled - skills not transferable	Not disabled

		work		
203.16	Advanced age	High school graduate or more - does not provide for direct entry into skilled work	Skilled or semiskilled - skills transferable	Not disabled
203.17	Advanced age	High school graduate or more - provides for direct entry into skilled work	Skilled or semiskilled - skills not transferable	Not disabled
203.18	Closely approaching advanced age	Limited or less	Unskilled or none	Not disabled
203.19	Closely approaching advanced age	Limited or less	Skilled or semiskilled - skills not transferable	Not disabled
203.20	Closely	Limited or	Skilled or	Not

	approaching advanced age	less	semiskilled - skills transferable	disabled
203.21	Closely approaching advanced age	High school graduate or more	Unskilled or none	Not disabled
203.22	Closely approaching advanced age	High school graduate or more - does not provide for direct entry into skilled work	Skilled or semiskilled - skills not transferable	Not disabled
203.23	Closely approaching advanced age	High school graduate or more - does not provide for direct entry into skilled work	Skilled or semiskilled - skills transferable	Not disabled
203.24	Closely approaching advanced	High school graduate or more -	Skilled or semiskilled - skills not	Not disabled

	age	provides for direct entry into skilled work	transferable	
203.25	Younger individual	Limited or less	Unskilled or none	Not disabled
203.26	Younger individual	Limited or less	Skilled or semiskilled - skills not transferable	Not disabled
203.27	Younger individual	Limited or less	Skilled or semiskilled - skills transferable	Not disabled
203.28	Younger individual	High school graduate or more	Unskilled or none	Not disabled
203.29	Younger individual	High school graduate or more - does not provide for direct entry into skilled work	Skilled or semiskilled - skills not transferable	Not disabled

203.30	Younger individual	High school graduate or more - does not provide for direct entry into skilled work	Skilled or semiskilled - skills transferable	Not disabled
203.31	Younger individual	High school graduate or more - provides for direct entry into skilled work	Skilled or semiskilled - skills not transferable	Not disabled

APPENDIX D

FUNCTION REPORT - ADULT - FORM - SSA-3373-BK

SOCIAL SECURITY ADMINISTRATION

Form Approved
OMB No. 0960-0681

FUNCTION REPORT - ADULT

How your illnesses, injuries, or conditions limit your activities

For SSA Use Only
Do not write in this box.

Anyone who makes or causes to be made a false statement or representation of material fact for use in determining a payment under the Social Security Act, or knowingly conceals or fails to disclose an event with an intent to affect an initial or continued right to payment, commits a crime punishable under Federal law by fine, imprisonment, or both, and may be subject to administrative sanctions.

SECTION A - GENERAL INFORMATION

1. **NAME OF DISABLED PERSON** *(First, Middle Initial, Last)*

2. **SOCIAL SECURITY NUMBER**

3. **YOUR DAYTIME TELEPHONE NUMBER** *(If there is no telephone number where you can be reached, please give us a daytime number where we can leave a message for you.)*

_____ *Area Code* _____ *Phone Number* ☐ Your Number ☐ Message Number ☐ None

4. a. Where do you live? *(Check one.)*

☐ House ☐ Apartment ☐ Boarding House ☐ Nursing Home
☐ Shelter ☐ Group Home ☐ Other *(What?)* _____

b. With whom do you live? *(Check one.)*

☐ Alone ☐ With Family ☐ With Friends
☐ Other *(Describe relationship.)* _____

SECTION B - INFORMATION ABOUT YOUR ILLNESSES, INJURIES, OR CONDITIONS

5. How do your illnesses, injuries, or conditions limit your ability to work?

Form SSA-3373-BK (10-2015) UF (10-2015)
Use (01-2013) ef (01-2013) Edition until Stock is Exhausted

Page 1

SECTION C - INFORMATION ABOUT DAILY ACTIVITIES

6. Describe what you do from the time you wake up until going to bed.

7. Do you take care of anyone else such as a wife/husband, children, grandchildren, parents, friend, other? ☐ Yes ☐ No

   If "YES," for whom do you care, and what do you do for them?

8. Do you take care of pets or other animals? ☐ Yes ☐ No

   If "YES," what do you do for them?

9. Does anyone help you care for other people or animals? ☐ Yes ☐ No

   If "YES," who helps, and what do they do to help?

10. What were you able to do before your illnesses, injuries, or conditions that you can't do now?

11. Do the illnesses, injuries, or conditions affect your sleep? ☐ Yes ☐ No

    If "YES," how?

12. **PERSONAL CARE** (Check here ☐ if **NO PROBLEM** with personal care.)

    a. Explain how your illnesses, injuries, or conditions affect your ability to:

    Dress

    Bathe

    Care for hair

    Shave

    Feed self

    Use the toilet

    Other

b. Do you need any special reminders to take care of personal needs and grooming? ☐ Yes ☐ No

If "YES," what type of help or reminders are needed?

c. Do you need help or reminders taking medicine? ☐ Yes ☐ No

If "YES," what kind of help do you need?

13. **MEALS**

a. Do you prepare your own meals? ☐ Yes ☐ No

If "Yes," what kind of food do you prepare? (For example, sandwiches, frozen dinners, or complete meals with several courses.)

How often do you prepare food or meals? (For example, daily, weekly, monthly.)

How long does it take you?

Any changes in cooking habits since the illness, injuries, or conditions began?

b. If "No," explain why you cannot or do not prepare meals.

14. **HOUSE AND YARD WORK**

a. List household chores, both indoors and outdoors, that you are able to do. (For example, cleaning, laundry, household repairs, ironing, mowing, etc.)

b. How much time does it take you, and how often do you do each of these things?

c. Do you need help or encouragement doing these things? ☐ Yes ☐ No

If "YES," what help is needed?

d. If you don't do house or yard work, explain why not.

15. **GETTING AROUND**

a. How often do you go outside? ____________

If you don't go out at all, explain why not.

b. When going out, how do you travel? *(Check all that apply.)*

☐ Walk ☐ Drive a car ☐ Ride in a car ☐ Ride a bicycle

☐ Use public transportation ☐ Other *(Explain)* ____________

c. When going out, can you go out alone? ☐ Yes ☐ No

If "NO," explain why you can't go out alone.

d. Do you drive? ☐ Yes ☐ No

If you don't drive, explain why not.

16. **SHOPPING**

a. If you do any shopping, do you shop: *(Check all that apply.)*

☐ In stores ☐ By phone ☐ By mail ☐ By computer

b. Describe what you shop for.

c. How often do you shop and how long does it take?

17. **MONEY**

a. Are you able to:

Pay bills	☐ Yes	☐ No	Handle a savings account	☐ Yes	☐ No
Count change	☐ Yes	☐ No	Use a checkbook/money orders	☐ Yes	☐ No

Explain all "NO" answers.

b. Has your ability to handle money changed since the illnesses, injuries, or conditions began? ☐ Yes ☐ No

If "YES," explain how the ability to handle money has changed.

18. **HOBBIES AND INTERESTS**

a. What are your hobbies and interests? (For example, reading, watching TV, sewing, playing sports, etc.)

b. How often and how well do you do these things?

c. Describe any changes in these activities since the illnesses, injuries, or conditions began.

19. **SOCIAL ACTIVITIES**

a. Do you spend time with others? *(In person, on the phone, on the computer, etc.)* ☐ Yes ☐ No

If "YES," describe the kinds of things you do with others.

How often do you do these things?

b. List the places you go on a regular basis. (For example, church, community center, sports events, social groups, etc.)

Do you need to be reminded to go places? ☐ Yes ☐ No

How often do you go and how much do you take part?

Do you need someone to accompany you? ☐ Yes ☐ No

c. Do you have any problems getting along with family, friends, neighbors, or others? ☐ Yes ☐ No

If "YES," explain.

d. Describe any changes in social activities since the illnesses, injuries, or conditions began.

SECTION D - INFORMATION ABOUT ABILITIES

20. a. Check any of the following items that your illnesses, injuries, or conditions affect:

☐ Lifting	☐ Walking	☐ Stair Climbing	☐ Understanding
☐ Squatting	☐ Sitting	☐ Seeing	☐ Following Instructions
☐ Bending	☐ Kneeling	☐ Memory	☐ Using Hands
☐ Standing	☐ Talking	☐ Completing Tasks	☐ Getting Along With Others
☐ Reaching	☐ Hearing	☐ Concentration	

Please explain how your illnesses, injuries, or conditions affect each of the items you checked. (For example, you can only lift [how many pounds], or you can only walk [how far])

b. Are you: ☐ Right Handed? ☐ Left Handed?

c. How far can you walk before needing to stop and rest?

If you have to rest, how long before you can resume walking?

d. For how long can you pay attention?

e. Do you finish what you start? *(For example, a conversation, chores, reading, watching a movie.)* ☐ Yes ☐ No

f. How well do you follow written instructions? (For example, a recipe.)

g. How well do you follow spoken instructions?

h. How well do you get along with authority figures? (For example, police, bosses, landlords or teachers.)

____

i. Have you ever been fired or laid off from a job because of problems getting along with other people? ☐ Yes ☐ No

If "YES," please explain.

____

If "YES," please give name of employer. ______________________________

j. How well do you handle stress?

____

k. How well do you handle changes in routine?

____

l. Have you noticed any unusual behavior or fears? ☐ Yes ☐ No

If "YES," please explain.

____

!1. Do you use any of the following? *(Check all that apply.)*

☐ Crutches ☐ Cane ☐ Hearing Aid
☐ Walker ☐ Brace/Splint ☐ Glasses/Contact Lenses
☐ Wheelchair ☐ Artificial Limb ☐ Artificial Voice Box
☐ Other (Explain) ______________________________

Which of these were prescribed by a doctor?

____

When was it prescribed?

____

When do you need to use these aids?

____

22. Do you currently take any medicines for your illnesses, injuries, or conditions? ☐ Yes ☐ No

If "YES, "do any of your medicines cause side effects? ☐ Yes ☐ No

If "YES," please explain. (Do not list all of the medicines that you take. List only the medicines that cause side effects.)

NAME OF MEDICINE	SIDE EFFECTS YOU HAVE

SECTION E - REMARKS

Use this section for any added information you did not show in earlier parts of this form. When you are done with this section (or if you didn't have anything to add), be sure to complete the fields at the bottom of this page.

Name of person completing this form (Please print)		Date *(month, day, year)*
Address (Number and Street)	Email address (optional)	
City	State	ZIP Code

APPENDIX E

PHYSICAL RESIDUAL FUNCTIONAL CAPACITY ASSESSMENT - FORM SSA-4734-U8

FORM APPROVED
OMB NO. 0960-0431

PHYSICAL RESIDUAL FUNCTIONAL CAPACITY ASSESSMENT

CLAIMANT:

SOCIAL SECURITY NUMBER:
– –

NUMBERHOLDER (IF CDB CLAIM):

PRIMARY DIAGNOSIS:

SECONDARY DIAGNOSIS:

OTHER ALLEGED IMPAIRMENTS:

RFC ASSESSMENT IS FOR:

☐ Current Evaluation

☐ Date Last Insured: ________ (Date)

☐ Date 12 Months After Onset: ________ (Date)

☐ Other (Specify): ________

PRIVACY ACT NOTICE: The information requested on this form is authorized by Section 223 and Section 1633 of the Social Security Act. The information provided will be used in making a decision of this claim. Failure to complete this form may result in a delay in processing the claim. Information furnished on this form may be disclosed by the Social Security Administration to another person or governmental agency only with respect to Social Security programs and to comply with Federal laws requiring the exchange of information between Social Security and other agencies.

PAPERWORK REDUCTION ACT: This information collection meets the requirements of 44 U.S.C. § 3507, as amended by Section 2 of the Paperwork Reduction Act of 1995. You do not need to answer these questions unless we display a valid Office of Management and Budget control number. We estimate that it will take about 20 minutes to read the instructions, gather the facts, and answer the questions. *You may send comments on our time estimate above to: SSA, 1338 Annex Building, Baltimore, MD 21235-0401. Send only comments relating to our time estimate to this address, not the completed form.*

I. LIMITATIONS:

For Each Section A - F

➡ Base your conclusions on **all evidence** in file (clinical and laboratory findings; symptoms; observations, lay evidence; reports of daily activities; etc.).

➡ Check the blocks which reflect your **reasoned judgement**.

➡ Describe how the evidence **substantiates your conclusions** (Cite specific clinical and laboratory findings, observations, lay evidence, etc.).

➡ Ensure that you have:

- Requested appropriate treating and examining source statements regarding the individual's capacities (DI 22505.000ff. and DI 22510.000ff.) and that you have given appropriate **weight to treating source conclusions** (See Section III.).
- Considered and responded to **any alleged limitations imposed by symptoms** (pain, fatigue, etc.) attributable, in your judgement, to a medically determinable impairment. Discuss your assessment of symptom-related limitations in the explanation for your conclusions in A - F below (See also Section II.).
- Responded to all allegations of physical limitations or factors which can cause physical limitations.

➡ **Frequently** means occurring one-third to two-thirds of an 8-hour workday (cumulative, not continuous). **Occasionally** means occurring from very little up to one-third of an 8-hour workday (cumulative, not continuous).

☐ Continued on Page 2

A. EXERTIONAL LIMITATIONS

☐ None established. (Proceed to section B.)

1. **Occasionally** lift and/or carry (including upward pulling)
   (maximum) - when less than one-third of the time or less than 10 pounds, explain the amount (time/pounds) in item 6.

   ☐ less than 10 pounds
   ☐ 10 pounds
   ☐ 20 pounds
   ☐ 50 pounds
   ☐ 100 pounds or more

2. **Frequently** lift and/or carry (including upward pulling)
   (maximum) - when less than two-thirds of the time or less than 10 pounds, explain the amount (time/pounds) in item 6

   ☐ less than 10 pounds
   ☐ 10 pounds
   ☐ 25 pounds
   ☐ 50 pounds or more

3. Stand and/or walk (with normal breaks) for a total of -

   ☐ less than 2 hours in an 8-hour workday
   ☐ at least 2 hours in an 8-hour workday
   ☐ about 6 hours in an 8-hour workday
   ☐ medically required hand-held assistive device is necessary for ambulation

4. Sit (with normal breaks) for a total of -

   ☐ less than about 6 hours in an 8-hour workday
   ☐ about 6 hours in an 8-hour workday
   ☐ must periodically alternate sitting and standing to relieve pain or discomfort. (If checked, explain in 6.)

5. Push and/or pull (including operation of hand and/or foot controls) -

   ☐ unlimited, other than as shown for lift and/or carry
   ☐ limited in upper extremities (describe nature and degree)
   ☐ limited in lower extremities (describe nature and degree)

6. Explain how and why the evidence supports your conclusions in item 1 through 5.
   Cite the specific facts upon which your conclusions are based.

☐ Continued on Page 3

6. Continue (NOTE: MAKE ADDITIONAL COMMENTS IN SECTION IV)

B. POSTURAL LIMITATIONS

☐ None established. (Proceed to section C.)

	Frequently	Occasionally	Never
1. Climbing - ramp/stairs →	☐	☐	☐
- ladder/rope/scaffolds →	☐	☐	☐
2. Balancing →	☐	☐	☐
3. Stooping →	☐	☐	☐
4. Kneeling →	☐	☐	☐
5. Crouching →	☐	☐	☐
6. Crawling →	☐	☐	☐

7. When less than two-thirds of the time for frequently or less than one-third for occasionally, fully describe and explain. Also explain how and why the evidence supports your conclusions in items 1 through 6. Cite the specific facts upon which your conclusions are based.

☐ Continued on Page 4

C. MANIPULATIVE LIMITATIONS

☐ None established. (Proceed to section D.)

	LIMITED	UNLIMITED
1. Reaching all directions (including overhead)	☐	☐
2. Handling (gross manipulation)	☐	☐
3. Fingering (fine manipulation)	☐	☐
4. Feeling (skin receptors)	☐	☐

5. Describe how the activities checked "limited" are impaired. Also, explain how and why the evidence supports your conclusions in item 1 through 4. Cite the specific facts upon which your conclusions are based.

D. VISUAL LIMITATIONS

☐ None established. (Proceed to section E.)

	LIMITED	UNLIMITED
1. Near acuity	☐	☐
2. Far acuity	☐	☐
3. Depth perception	☐	☐
4. Accommodation	☐	☐
5. Color vision	☐	☐
6. Field of vision	☐	☐

7. Describe how the faculties checked "limited" are impaired. Also explain how and why the evidence supports your conclusions in items 1 through 6. Cite the specific facts upon which your conclusions are based.

☐ Continued on Page 5

E. COMMUNICATIVE LIMITATIONS

☐ None established. (Proceed to section F.)

	LIMITED	UNLIMITED
1. Hearing	☐	☐
2. Speaking	☐	☐

3. Describe how the faculties checked "limited" are impaired. Also, explain how and why the evidence supports your conclusions in items 1 and 2. Cite the specific facts upon which your conclusions are based.

F. ENVIRONMENTAL LIMITATIONS

☐ None established. (Proceed to section II.)

	UNLIMITED	AVOID CONCENTRATED EXPOSURE	AVOID EVEN MODERATE EXPOSURE	AVOID ALL EXPOSURE
1. Extreme cold	☐	☐	☐	☐
2. Extreme heat	☐	☐	☐	☐
3. Wetness	☐	☐	☐	☐
4. Humidity	☐	☐	☐	☐
5. Noise	☐	☐	☐	☐
6. Vibration	☐	☐	☐	☐
7. Fumes, odors, dusts, gases, poor ventilation, etc.	☐	☐	☐	☐
8. Hazards (machinery, heights, etc.)	☐	☐	☐	☐

9. Describe how these environmental factors impair activities and identify hazards to be avoided. Also, explain how and why the evidence supports your conclusions in items 1through 8. Cite the specific facts upon which your conclusions are based.

☐ Continued on Page 6

9. Continue (NOTE: MAKE ADDITIONAL COMMENTS IN SECTION IV)

II. SYMPTOMS

For symptoms alleged by the claimant to produce physical limitations, and for which the following have not previously been addressed in section I, discuss whether:

A. The symptom(s) is attributable, in your judgment, to a medically determinable impairment.

B. The severity or duration of the symptom(s), in your judgment, is disproportionate to the expected severity or expected duration on the basis of the claimant's medically determinable impairment(s).

C. The severity of the symptom(s) and its alleged effect on function is consistent, in your judgment, with the total medical and nonmedical evidence, including statements by the claimant and others, observations regarding activities of daily living, and alterations of usual behavior or habits.

☐ Continued on Page 7

III. TREATING OR EXAMINING SOURCE STATEMENT(S)

A. Is a treating or examining source statement(s) regarding the claimant's physical capacities in file?

☐ Yes

☐ No (Includes situations in which there was no source or when the source(s) did not provide a statement regarding the claimant's physical capacities.)

B. If yes, are there treating/examining source conclusions about the claimant's limitations or restrictions which are significantly different from your findings?

☐ Yes

☐ No

C. If yes, explain why those conclusions are not supported by the evidence in file. Cite the source's name and the statement date.

☐ Continued on Page 8

IV. ADDITIONAL COMMENTS:

☐ THESE FINDINGS COMPLETE THE MEDICAL PORTION OF THE DISABILITY DETERMINATION.

MEDICAL CONSULTANT'S SIGNATURE:	MEDICAL CONSULTANT'S CODE:	DATE:

APPENDIX F

Mental Residual Functional Capacity Assessment - Form SSA-4734-F4-SUP

MENTAL RESIDUAL FUNCTIONAL CAPACITY ASSESSMENT

NAME

SOCIAL SECURITY NUMBER

CATEGORIES (*From IB of the PRTF*)

ASSESSMENT IS FOR:

☐ Current Evaluation

☐ Date Last Insured: ____________ (*Date*)

☐ Other: ____________ (*Date*) to ____________ (*Date*)

☐ 12 Months After Onset: ____________ (*Date*)

I. **SUMMARY CONCLUSIONS**

This section is for recording summary conclusions derived from the evidence in file. Each mental activity is to be evaluated within the context of the individual's capacity to sustain that activity over a normal workday and workweek, on an ongoing basis. Detailed explanation of the degree of limitation for each category (A through D), as well as any other assessment information you deem appropriate, is to be recorded in Section III (Functional Capacity Assessment).

If rating Category 5 is checked for any of the following items, you MUST specify in Section II the evidence that is needed to make the assessment. If you conclude that the record is so inadequately documented that no accurate functional capacity assessment can be made, indicate in Section II what development is necessary, but DO NOT COMPLETE SECTION III.

	Not Significantly Limited	Moderately Limited	Markedly Limited	No Evidence of Limitation in this Category	Not Ratable on Available Evidence
A. UNDERSTANDING AND MEMORY					
1. The ability to remember locations and work-like procedures.	1. ☐	2. ☐	3. ☐	4. ☐	5. ☐
2. The ability to understand and remember very short and simple instructions.	1. ☐	2. ☐	3. ☐	4. ☐	5. ☐
3. The ability to understand and remember detailed instructions.	1. ☐	2. ☐	3. ☐	4. ☐	5. ☐
B. SUSTAINED CONCENTRATION AND PERSISTENCE					
4. The ability to carry out very short and simple instructions.	1. ☐	2. ☐	3. ☐	4. ☐	5. ☐
5. The ability to carry out detailed instructions.	1. ☐	2. ☐	3. ☐	4. ☐	5. ☐
6. The ability to maintain attention and concentration for extended periods.	1. ☐	2. ☐	3. ☐	4. ☐	5. ☐
7. The ability to perform activities within a schedule, maintain regular attendance, and be punctual within customary tolerances.	1. ☐	2. ☐	3. ☐	4. ☐	5. ☐
8. The ability to sustain an ordinary routine without special supervision.	1. ☐	2. ☐	3. ☐	4. ☐	5. ☐
9. The ability to work in coordination with or proximity to others without being distracted by them.	1. ☐	2. ☐	3. ☐	4. ☐	5. ☐
10. The ability to make simple work-related decisions.	1. ☐	2. ☐	3. ☐	4. ☐	5. ☐

	Not Significantly Limited	Moderately Limited	Markedly Limited	No Evidence of Limitation in this Category	Not Ratable on Available Evidence
Continued—SUSTAINED CONCENTRATION AND PERSISTENCE					
11. The ability to complete a normal work-day and workweek without interruptions from psychologically based symptoms and to perform at a consistent pace without an unreasonable number and length of rest periods.	1. ☐	2. ☐	3. ☐	4. ☐	5. ☐
C. SOCIAL INTERACTION					
12. The ability to interact appropriately with the general public.	1. ☐	2. ☐	3. ☐	4. ☐	5. ☐
13. The ability to ask simple questions or request assistance.	1. ☐	2. ☐	3. ☐	4. ☐	5. ☐
14. The ability to accept instructions and respond appropriately to criticism from supervisors.	1. ☐	2. ☐	3. ☐	4. ☐	5. ☐
15. The ability to get along with coworkers or peers without distracting them or exhibiting behavioral extremes.	1. ☐	2. ☐	3. ☐	4. ☐	5. ☐
16. The ability to maintain socially appropriate behavior and to adhere to basic standards of neatness and cleanliness.	1. ☐	2. ☐	3. ☐	4. ☐	5. ☐
D. ADAPTATION					
17. The ability to respond appropriately to changes in the work setting.	1. ☐	2. ☐	3. ☐	4. ☐	5. ☐
18. The ability to be aware of normal hazards and take appropriate precautions.	1. ☐	2. ☐	3. ☐	4. ☐	5. ☐
19. The ability to travel in unfamiliar places or use public transportation.	1. ☐	2. ☐	3. ☐	4. ☐	5. ☐
20. The ability to set realistic goals or make plans independently of others.	1. ☐	2. ☐	3. ☐	4. ☐	5. ☐

II. **REMARKS:** If you checked box 5 for any of the preceding items or if any other documentation deficiencies were identified, you must specify what additional documentation is needed. Cite the item number(s), as well as any other specific deficiency and indicate the development to be undertaken.

☐ Continued on Page 3

III. **FUNCTIONAL CAPACITY ASSESSMENT**

☐ Continued on Page 4

Record in this section the elaborations on the preceding capacities. Complete this section ONLY after the SUMMARY CONCLUSIONS section has been completed. Explain your summary conclusions in narrative form. Include any information which clarifies limitation or function. Be especially careful to explain conclusions that differ from those of treating medical sources or from the individual's allegations.

☐ Continued on Page 4

MEDICAL CONSULTANT'S SIGNATURE	DATE

Continuation Sheet—Indicate section(s) being continued.

*U.S. Government Printing Office: 1989-241-312/80099

APPENDIX G

Sample Letter From Doctor About Disability

Naturally, the letter from the physician will vary depending on the underlying condition. However, here is one in which the claimant has been diagnosed with Multiple Sclerosis. Since that particular medical condition can have a wide variety of symptoms as well as severity, the letter below is one that takes the diagnosis and explains how this particular patient's/claimant's symptoms are viewed in light of the SSAs definition of disability.

The letter should be printed on paper with the physician's letterhead. Where you send this letter depends on which stage of the application process you are going through.

Social Security Administration
Address of Your Local Social Security Office
RE: James Cobb, D.O.B. 10-09-1972, SSN 123-45-6789

To Whom It May Concern:

My patient, James Cobb, has a diagnosis of Multiple Sclerosis which is severe. He is limited in daily activities and is unable to work on a sustained basis. This diagnosis has been confirmed through physical examination, medical history, MRI, and a standard neurological examination. Mr. Cobb was first diagnosed with MS on January 18, 2012.

Mr. Cobb's symptoms include:

Chronic fatigue
Weakness
Bowel Problems
Difficulty Remembering
Depression
Sensitivity to heat
Unstable walking
Pain
Poor coordination

In an 8-hour work day, Mr. Cobb may:

Stand less than two hours ,
Sit less than four hours,
Require the ability to change position at-will,
Require frequent breaks to rest,
Occasionally lift less than 10 pounds,
Avoid lifting more than 10 pounds,
Frequently be off-task due to difficulty concentrating,
Be capable of low work stress, and

Miss at least 4 days of work per month as a result of impairment although the amount of time required to be off from work will likely increase as his condition worsens.

I am enclosing all medical records, medical history, specific tests used, lab results, and relevant clinical findings.

In my opinion, Mr. Cobb is unable to resume any type of gainful employment due to physical impairment. His fatigue, pain, weakness, and other symptoms will significantly and consistently interfere with work performance and attendance. MS is a progressive neurological disorder without a cure. My expectation is that Mr. Cobb will see a continued decline in function over time, lasting longer than 12 months.

Sincerely,

Dr. Samuel Watkins

There is an interesting website which contains additional samples of letters pertaining to other conditions at https://howtogeton.wordpress.com/2017/05/01/sample-doctor-letters-for-disability/ . Please note that this website is not affiliated in any way with our Guerrilla Guides to the Law series or www.RebellionBooks.com.

APPENDIX H

Roles and Responsibilities of the DE, MC, PC, and MA

DI 24501.001 - The Disability Determination Services (DDS) Disability Examiner (DE), Medical Consultant (MC), and Psychological Consultant (PC) Team, and the Role of the Medical Advisor (MA)

A. Introduction To The Roles And Responsibilities Of The DE, MC, PC, And MA

A disability determination requires the DE, MC, and PC to collaborate as the adjudicative team. Not all team members participate in the development and evaluation of all claims, as outlined in this section.

All team members have training in the disability process. MAs are not part of the adjudicative team but can provide analysis of medical issues.

B. Adjudicative Roles And Responsibilities Of The DE, MC, PC, And MA

1. General role of the DE

The role of the DE in the disability determination process includes, but is not limited to a responsibility to:

a. Develop the case

- Obtain evidence from the claimant, medical sources, entities that maintain medical sources' evidence, and nonmedical sources;

- Contact claimants, applicants, appointed representatives, and other appropriate parties for additional information;
- Consult with MCs, PCs, and other staff members to resolve problems in getting evidence from medical sources, entities that maintain medical sources' evidence, and nonmedical sources;
- Initiate requests for consultative examinations (CE) when medical evidence of record (MER) is not sufficient to make a determination of disability and all available medical information has been obtained; and
- Follow up to obtain CE reports when necessary.

b. Prepare the case for MC, PC, or MA review

- Prepare cases for MC, PC, and MA review, including highlighting the relevant period to consider such as the date last insured, prescribed periods, or prior adjudicated periods; and
- Assist MCs and PCs with the completion of any applicable residual functional capacity (RFC) assessments as appropriate.

c. Evaluate the vocational aspects of the case

- Determine whether a claimant can perform past relevant work given his or her RFC at step 4 of the sequential evaluation process; and
- Determine whether a claimant can adjust to other work given the applicant's RFC, age, education, and work

experience at step 5 of the sequential evaluation process.

d. Prepare the determination

1. Prepare rationales and determinations, including Forms SSA-831 (Disability Determination and Transmittal) or Title XVI SSA-832 and Title II SSA-833 (Cessation or Continuance of Disability or Blindness Determination and Transmittal;
2. Prepare disability determination notices; and
3. Make every reasonable effort to ensure that the following sources completed the medical portion of the case review and completed all applicable RFC assessment:
   - A qualified physician (where a physical impairment is alleged);
   - A psychiatrist or psychologist (where a mental impairment is alleged); or
   - Both (where both a physical impairment and mental impairment are alleged).

2. Signature responsibilities of the DE

The DE alone may make the disability determination without an MC or PC signature in the following situations:

A. The DE has single decision-maker (SDM) authority in a prototype or SDM II DDS and the claimant meets SDM requirements.

B. The DE has the authority to use the procedures for the quick disability determination (QDD) process or the compassionate allowance process (CAL) determinations; and

C. The current file or any prior file contains no medical evidence and despite making every reasonable effort, the DDS is unable to obtain medical evidence that exists and one or more of the following situations exists:
   - The claimant refuses or fails without good reason to attend a CE;
   - The DDS curtails CE development after establishing the claimant's failure or refusal to cooperate; or
   - The date last insured or other technical factor is in the past, and there is no possibility of setting an onset prior to the end of the entitlement period.

NOTE: Effective December 28, 2018, SDM, QDD, and CAL authority ends.

3. General role of the MC and PC

This section provides information about the MC or PC role in the disability process. The MC or PC role in the determination process includes, but is not limited to the responsibility to:

a. Evaluate the sufficiency of the evidence and need for further testing

- Evaluate the evidence in the case to determine its adequacy to complete the medical portion of the case review;
- Review requests for CEs in specific claims to ensure they are necessary, are not contraindicated based on the evidence in file, and resolve the issues as intended; and
- Provide alternatives to the purchase of a CE.

b. Act as a liaison between the DDS and the medical community

- Resolve problems in obtaining MER through discussions with DEs and other staff members;
- Review CE reports for deficiencies in content and recommend ways to avoid deficient reports;
- Evaluate and respond to medical questions;
- Improve relations with the medical community, enlarging consultative examiner panels, and minimizing CE processing time by working closely with staff members and CE providers; and
- Improve DE understanding and use of medical evidence by working with training staff.

c. Determine severity, whether the claimant meets or equals a listing, or for a Title XVI child whether the claimant's impairment functionally equals the listings

- Assess the existence and severity of impairments at **step 2** of the sequential evaluation process;

- Determine whether an impairment meets or equals the requirements of a listing in the Listing of Impairments (Listings) at **step 3** of the sequential evaluation process; and
- Determining whether a claimant's impairment(s) functionally equals the Listings at **step**
- **3** of the sequential evaluation process in childhood disability claims.

d. Assess RFC and other specific medical issues

- Assess and determine RFC in adult disability determinations;
- Participate in other specific medical determinations in a claim (such as whether drug addiction or alcoholism is material to the determination), as appropriate; and
- Review determinations to ensure their integrity.

4. Signature responsibilities of the MC and PC

The MC and PC:

- Sign assessments and determinations; and
- Indicate that his or her signature completes the medical portion of the disability determination.

An MC who is a physician takes responsibility for the medical portion of the determination, except in cases where a PC may perform this function.

A PC may perform this function when:

- a mental impairment is the only impairment in the claim; or
- there is a combination of a mental impairment with a physical impairment, but the mental impairment alone justifies a finding of disability.

The MC or PC who is taking responsibility for the medical portion of the determination signs the disability determination forms and all supporting documents relevant to the determination that require a signature.

In cases where there is evidence of mental and physical impairment(s), and a PC reviews the case, the PC evaluates only the mental impairment(s) and the MC evaluates the physical impairment(s).

In cases where the combination of physical and mental impairments may be equivalent to a medical listing, the MC and PC confer, both complete and sign an SSA-416 (Medical Evaluation), and one of the consultants takes overall responsibility to sign the rationale supporting the equivalence.

5. Handle adjudicative team conflicts of interest

If a DDS MC or PC furnishes any of the MER, he or she does not participate in the disability determination of that claim.

6. The general role of the MA

The MA's role in the determination process includes:

- Help DEs, MCs, and PCs understand specialized issues or evidence in claims; and
- Provide analysis about medical issues related to impairments for which they are qualified to evaluate.

  EXAMPLE: A speech-language pathologist (SLP) provides advice in a claim about an issue or evidence related to a speech or language impairment.

The adjudicative team must consider the MA analysis as evidence from an acceptable medical source.

NOTE: Because an MA is an independent medical source that provides evidence in a claim, an MA may provide analyses of the same case at both the initial and

7. Signature requirements for MA

The statute prohibits MAs from signing or otherwise taking responsibility for the medical portion of the disability determination.

C. Qualifications For MC, PC, And MA

1. MC

An MC is a licensed physician (medical or osteopathic doctor) who is a member of a DDS or Social Security Administration (SSA) team that makes disability determinations.

2. PC

A PC is a licensed psychiatrist or a psychologist who is a member of a DDS or Social Security Administration (SSA) team that makes disability determinations and:

- is licensed or certified as a psychologist at the independent practice level of psychology by the State in which he or she practices;
- possesses a doctorate degree in psychology from a program in clinical psychology of an educational institution accredited by an organization recognized by the Council for Higher Education Accreditation, formerly the Council on Post-Secondary Accreditation; or
- is listed in a national register of health service providers in psychology that the Commissioner of Social Security deems appropriate; and
- possesses two years of supervised clinical experience as a psychologist in health service, at least one year of which is post master's degree.

NOTE: The Commissioner has not identified an appropriate national register of health service providers, so a PC must meet the criteria in the first two bullets, or the DDS must be able to check a registry to ensure the psychologist is properly credentialed.

3. MA

An MA is an acceptable medical source who is not an MC or PC.

For claims filed before March 27, 2017, this includes:

- Licensed optometrists, for impairments of visual disorders only (except, in the United States Virgin Islands, licensed optometrists, for the measurement of visual acuity and visual fields only).
- Licensed podiatrists, for impairments of the foot, or the foot and ankle only, depending on whether the State in which the podiatrist practices permits the practice of podiatry on the foot only, or the foot and ankle.
- Qualified speech-language pathologists, for impairments of speech or language only.
- For claims with a filing date on or after March 27, 2017, this additionally includes:
- Licensed physician assistants for impairments within the licensed scope of practice only.
- Licensed audiologists for impairments of hearing loss, auditory processing disorders, and balance disorders within the licensed scope of practice only.
  NOTE: Audiologists' scope of practice generally includes evaluation, examination, and treatment of certain balance impairments that result from the audio-vestibular system. However, some balance impairments involve several body systems that are outside the scope of practice for audiologists, such as those involving muscles, bones, joints, vision, nerves, heart, and blood vessels.

- Licensed Advanced Practice Registered Nurses (APRN), also known in some States as Advanced Practice Nurse (APN), and Advanced Registered Nurse Practitioner (ARNP) for impairments within his or her licensed scope of practice.

APPENDIX I

MONTHLY SUBSTANTIAL GAINFUL ACTIVITY AMOUNTS BY DISABILITY TYPE

Note: Monthly Substantial Gainful Employment amounts change yearly. See table below.

Year	Blind	Non-blind
2019	$2,040	$1,220
2018	$1,970	$1,180
2017	$1,950	$1,170
2016	$1,820	$1,130
2015	$1,820	$1,090
2014	$1,800	$1,070
2013	$1,740	$1,040
2012	$1,690	$1,010
2011	$1,640	$1,000
2010	$1,640	$1,000

APPENDIX J

** The following information in this appendix is quoted directly from the SSA website at this link: https://www.ssa.gov/ssi/text-income-ussi.htm. At the time of this printing the information is correct but the information changes frequently so always check the direct link on the SSA website.*

Supplemental Security Income (SSI Income)

What is Income?

Income is any item an individual receives in cash or in-kind that can be used to meet his or her need for food or shelter. Income includes, for the purposes of SSI, the receipt of any item which can be applied, either directly or by sale or conversion, to meet basic needs of food or shelter.

Types of income for SSI purposes:

- **Earned Income** is wages, net earnings from self–employment, certain royalties, honoraria, and sheltered workshop payments.
- **Unearned Income** is all income that is not earned such as Social Security benefits, pensions, State disability payments, unemployment benefits, interest income, dividends and cash from friends and relatives.
- **In–Kind Income** is food or shelter that you get for free or less than its fair market value.
- **Deemed Income** is the part of the income of your spouse with whom you live, your parent(s) with whom you live, or

your sponsor (if you are an alien), which we use to compute your SSI benefit amount.

Why Is Income Important in the SSI Program?

Generally, the more countable income you have, the less your SSI benefit will be. If your countable income is over the allowable limit, you cannot receive SSI benefits. Some of your income may not count as income for the SSI program.

What Income Does Not Count For SSI?

Examples of payments or services we do **not** count as income for the SSI program include but are not limited to:

- the first $20 of most income received in a month;
- the first $65 of earnings and one-half of earnings over $65 received in a month;
- the value of Supplemental Nutrition Assistance Program (food stamps) received;
- income tax refunds;
- home energy assistance;
- assistance based on need funded by a State or local government, or an Indian tribe;

- small amounts of income received irregularly or infrequently;
- interest or dividends earned on countable resources or resources excluded under other Federal laws;
- grants, scholarships, fellowships or gifts used for tuition and educational expenses;
- food or shelter based on need provided by nonprofit agencies;
- loans to you (cash or in–kind) that you have to repay;
- money someone else spends to pay your expenses for items other than food or shelter (for example, someone pays your telephone or medical bills);
- income set aside under a Plan to Achieve Self–Support (PASS);
- earnings up to $1,820 per month to a maximum of $7,350 per year (effective January 2018) for a student under age 22;
- the cost of impairment–related work expenses for items or services that a disabled person needs in order to work;
- the cost of work expenses that a blind person incurs in order to work;
- disaster assistance;

- the first $2,000 of compensation received per calendar year for participating in certain clinical trials;
- refundable Federal and advanced tax credits received on or after January 1, 2010; and
- certain exclusions on Indian trust fund payments paid to American Indians who are members of a federally recognized tribe.

How Does Your Income Affect Your SSI Benefit?

Step 1: SSA will subtract any income that does not count from your total gross income. The remaining amount is the "**countable income**".

Step 2: SSA will subtract the "countable income" from the SSI Federal benefit rate. The result is the monthly SSI Federal benefit as follows:

1) Your Total Income
<u>- the income that is not counted</u>
= the countable income

2) SSI Federal benefit rate
<u>- the countable income</u>
= SSI Federal benefit

The Following Examples are Based on Sample Dollar Amounts:

EXAMPLE A – SSI Federal Benefit with only UNEARNED INCOME

Total monthly income = $300 (Social Security benefit)

1) $300 (Social Security benefit)
   -20 (Not counted)
   =$280 (Countable income)

2) $750 (SSI Federal benefit rate)
   -280 (Countable income)
   =$470 (SSI Federal benefit)

EXAMPLE B – SSI Federal Benefit with only EARNED INCOME

Total monthly income = $317 (Gross wages)

1) $317 (Gross wages)
   -20 (Not counted)
   $297
   -65 (Not counted)
   =$232 divided by 1/2 =$116 (Countable income)

2) $750 (SSI Federal benefit rate)
   -116 (Countable income)
   =$634 (SSI Federal benefit)

EXAMPLE C – SSI Federal Benefit and STATE SUPPLEMENT with only UNEARNED INCOME

The facts are the same as example A, but with federally administered State supplementation.

1) $300 (Social Security benefit)
   -20 (Not counted)
   =$280 (Countable income)

2) $750 (SSI Federal benefit rate)

-280 (Countable Income)

=$470 (SSI Federal benefit)

3) $470 (SSI Federal benefit)

+15 (State supplement payment for an individual living alone)

=$485 (Total Federal and State SSI benefit)

EXAMPLE D – SSI Federal Benefit and STATE SUPPLEMENT with only EARNED INCOME

Total monthly income = $317 (Gross wages)

1) $317 (Gross wages)

-20 (Not counted)

$297

-65 (Not counted)

$232 divided by 1/2 =$116 (Countable income)

2) $750 (SSI Federal benefit rate)

-116 (Countable Income)

=$634 (SSI Federal benefit)

3) $634 (SSI Federal benefit)

+15 (State supplement payment for an individual living alone)

=$649 (Total Federal and State SSI benefit)

How Will Windfall Offset Affect My Benefit?

Windfall offset occurs when we the SSA reduce the retroactive Social Security benefits if you are eligible for Social Security and SSI benefits for the same months.

The SSA will reduce your Social Security benefits by the amount of SSI you would not have received if we had paid you Social Security benefits when they were due.

When Does Deemed Income Apply?

- When a person who is eligible for SSI benefits lives with a spouse who is not eligible for SSI benefits, the SSA may count some of the spouse's income in determining the SSI benefit.
- When a disabled or blind child under age 18 lives with parent(s), (or a parent and a stepparent), and at least one parent does not receive SSI benefits, SSA may count some of the parents' income in figuring the child's SSI benefit.

- When an alien has a sponsor, with certain exceptions, SSA may count some or all of the sponsor's income in figuring the SSI benefit.

When Does Deemed Income Not Apply?

- When you no longer live with a spouse or parent.
- When a disabled or blind child attains age 18.
- When an alien's sponsorship ends.

APPENDIX K

MONTHLY EARNINGS THAT TRIGGER A TRIAL WORK PERIOD

Year	Monthly Earnings
1978 & Prior	$50
1979-1989	$75
1990-2000	$200
2001	$530
2002	$560
2003	$570
2004	$580
2005	$590
2006	$620
2007	$640
2008	$670
2009	$700
2010	$720
2011	$720
2012	$720
2013	$750
2014	$770
2015	$780

2016	$810
2017	$840
2018	$850
2019	$880

APPENDIX L

Request For Reconsideration - Form - SSA-561-U2

Form **SSA-561-U2** (12-2016) uf (12-2016)
Prior Edition May Be Used Until Exhausted
Social Security Administration

Page 1 of 4
OMB No. 0960-0622

REQUEST FOR RECONSIDERATION

NAME OF CLAIMANT:	CLAIMANT SSN:	CLAIM NUMBER: *(If different than SSN)*

ISSUE BEING APPEALED: *(Specify if retirement, disability, hospital or medical, SSI, SVB, overpayment, etc.)*

I do not agree with the Social Security Administration's (SSA) determination and request reconsideration.
My reasons are:

SUPPLEMENTAL SECURITY INCOME (SSI) OR SPECIAL VETERANS BENEFITS (SVB) RECONSIDERATION ONLY

THREE WAYS TO APPEAL

I want to appeal your determination about my claim for **SSI** or **SVB**. I have read about the three ways to appeal. I have checked the box below:

- ☐ **CASE REVIEW** - **You can pick this kind of appeal in all cases**. You can give us more facts to add to your file. Then we will decide your case again. You do not meet with the person who decides your case.
- ☐ **INFORMAL CONFERENCE** - **You can pick this kind of appeal in all SSI cases except for medical issues. In SVB cases, you can pick this kind of appeal only if we are stopping or lowering your SVB payment.** You will meet with a person who will decide your case. You can tell that person why you think you are right. You can give us more facts to help prove you are right. You can bring other people to help explain your case.
- ☐ **FORMAL CONFERENCE** - **You can pick this kind of appeal only if we are stopping or lowering your SSI or SVB payment.** This meeting is like an informal conference, but we can also get people to come in and help prove you are right. We can do this even if they do not want to help you. You can question these people at your meeting.

CONTACT INFORMATION

CLAIMANT SIGNATURE - *OPTIONAL*:			NAME OF CLAIMANT'S REPRESENTATIVE: *(If any)*		
MAILING ADDRESS:			MAILING ADDRESS:		
CITY:	STATE:	ZIP CODE:	CITY:	STATE:	ZIP CODE:
TELEPHONE NUMBER: *(Include area code)*	DATE:		TELEPHONE NUMBER: *(Include area code)*	DATE:	

TO BE COMPLETED BY SOCIAL SECURITY ADMINISTRATION

1. HAS INITIAL DETERMINATION BEEN MADE? ☐ Yes ☐ No 2. IS THIS REQUEST FILED TIMELY? ☐ Yes ☐ No *(If "NO", attach claimant's explanation for delay. Refer to GN 03102.125)*	**FIELD OFFICE DEVELOPMENT (GN 03102.300)** ☐ NO FURTHER DEVELOPMENT REQUIRED ☐ REQUIRED DEVELOPMENT ATTACHED ☐ REQUIRED DEVELOPMENT PENDING, WILL FORWARD OR ADVISE STATUS WITHIN 30 DAYS
SOCIAL SECURITY OFFICE ADDRESS AND DATE APPEAL RECEIVED:	**SSI CASES ONLY - GOLDBERG KELLY (GK) (SI 02301.310)** RECIPIENT APPEALED AN ADVERSE ACTION: ☐ WITHIN 10 DAYS AFTER RECEIVING THE ADVANCE NOTICE; ☐ AFTER THE 10-DAY PERIOD AND GOOD CAUSE EXISTS FOR EXTENDING THE TIME LIMIT ☐ PAYMENT CONTINUATION APPLIES AND INPUT MADE TO SYSTEM

NOTE: Take or mail the **completed original** to your local Social Security office, the Veterans Affairs Regional Office in Manila, or any U.S. Foreign Service post and keep a copy for your records.

Claims Folder

ADMINISTRATIVE ACTIONS THAT ARE INITIAL DETERMINATIONS (See GN03101.070, GN03101.080, and SI04010.010)

NOTE: These lists cover the vast majority of administrative actions that are initial determinations. However, they are not all inclusive.

Title II

1. Entitlement or continuing entitlement to benefits;
2. Reentitlement to benefits;
3. The amount of benefit;
4. A recomputation of benefit;
5. A reduction in disability benefits because benefits under a worker's compensation law were also received;
6. A deduction from benefits on account of work;
7. A deduction from disability benefits because of claimant's refusal to accept rehabilitation services;
8. Termination of benefits;
9. Penalty deductions imposed because of failure to report certain events;
10. Any overpayment or underpayment of benefits;
11. Whether an overpayment of benefits must be repaid;
12. How an underpayment of benefits due a deceased person will be paid;
13. The establishment or termination of a period of disability;
14. A revision of an earnings record;
15. Whether the payment of benefits will be made, on the claimant's behalf to a representative payee, u unless the claimant is under age 18 or legally incompetent;
16. Who will act as the payee if we determine that representative payment will be made;
17. An offset of benefits because the claimant previously received Supplemental Security Income payments for the same period;
18. Whether completion of or continuation for a specified period of time in an appropriate v vocational rehabilitation program will significantly increase the likelihood that the claimant will not have to return to the disability benefit rolls and thus, whether the claimant's benefits may be continued even though the claimant is not disabled;
19. Nonpayment of benefits because of claimant's confinement for more than 30 continuous days in a jail, prison, or other correctional institution for conviction of a criminal offense;
20. Nonpayment of benefits because of claimant's confinement for more than 30 continuous days in a mental health institution or other medical facility because a court found the individual was not guilty for reason of insanity; a court found that he/she was incompetent to stand trial or was unable to stand trial for some other similar mental defect, or, a court found that he/she was sexually dangerous.

Title XVI

1. Eligibility for, or the amount of, Supplemental Security Income benefits;
2. Suspension, reduction, or termination of Supplemental Security Income benefits;
3. Whether an overpayment of benefits must be repaid;
4. Whether payments will be made, on claimant's behalf to a representative payee, unless the claimant is under age 18, legally incompetent, or determined to be a drug addict or alcoholic;
5. Who will act as payee if we determine that representative payment will be made;
6. Imposing penalties for failing to report important information;
7. Drug addiction or alcoholism;
8. Whether claimant is eligible for special SSI cash benefits;
9. Whether claimant is eligible for special SSI eligibility status;
10. Claimant's disability; and
11. Whether completion of or continuation for a specified period of time in an appropriate vocational rehabilitation program will significantly increase the likelihood that claimant will not have to return to the disability benefit rolls and thus, whether claimant's benefits may be continued even though he or she is not disabled.

NOTE: Every redetermination which gives an individual the right of further review constitutes an initial determination.

Title VIII (See VB 02501.035)

1. Meeting or failing to meet the qualifying and/or entitlement factors for special veterans benefits (SVB);
2. Reduction, suspension or termination of SVB payments;
3. Applicability of a disqualifying event prior to SVB entitlement;
4. Administrative actions in SVB cases similar to those listed under Title II-items 3, 4, 10, 11 & 16.

Title XVIII

1. Entitlement to hospital insurance benefits and to enrollment for supplementary medical insurance benefits;
2. Disallowance (including denial of application for HIB and denial of application for enrollment for SMIB);
3. Termination of benefits (including termination of entitlement to HI and SMI);
4. Initial determinations regarding Medicare Part B income-related premium subsidy reductions.

REQUEST FOR RECONSIDERATION

NAME OF CLAIMANT:	CLAIMANT SSN:	CLAIM NUMBER: *(If different than SSN)*

ISSUE BEING APPEALED: *(Specify if retirement, disability, hospital or medical, SSI, SVB, overpayment, etc.)*

I do not agree with the Social Security Administration's (SSA) determination and request reconsideration.
My reasons are:

SUPPLEMENTAL SECURITY INCOME (SSI) OR SPECIAL VETERANS BENEFITS (SVB) RECONSIDERATION ONLY

THREE WAYS TO APPEAL

I want to appeal your determination about my claim for **SSI** or **SVB**. I have read about the three ways to appeal. I have checked the box below:

- ☐ CASE REVIEW - **You can pick this kind of appeal in all cases.** You can give us more facts to add to your file. Then we will decide your case again. You do not meet with the person who decides your case.
- ☐ INFORMAL CONFERENCE - **You can pick this kind of appeal in all SSI cases except for medical issues. In SVB cases, you can pick this kind of appeal only if we are stopping or lowering your SVB payment.** You will meet with a person who will decide your case. You can tell that person why you think you are right. You can give us more facts to help prove you are right. You can bring other people to help explain your case.
- ☐ FORMAL CONFERENCE - **You can pick this kind of appeal only if we are stopping or lowering your SSI or SVB payment.** This meeting is like an informal conference, but we can also get people to come in and help prove you are right. We can do this even if they do not want to help you. You can question these people at your meeting.

CONTACT INFORMATION

CLAIMANT SIGNATURE - *OPTIONAL:*		NAME OF CLAIMANT'S REPRESENTATIVE: *(If any)*	
MAILING ADDRESS:		MAILING ADDRESS:	
CITY: STATE: ZIP CODE:		CITY: STATE: ZIP CODE:	
TELEPHONE NUMBER: *(Include area code)*	DATE:	TELEPHONE NUMBER: *(Include area code)*	DATE:

TO BE COMPLETED BY SOCIAL SECURITY ADMINISTRATION

1. HAS INITIAL DETERMINATION BEEN MADE? ☐ Yes ☐ No 2. IS THIS REQUEST FILED TIMELY? ☐ Yes ☐ No *(If "NO", attach claimant's explanation for delay. Refer to GN 03102.125)*	**FIELD OFFICE DEVELOPMENT** (GN 03102.300) ☐ NO FURTHER DEVELOPMENT REQUIRED ☐ REQUIRED DEVELOPMENT ATTACHED ☐ REQUIRED DEVELOPMENT PENDING, WILL FORWARD OR ADVISE STATUS WITHIN 30 DAYS
SOCIAL SECURITY OFFICE ADDRESS AND DATE APPEAL RECEIVED:	**SSI CASES ONLY - GOLDBERG KELLY (GK) (SI 02301.310)** RECIPIENT APPEALED AN ADVERSE ACTION: ☐ WITHIN 10 DAYS AFTER RECEIVING THE ADVANCE NOTICE; ☐ AFTER THE 10-DAY PERIOD AND GOOD CAUSE EXISTS FOR EXTENDING THE TIME LIMIT ☐ PAYMENT CONTINUATION APPLIES AND INPUT MADE TO SYSTEM

NOTE: Take or mail the **completed original** to your local Social Security office, the Veterans Affairs Regional Office in Manila, or any U.S. Foreign Service post and keep a copy for your records.

Claimant

HOW TO APPEAL YOUR SUPPLEMENTAL SECURITY INCOME (SSI) OR SPECIAL VETERANS BENEFIT (SVB) DECISION

Now that you picked the kind of appeal that fits your case, fill out this form or we'll help you fill it out. You can have a lawyer, friend, or someone else help you with your appeal. There are groups that can help you with your appeal. Some can give you a free lawyer. We can give you the names of these groups.

NOTE: DON'T FILL OUT THIS FORM IF WE SAID WE'LL STOP YOUR DISABILITY CHECK FOR MEDICAL REASONS OR BECAUSE YOU'RE NO LONGER BLIND. WE'LL GIVE YOU THE RIGHT FORM (SSA-789-U4) FOR YOUR APPEAL.

The information on this form is authorized by regulation (20 CFR 404.907 - 404.921 and 416.1407 - 416.1421) and Public Law 106-169 (section 809(a)(1) of section 251(a)). While your response to these questions is voluntary, the Social Security Administration cannot reconsider the decision on this claim unless the information is furnished.

Privacy Act Statement
Request for Reconsideration

Sections 205, 702(a)(5), 809(a), 809(b), 1631, 1633, and 1869(b) allow us to collect this information. Furnishing us this information is voluntary. However, failing to provide all or part of the information may prevent us from re-evaluating the decision on your claim.

We will use the information to determine your eligibility for benefits and administer our programs. We may also share your information for the following purposes, called routine uses:

1. To third party contacts in situations where the party to be contacted has, or is expected to have, information relating to the individual's capability to manage his/her affairs or his/her eligibility for or entitlement to benefits under the Social Security program.

2. To contractors and other Federal agencies, as necessary, for the purpose of assisting the Social Security Administration in the efficient administration of its programs.

3. To the Center for Medicare & Medicaid Services (CMS), for the purpose of administering Medicare Part A, Part B, Medicare Advantage Part C, and Medicare Part D, including but not limited to: Medicare Pa rt C enrollment and premium collection processes; Part D enrollment and premium collection processes; Medicare Part B premium reduction based on participation in a Part C plan; and Medicare Part B enrollment and income-related monthly adjustment amount determinations, appeals of determinations, and premium collections.

In addition, we may share this information in accordance with the Privacy Act and other Federal laws. For example, where authorized, we may use and disclose this information in computer matching programs, in which our records are compared with other records to establish or verify a person's eligibility for Federal benefit programs and for repayment of incorrect or delinquent debts under these programs.

A list of additional routine uses is available in our Privacy Act System of Records Notices (SORNs). There are several SORNs that govern the collection of this information, including 60-0089, entitled Claims Folder System, and 60-0321, entitled Medicare Database File. Additional information and a full listing of all our SORNs and applicable routine uses are available on our website at www.socialsecurity.gov/foia/bluebook.

Paperwork Reduction Act Statement - This information collection meets the requirements of 44 U.S.C. § 3507, as amended by Section 2 of the Paperwork Reduction Act of 1995. You do not need to answer these questions unless we display a valid Office of Management and Budget control number. We estimate that it will take about 8 minutes to read the instructions, gather the facts, and answer the questions.

SEND THE COMPLETED FORM TO YOUR LOCAL SOCIAL SECURITY OFFICE. The office is listed under U.S. Government agencies in your telephone directory or you may call Social Security at 1-800-772-1213 (TTY 1-800-325-0778). *You may send comments on our time estimate above to: SSA, 6401 Security Blvd., Baltimore, MD 21235-6401.* ***Send only comments relating to our time estimate to this address, not the completed form.***

Disability Report-Appeal - Form SSA-3441-BK

DISABILITY REPORT – APPEAL

For SSA use only. Please do not write in this box.

Related SSN ____________________ Number Holder ____________________

If you are filling out this report for someone else, please provide information about him or her. When a question refers to "you" or "your," it refers to the person who is applying for disability benefits.

SECTION 1 – INFORMATION ABOUT THE DISABLED PERSON

1. A. Name (First, Middle, Last, Suffix)	**1. B.** Social Security Number

1. C. Daytime Phone Number, including area code (include IDD and country codes if outside the U.S. or Canada)

☐ Check this box if you do not have a phone number where we can leave a message.

1. D. Alternate Phone Number – another number where we may reach you, if any

1. E. Email Address (Optional)

SECTION 2 – CONTACTS

Give the name of someone **(other than your doctors)** we can contact who knows about your medical conditions, and can help you with your claim. (e.g., friend or relative)

2. A. Name (First, Middle, Last)	**2. B.** Relationship to Disabled Person

2. C. Mailing Address (Street or PO Box), include apartment number or unit if applicable.

City	State/Province	ZIP/Postal Code	Country (if not U.S.)

2. D. Daytime Phone Number, including area code (include IDD and country codes if outside the U.S. or Canada)

2. E. Can this person speak and understand English?

☐ Yes ☐ No

If no, what language does the contact person prefer? ____________________

2. F. Who is completing this form?

☐ The person who is applying for disability (Go to SECTION 3 - MEDICAL CONDITIONS).
☐ The person listed in 2.A. (Go to SECTION 3 - MEDICAL CONDITIONS).
☐ Someone else (Please complete the information below).

2. G. Name (First, Middle, Last)	**2. H.** Relationship to Disabled Person

2. I. Mailing Address (Street or PO Box) Include apartment number or unit if applicable.

City	State/Province	ZIP/Postal Code	Country (if not U.S.)

2. J. Daytime Phone Number, including area code (include IDD and country codes if outside the U.S. or Canada)

SECTION 3 – MEDICAL CONDITIONS

3. A. **Since you last told us about your medical conditions**, has there been any **CHANGE** (for better or worse) in your physical or mental conditions?

☐ Yes, approximate date change occurred: ______________ ☐ No

If yes, please describe in detail: ______________

____

____

3. B. **Since you last told us about your medical conditions**, do you have any **NEW** physical or mental conditions?

☐ Yes, approximate date of new conditions: ______________ ☐ No

If yes, please describe in detail: ______________

____

____

If you need more space, use SECTION 10 – REMARKS on the last page.

SECTION 4 – MEDICAL TREATMENT

4. A. Have you used any other names on your medical or educational records? Examples are maiden name, other married name, or nickname.

☐ Yes ☐ No

If yes, please list the other names used: ______________

____

4. B. **Since you last told us about your medical treatment**, have you seen a doctor or other health care provider, received treatment at a hospital or clinic, or **do you have a future appointment scheduled?**

☐ Yes ☐ No (Go to SECTION 6 – MEDICINES)

4. C. What type(s) of condition(s) were you treated for, or will you be seen for?

☐ Physical ☐ Mental (including emotional or learning problems)

If you answered "Yes" to 4.B., please tell us who may have **NEW** medical records about any of your **physical** or **mental** conditions (including emotional or learning problems).

Use the following pages to provide information for up to three (3) providers. **Complete one page for each provider.** If you have more than three providers, list them in SECTION 10 - REMARKS on the last page.

Please include:

- doctors' offices
- hospitals (including emergency room visits)
- clinics
- mental health center
- other health care facilities.

Only list the providers you have seen since you last told us about your medical treatment.

SECTION 4 – MEDICAL TREATMENT (continued)

Provider 1

4. D. Name of facility or office	Name of health care provider who treated you

ALL OF THE QUESTIONS ON THIS PAGE REFER TO THE HEALTH CARE PROVIDER ABOVE.

Phone Number	Patient ID# (if known)

Address

City	State/Province	ZIP/Postal Code	Country (if not U.S.)

Dates of Treatment (approximate date, if exact date is unknown)

Office, Clinic or Outpatient visits at this facility	**Emergency Room visits at this facility**	**Overnight hospital stays at this facility**
First Visit ______	Date ______	Date in ______ Date out ______
Last Visit ______	Date ______	Date in ______ Date out ______
Next scheduled appointment (if any) ______	Date ______	Date in ______ Date out ______
	☐ None	☐ None

What medical conditions were treated or evaluated?

What treatment did you receive for the above conditions? (Do not list medicines or tests in this box.)

Has this provider performed or sent you to any tests? Please include tests you are scheduled to have in the future. ☐ Yes (Please complete the information below.) ☐ No (Go to the next page.)

KIND OF TEST	DATES OF TESTS	KIND OF TEST	DATES OF TESTS
☐ Biopsy (list body part) ______		☐ MRI/CT Scan (list body part) ______	
☐ Blood Test (not HIV)		☐ Speech/Language Test	
☐ Breathing Test		☐ Treadmill (exercise test)	
☐ Cardiac Catheterization		☐ Vision Test	
☐ EEG (brain wave test)		☐ X-ray (list body part) ______	
☐ EKG (heart test)			
☐ Hearing Test		☐ Other (please describe) ______	
☐ HIV Test			
☐ IQ Testing			

If you need to list more tests, use SECTION 10 - REMARKS on the last page.

If you do not have any more providers to describe,

go to SECTION 5 – OTHER MEDICAL INFORMATION on page 6.

SECTION 4 – MEDICAL TREATMENT (continued)

Provider 2

4. D. Name of facility or office	Name of health care provider who treated you

ALL OF THE QUESTIONS ON THIS PAGE REFER TO THE HEALTH CARE PROVIDER ABOVE.

Phone Number	Patient ID# (if known)

Address

City	State/Province	ZIP/Postal Code	Country (if not U.S.)

Dates of Treatment (approximate date, if exact date is unknown)

Office, Clinic or Outpatient visits at this facility	Emergency Room visits at this facility	Overnight hospital stays at this facility
First Visit ______	Date ______	Date in ______ Date out ______
Last Visit ______	Date ______	Date in ______ Date out ______
Next scheduled appointment (if any) ______	Date ______	Date in ______ Date out ______
	☐ None	☐ None

What medical conditions were treated or evaluated?

What treatment did you receive for the above conditions? (Do not list medicines or tests in this box.)

Has this provider performed or sent you to any tests? Please include tests you are scheduled to have in the future. ☐ Yes (Please complete the information below.) ☐ No (Go to the next page.)

KIND OF TEST	DATES OF TESTS	KIND OF TEST	DATES OF TESTS
☐ Biopsy (list body part) ______		☐ MRI/CT Scan (list body part) ______	
☐ Blood Test (not HIV)		☐ Speech/Language Test	
☐ Breathing Test		☐ Treadmill (exercise test)	
☐ Cardiac Catheterization		☐ Vision Test	
☐ EEG (brain wave test)		☐ X-ray (list body part) ______	
☐ EKG (heart test)			
☐ Hearing Test		☐ Other (please describe) ______	
☐ HIV Test			
☐ IQ Testing			

If you need to list more tests, use SECTION 10 - REMARKS on the last page.

If you do not have any more providers to describe,

go to SECTION 5 – OTHER MEDICAL INFORMATION on page 6.

SECTION 4 – MEDICAL TREATMENT (continued)

Provider 3

4. D. Name of facility or office	Name of health care provider who treated you

ALL OF THE QUESTIONS ON THIS PAGE REFER TO THE HEALTH CARE PROVIDER ABOVE.

Phone Number	Patient ID# (if known)

Address

City	State/Province	ZIP/Postal Code	Country (if not U.S.)

Dates of Treatment (approximate date, if exact date is unknown)

Office, Clinic or Outpatient visits at this facility	Emergency Room visits at this facility	Overnight hospital stays at this facility
First Visit ______	Date ______	Date in ______ Date out ______
Last Visit ______	Date ______	Date in ______ Date out ______
Next scheduled appointment	Date ______	Date in ______ Date out ______
(if any) ______	☐ None	☐ None

What medical conditions were treated or evaluated?

What treatment did you receive for the above conditions? (Do not list medicines or tests in this box.)

Has this provider performed or sent you to any tests? Please include tests you are scheduled to have in the future. ☐ Yes (Please complete the information below.) ☐ No (Go to the next page.)

KIND OF TEST	DATES OF TESTS	KIND OF TEST	DATES OF TESTS
☐ Biopsy (list body part) ______		☐ MRI/CT Scan (list body part) ______	
☐ Blood Test (not HIV)		☐ Speech/Language Test	
☐ Breathing Test		☐ Treadmill (exercise test)	
☐ Cardiac Catheterization		☐ Vision Test	
☐ EEG (brain wave test)		☐ X-ray (list body part) ______	
☐ EKG (heart test)			
☐ Hearing Test		☐ Other (please describe) ______	
☐ HIV Test			
☐ IQ Testing			

If you need to list more tests, use **SECTION 10 - REMARKS** on the last page.

If you have been treated by more providers, use section 10 - REMARKS on the last page.

SECTION 5 – OTHER MEDICAL INFORMATION

5. **Since you last told us about your other medical information,** does anyone else have medical information about any of your **physical** or **mental** conditions (including emotional and learning problems) or are you scheduled to see anyone else?

This may include:

- workers' compensation
- vocational rehabilitation services
- insurance companies who have paid you disability benefits
- prisons and correctional facilities
- attorneys
- social service agencies
- welfare agencies
- school/education records

☐ Yes (Please complete the information below.)
☐ No (Go to SECTION 6 – MEDICINES)

Name of Organization			Claim or ID Number (if any)
Address			
City	State/Province	ZIP/Postal Code	Country (if not U.S.)
Name of Contact Person			Phone Number
Date of First Contact	Date of Last Contact	Date of Next Contact (if any)	
Reasons for Contacts			

If you need to list more people or organizations, use **SECTION 10 – REMARKS** on the last page.

SECTION 6 – MEDICINES

6. Are you <u>currently</u> taking any medicines (prescription or non-prescription)?

☐ Yes (Please complete the information below. You may need to look at your medicine containers.)
☐ No (Go to SECTION 7 – ACTIVITIES)

NAME OF MEDICINE	IF PRESCRIBED, NAME OF DOCTOR	REASON FOR MEDICINE	SIDE EFFECTS YOU HAVE

If you need to list more medicines, use **SECTION 10 – REMARKS** on the last page.

SECTION 7 - ACTIVITIES

7. **Since you last told us about your activities,** has there been any **change** (for better or worse) in your daily activities due to your **physical** or **mental** conditions? (Examples of daily activities are household tasks, personal care, getting around, hobbies and interests, social activities, etc.)

☐ Yes ☐ No

If yes, please describe in detail: ____________________

____

____

____

If you need more space, use SECTION 10 – REMARKS on the last page.

SECTION 8 – WORK AND EDUCATION

8. A. **Since you last told us about your work,** have you worked or has your work changed?

☐ Yes ☐ No

If yes, you will be asked to provide additional information.

8. B. **Since you last told us about your education,** have you completed or are you enrolled in any type of specialized job training, trade school, or vocational school?

☐ Yes ☐ No

If yes, what type? ____________________

Date(s) attended: ____________________

If you need more space, use SECTION 10 – REMARKS on the last page.

SECTION 9 – VOCATIONAL REHABILITATION, EMPLOYMENT, OR OTHER SUPPORT SERVICES

9. Since you last told us about your vocational rehabilitation, have you participated, or are you participating in:

- an individual work plan with an employment network under the Ticket to Work Program?
- an individualized plan for employment with a vocational rehabilitation agency or any other organization?
- a Plan to Achieve Self-Support (PASS)?
- an individualized education program (IEP) through an educational institution (if a student age 18-21)?
- any program providing vocational rehabilitation, employment services, or other support services to help you go to work?

☐ Yes (Please complete the information below.)
☐ No (Go to SECTION 10 – REMARKS)

Name of Organization or School			
Name of Counselor, Instructor, or Job Coach			Phone Number
Address			
City	State/Province	ZIP/Postal Code	Country (if not U.S.)

Date when you started participating in the plan or program:

If you need more space, use SECTION 10 – REMARKS on the last page.

SECTION 10 – REMARKS

Use this space to provide any information you could not show in earlier sections of this form or any additional information you feel we should know about. Please be sure to include the number of the question you are answering (For example, 3A, 4D, etc.).

Date Report Completed MM/DD/YYYY: ______________________

Authorization to Disclose Information to the Social Security Administration - Form - SSA-827

WHOSE *Records to be Disclosed*

Form Approved
OMB No. 0960-0623

NAME *(First, Middle, Last, Suffix)*	
SSN	Birthday *(mm/dd/yy)*

AUTHORIZATION TO DISCLOSE INFORMATION TO THE SOCIAL SECURITY ADMINISTRATION (SSA)

**** PLEASE READ THE ENTIRE FORM, BOTH PAGES, BEFORE SIGNING BELOW ****

I voluntarily authorize and request disclosure (including paper, oral, and electronic interchange):

OF WHAT ***All my medical records;* also education records and other information related to my ability to perform tasks. This includes specific permission to release:**

1. **All records and other information regarding my treatment, hospitalization, and outpatient care for my impairment(s) *including*, and not limited to :**
   - Psychological, psychiatric or other mental impairment(s) (excludes "psychotherapy notes" as defined in 45 CFR 164.501)
   - Drug abuse, alcoholism, or other substance abuse
   - Sickle cell anemia
   - Records which may indicate the presence of a communicable or noncommunicable disease, and tests for or records of HIV/AIDS
   - Gene-related impairments (including genetic test results)
2. **Information about how my impairment(s) affects my ability to complete tasks and activities of daily living, and affects my ability to work.**
3. **Copies of educational tests or evaluations, including Individualized Educational Programs, triennial assessments, psychological and speech evaluations, and any other records that can help evaluate function; also teachers' observations and evaluations.**
4. **Information created within 12 months after the date this authorization is signed, as well as past information.**

FROM WHOM

- **All medical sources** (hospitals, clinics, labs, physicians, psychologists, etc.) including mental health, correctional, addiction treatment, and VA health care facilities
- All educational sources (schools, teachers, records administrators, counselors, etc.)
- Social workers/rehabilitation counselors
- Consulting examiners used by SSA
- Employers, insurance companies, workers' compensation programs
- Others who may know about my condition (family, neighbors, friends, public officials)

THIS BOX TO BE COMPLETED BY SSA/DDS (as needed) Additional information to identify the subject (e.g., other names used), the specific source, or the material to be disclosed:

TO WHOM **The Social Security Administration and to the State agency authorized to process my case** (usually called "disability determination services"), **including contract copy services, and doctors or other professionals consulted during the process.** [Also, for international claims, to the U.S. Department of State Foreign Service Post.]

PURPOSE Determining my **eligibility for benefits**, including looking at the combined effect of any impairments that by themselves would not meet SSA's definition of disability; and whether I can manage such benefits.

☐ Determining whether I am **capable of managing benefits ONLY** (check only if this applies)

EXPIRES WHEN This authorization is good for 12 months from the date signed (below my signature).

- I authorize the use of a copy (including electronic copy) of this form for the disclosure of the information described above.
- I understand that there are some circumstances in which this information may be redisclosed to other parties (see page 2 for details).
- I may write to SSA and my sources to revoke this authorization at any time (see page 2 for details).
- SSA will give me a copy of this form if I ask; I may ask the source to allow me to inspect or get a copy of material to be disclosed.
- **I have read both pages of this form and agree to the disclosures above from the types of sources listed.**

PLEASE SIGN USING BLUE OR BLACK INK ONLY	IF not signed by subject of disclosure, specify basis for authority to sign
INDIVIDUAL authorizing disclosure	☐ **Parent of minor** ☐ **Guardian** ☐ **Other personal representative (explain)**
SIGN ▶	(Parent/guardian/personal representative sign here if two signatures required by State law) ▶

Date Signed	Street Address		
Phone Number (with area code)	City	State	ZIP

WITNESS *I know the person signing this form or am satisfied of this person's identity:*

SIGN ▶	IF needed, second witness sign here (e.g., if signed with "X" above) **SIGN ▶**
Phone Number (or Address)	Phone Number (or Address)

This general and special authorization to disclose was developed to comply with the provisions regarding disclosure of medical, educational, and other information under P.L. 104-191 ("HIPAA"); 45 CFR parts 160 and 164; 42 U.S. Code section 290dd-2; 42 CFR part 2; 38 U.S. Code section 7332; 38 CFR 1.475; 20 U.S. Code section 1232g ("FERPA"); 34 CFR parts 99 and 300; and State law.

Form **SSA-827** (11-2012) ef (11-2012) Use 4-2009 and Later Editions Until Supply is Exhausted — Page 1 of 2

Explanation of Form SSA-827, "Authorization to Disclose Information to the Social Security Administration (SSA)"

We need your written authorization to help get the information required to process your claim, and to determine your capability of managing benefits. Laws and regulations require that sources of personal information have a signed authorization before releasing it to us. Also, laws require specific authorization for the release of information about certain conditions and from educational sources.

You can provide this authorization by signing a form SSA-827. Federal law permits sources with information about you to release that information if you sign a single authorization to release all your information from all your possible sources. We will make copies of it for each source. A covered entity (that is, a source of medical information about you) may not condition treatment, payment, enrollment, or eligibility for benefits on whether you sign this authorization form. A few States, and some individual sources of information, require that the authorization specifically name the source that you authorize to release personal information. In those cases, we may ask you to sign one authorization for each source and we may contact you again if we need you to sign more authorizations.

You have the right to revoke this authorization at any time, except to the extent a source of information has already relied on it to take an action. To revoke, send a written statement to any Social Security Office. If you do, also send a copy directly to any of your sources that you no longer wish to disclose information about you. SSA can tell you if we identified any sources you didn't tell us about. SSA may use information disclosed prior to revocation to decide your claim.

It is SSA's policy to provide service to people with limited English proficiency in their native language or preferred mode of communication consistent with Executive Order 13166 (August 11, 2000) and the Individuals with Disabilities Education Act. SSA makes every reasonable effort to ensure that the information in the SSA-827 is provided to you in your native or preferred language.

Privacy Act Statement
Collection and Use of Personal Information

Sections 205(a), 233(d)(5)(A), 1614(a)(3)(H)(i), 1631(d)(1) and 1631(e)(1)(A) of the Social Security Act as amended, [42 U.S.C. 405(a), 433(d)(5)(A), 1382c(a)(3)(H)(i), 1383(d)(1) and 1383(e)(1)(A)] authorize us to collect this information. We will use the information you provide to help us determine your eligibility, or continuing eligibility for benefits, and your ability to manage any benefits received. The information you provide is voluntary. However, failure to provide the requested information may prevent us from making an accurate and timely decision on your claim, and could result in denial or loss of benefits.

We rarely use the information you provide on this form for any purpose other than for the reasons explained above. However, we may use it for the administration and integrity of Social Security programs. We may also disclose information to another person or to another agency in accordance with approved routine uses, including but not limited to the following:

1. To enable a third party or an agency to assist us in establishing rights to Social Security benefits and/or coverage;

2. To comply with Federal laws requiring the release of information from our records (e.g., to the Government Accountability Office, General Services Administration, National Archives Records Administration, and the Department of Veterans Affairs);

3. To make determinations for eligibility in similar health and income maintenance programs at the Federal, State, and local level; and

4. To facilitate statistical research, audit, or investigative activities necessary to assure the integrity and improvement of our programs (e.g., to the U.S. Census Bureau and to private entities under contract with us).

We may also use the information you provide in computer matching programs. Matching programs compare our records with records kept by other Federal, State, or local government agencies. We use the information from these programs to establish or verify a person's eligibility for Federally funded or administered benefit programs and for repayment of incorrect payments or delinquent debts under these programs.

A complete list of routine uses of the information you gave us is available in our Privacy Act Systems of Records Notices entitled, Claims Folder System, 60-0089, Master Beneficiary Record, 60-0090, Supplemental Security Income record and Special Veterans benefits, 60-0103, and Electronic Disability (eDIB) Claims File, 60-0340. The notices, additional information regarding this form, and information regarding our systems and programs, are available on-line at www.socialsecurity.gov or at any Social Security office.

Paperwork Reduction Act Statement - This information collection meets the requirements of 44 U.S.C. § 3507, as amended by section 2 of the Paperwork Reduction Act of 1995. You do not need to answer these questions unless we display a valid Office of Management and Budget control number. We estimate that it will take about 10 minutes to read the instructions, gather the facts, and answer the questions. **SEND OR BRING THE COMPLETED FORM TO YOUR LOCAL SOCIAL SECURITY OFFICE.** You can find your local Social Security office through SSA's website at www.socialsecurity.gov. Offices are also listed under U.S. Government agencies in your telephone directory **or you may call Social Security at 1-800-772-1213 (TTY 1-800-325-0778).** *You may send comments on our time estimate above to: SSA, 6401 Security Blvd, Baltimore, MD 21235-6401.* ***Send only comments relating to our time estimate to this address, not the completed form.***

APPENDIX M

REQUEST FOR HEARING BY ALJ - FORM - HA-501-US

SOCIAL SECURITY ADMINISTRATION
OFFICE OF DISABILITY ADJUDICATION AND REVIEW

Form Approved
OMB No. 0960-0269

REQUEST FOR HEARING BY ADMINISTRATIVE LAW JUDGE

*(Take or mail the **completed original** to your local Social Security office, the Veterans Affairs Regional Office in Manila or any U.S. Foreign Service post and keep a copy for your records)*

See Privacy Act Notice

1. Claimant Name	2. Claimant SSN	3. Claim Number, if different

4. I REQUEST A HEARING BEFORE AN ADMINISTRATIVE LAW JUDGE. I disagree with the determination because:

An Administrative Law Judge of the Social Security Administration's Office of Disability Adjudication and Review or the Department of Health and Human Services will be appointed to conduct the hearing or other proceedings in your case. You will receive notice of the time and place of a hearing at least 20 days before the date set for a hearing.

5. I have additional evidence to submit. ☐ Yes ☐ No

Name and source of additional evidence, if not included

Submit your evidence to the hearing office within 10 days. Your servicing Social Security office will provide the hearing office's address. Attach an additional sheet if you need more space.

6. Do not complete if the appeal is a Medicare issue. Otherwise, check one of the blocks

☐ I wish to appear at a hearing

☐ I do not wish to appear at a hearing and I request that a decision be made based on the evidence in my case. (Complete Waiver Form HA-4608)

Representation: You have a right to be represented at the hearing. If you are not represented, your Social Security office will give you a list of legal referral and service organizations. If you are represented, complete and submit form SSA-1696 (Appointment of Representative) unless you are appealing a Medicare issue.

7. CLAIMANT SIGNATURE (OPTIONAL)		DATE	8. NAME OF REPRESENTATIVE (if any)		DATE
RESIDENCE ADDRESS			ADDRESS		
CITY	STATE	ZIP CODE	CITY	STATE	ZIP CODE
TELEPHONE NUMBER	FAX NUMBER		TELEPHONE NUMBER	FAX NUMBER	

TO BE COMPLETED BY SOCIAL SECURITY ADMINISTRATION- ACKNOWLEDGMENT OF REQUEST FOR HEARING

9. Request received on ________ (Date) by ________ (Print Name) ________ (Title)

________ (Address) ________ (Servicing FO Code) ________ (PC Code)

10. Was the request for hearing received within 65 days of the reconsidered determination? ☐ Yes ☐ No
If no, attach claimant's explanation for delay and supporting documents if any.

11. If claimant is not represented, was a list of legal referral service organizations provided? ☐ Yes ☐ No

12. Interpreter needed ☐ Yes ☐ No

Language (including sign language)

13. Check one: ☐ Initial Entitlement Case
☐ Disability Cessation Case or ☐ Other Postentitlement Case

14. HO COPY SENT TO: ________ HO on ________
☐ Claims Folder (CF) Attached: ☐ Title (T) II; ☐ T XVI; ☐ T VIII; ☐ T XVIII; ☐ T II CF held in FO ☐ Electronic Folder
☐ CF requested ☐ T II; ☐ T XVI; ☐ T VIII; ☐ T XVIII
(Copy of email or phone report attached)

16. CF COPY SENT TO: ________ HO on ________
☐ CF Attached: ☐ Title (T) II; ☐ T XVI; ☐ T XVIII
☐ Other Attached: ________

15. Check all claim types that apply:

☐ Retirement and Survivors Insurance Only	(RSI)
☐ Title II Disability - Worker or child only	(DIWC)
☐ Title II Disability - Widow(er) only	(DIWW)
☐ Title XVI (SSI) Aged only	(SSIA)
☐ Title XVI Blind only	(SSIB)
☐ Title XVI Disability only	(SSID)
☐ Title XVI/Title II Concurrent Aged Claim	(SSAC)
☐ Title XVI/Title II Concurrent Blind	(SSBC)
☐ Title XVI/Title II Concurrent Disability	(SSDC)
☐ Title XVIII Hospital/Supplementary Insurance	(HI/SMI)
☐ Title VIII Only Special Veterans Benefits	(SVB)
☐ Title VIII/Title XVI	(SVB/SSI)
☐ Other - Specify:	

Form **HA-501-U5** (01-2015) ef (01-2015)
Use 08-2012 Edition Until Stock is Exhausted

TAKE OR SEND ORIGINAL TO SSA AND RETAIN A COPY FOR YOUR RECORDS

PRIVACY ACT STATEMENT
Request for Hearing by Administrative Law Judge

Sections 205(a) (42 U.S.C. 405 (a)), 702 (42 U.S.C. 902), 1631(e) (1) (A), and; (B) (42 U.S.C. 1383(e) (1) (A) and (B)), 1839(i) (42 U.S.C. 1395r), 1869(b) (1), and (c) (42 U.S.C. 1395ff) of the Social Security Act, as amended, authorize us to collect this information. We will use the information you provide to continue processing your claim.

Providing this information is voluntary. However, failing to provide us with all or part of the requested information may prevent us from making an accurate and timely decision on your claim.

We rarely use the information you supply for any purpose other than for determining problems in Social Security programs. However, we may use it for the administration and integrity of Social Security programs. We may also disclose information to another person or to another agency in accordance with approved routine uses, which include, but are not limited to the following:

1. To enable a third party or an agency to assist Social Security in establishing rights to Social Security benefits and/or coverage;
2. To comply with Federal laws requiring the release of information from Social Security records (e.g., to the Government Accountability Office and the Department of Veterans' Affairs);
3. To make determinations for eligibility in similar health and income maintenance programs at the Federal, State, and local level; and
4. To facilitate statistical research, audit, or investigate activities necessary to assure the integrity of Social Security programs.

We may also use the information you provide in computer matching programs. Matching programs compare our records with records kept by other Federal, State, or local government agencies. Information from these matching programs can be used to establish or verify a person's eligibility for Federally-funded or administered benefit programs and for repayment of payments or delinquent debts under these programs.

A complete list of routine uses for this information is available in System of Records Notices 60-0089, Claims Folder System and 60-0050, Completed Determination-Continuing Disablility Determinations. These notices, additional information regarding this form, and information regarding our programs and systems, are available on-line at www.socialsecurity.gov or any local Social Security office.

Paperwork Reduction Act Statement - This information collection meets the requirements of 44 U.S.C. § 3507, as amended by Section 2 of the Paperwork Reduction Act of 1995. You do not need to answer these questions unless we display a valid Office of Management and Budget control number. We estimate that it will take about 10 minutes to read the instructions, gather the facts, and answer the questions. **SEND OR BRING THE COMPLETED FORM TO YOUR LOCAL SOCIAL SECURITY OFFICE. You can find your local Social Security office through SSA's website at www.socialsecurity.gov. Offices are also listed under U. S. Government agencies in your telephone directory or you may call Social Security at 1-800-772-1213 (TTY 1-800-325-0778).** *You may send comments on our time estimate above to: SSA, 6401 Security Blvd, Baltimore, MD 21235-6401.* ***Send only comments relating to our time estimate to this address, not the completed form.***

Form **HA-501-U5** (01-2015) ef (01-2015)

REQUEST FOR REVIEW OF HEARING DECISION/ORDER - FORM HA-520-US

SOCIAL SECURITY ADMINISTRATION

Form Approved
OMB No. 0960-0277

REQUEST FOR REVIEW OF HEARING DECISION/ORDER

See Privacy Act Notice

(**Do not** use this form for objecting to a **recommended** ALJ decision.)

(Either mail the signed original form to the Appeals Council at the address shown below, or take or mail the signed original to your local Social Security office, the Department of Veterans Affairs Regional Office in Manila, or any U.S. Foreign Service Post and keep a copy for your records.)

1. CLAIMANT NAME	2. CLAIMANT SSN	3. CLAIM NUMBER (If different than SSN)

4. I request that the Appeals Council review the Administrative Law Judge's action on the above claim because:

☐ Please grant me an extension of time to submit evidence or argument.

ADDITIONAL EVIDENCE

If you have additional evidence that relates to the period on or before the date of the hearing decision, you must inform the Appeals Council about it or submit it. If you have a representative, then your representative must help you obtain the evidence unless the evidence falls under an exception. You may also submit any other additional evidence to the Appeals Council. If you need additional time to submit evidence or legal argument, you must request an extension of time in writing now. This will ensure that the Appeals Council has the opportunity to consider the additional evidence before taking its action. If you submit neither evidence nor legal argument now or within any extension of time the Appeals Council grants, the Appeals Council will take its action based on the evidence currently in your file.

IMPORTANT: WRITE YOUR SOCIAL SECURITY NUMBER ON ANY LETTER OR MATERIAL YOU SEND US. IF YOU RECEIVED A BARCODE FROM US, THE BARCODE SHOULD ACCOMPANY THIS DOCUMENT AND ANY OTHER MATERIAL YOU SUBMIT TO US.

SIGNATURE BLOCKS: You should complete No. 5 and your representative (if any) should complete No. 6. If you are represented and your representative is not available to complete this form, you should also print his or her name, address, etc. in No. 6.

I declare under penalty of perjury that I have examined all the information on this form, and on any accompanying statements or forms, and it is true and correct to the best of my knowledge.

5. CLAIMANT'S SIGNATURE		DATE	6. REPRESENTATIVE'S SIGNATURE		DATE
PRINT NAME			PRINT NAME ☐ ATTORNEY ☐ NON-ATTORNEY		
ADDRESS	CITY, STATE, ZIP		ADDRESS	CITY, STATE, ZIP	
TELEPHONE NUMBER	FAX NUMBER		TELEPHONE NUMBER	FAX NUMBER	

THE SOCIAL SECURITY ADMINISTRATION STAFF WILL COMPLETE THIS PART

7. Request received for the Social Security Administration on ______________ by: ______________
(Date) (Print Name)

(Title) (Address) (Servicing FO Code) (PC Code)

8. Is the request for review received within 65 days of the ALJ's Decision/Dismissal? ☐ Yes ☐ No

9. If "No" checked:
☐ (1) attach claimant's explanation for delay; and
☐ (2) attach copy of appointment notice, letter or other pertinent material or information in the Social Security Office.

10. Check one:
☐ Initial Entitlement
☐ Termination or other

11. Check all claim types that apply:

☐	Retirement or survivors	(RSI)
☐	Disability-Worker	(DIWC)
☐	Disability-Widow(er)	(DIWW)
☐	Disability-Child	(DIWC)
☐	SSI Aged	(SSIA)
☐	SSI Blind	(SSIB)
☐	SSI Disability	(SSID)
☐	Title VIII Only	(SVB)
☐	Title VIII/Title XVI	(SVB/SSI)
☐	Other - Specify:	

APPEALS COUNCIL
OFFICE OF DISABILITY ADJUDICATION
AND REVIEW, SSA
5107 Leesburg Pike
FALLS CHURCH, VA 22041 - 3255

Form HA-520-U5 (01-2016) UF (01-2016)
Destroy Prior Editions

TAKE OR SEND ORIGINAL TO SSA AND RETAIN A COPY FOR YOUR RECORDS

Privacy Act Statement
Request for Review of Hearing Decision/Order

Sections 205(a), 702, 1631(e), and 1869(b) and (c) of the Social Security Act, as amended, authorize us to collect this information. We will use the information you provide to complete our claims process.

Furnishing us this information is voluntary. However, failing to provide us with all or part of the information may prevent the continued processing of your claim.

We rarely use the information you supply for any purpose other than to complete our claims process. However, we may use the information for the administration of our programs including sharing information:

1. To comply with Federal laws requiring the release of information from our records (e.g., to the Government Accountability Office and Department of Veterans Affairs); and,

2. To facilitate statistical research, audit, or investigative activities necessary to assure the integrity and improvement of our programs (e.g., to the Bureau of the Census and to private entities under contract with us).

A complete list of when we may share your information with others, called routine uses, is available in our Privacy Act System of Records Notices 60-0005, entitled Administrative Law Judge Working Files and 60-0089, entitled Claims Folder. Additional information about these and other system of records notices and our programs is available from our Internet website at www.socialsecurity.gov or at your local Social Security office.

We may share the information you provide to other health agencies through computer matching programs. Matching programs compare our records with records kept by other Federal, State, or local government agencies. We use the information from these programs to establish or verify a person's eligibility for federally funded or administered benefit programs and for repayment of incorrect payments or delinquent debts under these programs.

Paperwork Reduction Act Statement - This information collection meets the requirements of 44 U.S.C. § 3507, as amended by section 2 of the Paperwork Reduction Act of 1995. You do not need to answer these questions unless we display a valid Office of Management and Budget (OMB) control number. We estimate that it will take about 10 minutes to read the instructions, gather the facts, and answer the questions. **SEND OR BRING THE COMPLETED FORM TO YOUR LOCAL SOCIAL SECURITY OFFICE**. You can find your local Social Security office through SSA's website at www.socialsecurity.gov. Offices are also listed under U. S. Government agencies in your telephone directory or you may call Social Security at 1-800-772-1213 (TTY 1-800-325-0778). ***Send only comments relating to our time estimate to this address, not the completed form.***

APPENDIX N

QUESTIONS ASKED BY ALJ

These are some example questions the Administrative Law Judge (ALJ) will ask. Each judge and each case is different. The judge will ask questions based on your specific case.

It is important that you listen to the question asked by the ALJ and answer only that specific question in just one or two sentences. Be specific in your answer and do not ramble or go off topic. If you do not understand or did not hear the question, ask the ALJ to restate or explain the question to you. The most common mistake made by claimants during a hearing is failing to answer the questions asked by the ALJ.

General Questions

What is your age?
What is your address and social security number?
What is your date of birth?
Are you currently married?
What is your height and weight?
What is your currently living situation?
Date of onset of disability?

If claimant is not fluent in English

Where were you born?
What language did you grow up speaking?
Where were you educated?
When did you come to the United States?
What language is spoken at your home today?
Who reads the mail at your house?
Are you able to read in another language?

Educational Questions

What is your level of education?
If you did not complete high school do you have a GED?
How well did you do in school?
Describe any vocational training you have completed or attempted.
Describe any on-the-job training. When?
Describe any training in the military. When?

Work History Questions

What is your work history?
Are you currently working? If so, in what capacity?
What are the approximate dates of employment?
Did you do this job long enough to learn the job and develop "the facility needed for average performance"?
Did you work full or part time?
What types of duties were performed?
Why did you leave your job?
Before you left this job, did your impairment cause you to miss work, do a poor job, change job duties, change hours of work, etc.?
Did you have periods in which your condition caused you to stop work?
How often did this occur?
Did you have times when you attempted to go back to work but were unable to stay on the job long?
Have you tried to work since the onset of your disabling condition? If so, what was the outcome?

What was your work environment like? (temperature, wet, humid, noise, vibration, fumes, odors, dusts, gases, hazards, height)
How long did it take to learn to do this job?
Describe machines, tools and equipment used.
Describe any technical knowledge or skill used on this job.
Describe any writing or completing reports.
How much independent judgment was required?
Describe any supervisory responsibilities: how many people? Did you complete work evaluations? Have any hiring/firing responsibilities?
What about your job made it stressful? e.g., speed, precision, complexity, deadlines, working within a schedule, making decisions, exercising independent judgment, working with other people, dealing with the public (strangers), dealing with supervisors, being criticized by supervisors, simply knowing that work is supervised, monotony of routine, getting to work regularly, remaining at work for a full day?
Why could you not do your job as of (date of last injury)?
Why can you not do your job now?

Daily Activities

What are your daily activities?
Are there things that you cannot do because of your disability that you use to do?
How does your disability affect your daily activities?
Do you have someone to help you with your activities?
What is the heaviest weight you can lift or carry?
How often did you lift/carry this much?
What objects weighed this much that you need to lift or carry?
How far did you carry them?
Average weight lifted/carried?

How much sitting and standing/walking in an eight-hour working day?
Did the nature of this job allow you to sit, stand or walk as you chose?
How much bending? Any crawling, climbing, balancing?
How much manipulative ability was required?

Medical Conditions

The medical history will be established by the medical records. Most ALJs have read the medical records and took notes to use at the hearing. Typically detailed testimony about medical history is not necessary in most cases. However, the ALJ may ask questions to clarify something or to establish a time frame.

What are your symptoms?
How does your medical condition affect your ability to care for yourself?
How does your medical condition affect your ability to perform routine activities like cleaning your home, cooking or shopping for yourself?
What is the date of diagnosis of your medical condition?
How has your medical condition progressed over time?
How long can you sit, stand, walk or move around?
How much can you lift, carry or move and how often?
Do you need extra bathroom break, or rest breaks? If so, how often and why?
Are you currently being treated for your condition? If not, why?
How often do you see your doctor?
What does your doctor do for you?

How much has the treatment helped?
What medications do you take now? How much and how often do you take them?
What treatments other than medication have you tried?
Are you in pain today? What type of pain and where?
Do you use assistive devices?
Do you get fatigued? Described when.
How well do you sleep?

Mental Health

The mental health history will be established by the medical records. Most ALJs have read the medical records and took notes to use at the hearing. Typically detailed testimony about your mental health is not necessary in most cases. However, the ALJ may ask questions to clarify something or to establish a time frame.

How often do you take breaks due to uncontrollable anger, tearfulness, or other problems?
Are you irritable, depressed, worried, anxious, have difficulty concentrating, or remembering or thinking clearly? If so, explain what they are.
Do you have issues which affect your ability to get along with coworkers, supervisors, friends, or family members?
Do you have a history of drug or alcohol problems?
Are you currently being treated for your condition? If not, why?
How often are you treated?
How much has the treatment helped?
What medications do you take now? How much and how often do you take them?

For those with Intellectual Disability

Did you attend regular classes or special education classes?
How well did you do in school?
If an 8th grade reading, level is average, would you say that you're at least an average reader?
If less than an average reader:
Can you read and understand a newspaper?
Can you "read or write a simple message such as instructions or inventory lists"?
Can you read by yourself or do you need help?
Can you complete a job applications?
Do you have a driver's license?
Did your or did you have someone help you complete the SSA forms?
Can you multiply and divide/add and subtract/make change?

Check with our site to view other books from The Guerrilla Guide to the Law series.

www.LessonsInLaw.com

www.RebellionBooks.com

www.amazon.com/author/robertdbennett

LessonsInLaw.com
Law without lawyers

Keep Up To Date

Keep up to date by going to LessonsinLaw.com/updates to sign up for free updates and discounts on The Guerrilla Guide to the Law products.

This book was published through the cooperation of www.RebellionBooks.com and www.LessonsInLaw.com.

Made in United States
Cleveland, OH
05 November 2026

47670545R00224